In this exploration of the significance of illness in the Victorian literary imagination, Miriam Bailin maps the cultural implications and narrative effects of the sickroom as an important symbolic space in nineteenth-century life and literature. Dr Bailin draws on non-fictional accounts of illness by Julia Stephen, Harriet Martineau, and others to illuminate the presentation of illness and ministration, patient and nurse in the fiction of Charlotte Brontë, Charles Dickens, and George Eliot. She argues that the sickroom functions as an imagined retreat from conflicts in Victorian society, and that fictional representations of illness serve to resolve both social conflict and aesthetic tension. Her concentration on the sickroom scene as a compositional response to insistent formal as well as social problems yields fresh readings of canonical works and new approaches to the constituent elements of Victorian realist narrative.

CAMBRIDGE STUDIES IN NINETEENTH-CENTURY
LITERATURE I

THE SICKROOM IN VICTORIAN FICTION

CAMBRIDGE STUDIES IN NINETEENTH-CENTURY
LITERATURE AND CULTURE

General editors
Gillian Beer, *Girton College, Cambridge*
Catherine Gallagher, *University of California Berkeley*

Editorial board
Isobel Armstrong, *Birkbeck College, London*
Terry Eagleton, *St Catherine's College, Oxford*
Leonore Davidoff, *University of Essex*
D. A. Miller, *Harvard University*
J. Hillis Miller, *University of California, Irvine*
Mary Poovey, *The Johns Hopkins University*
Elaine Showalter, *Princeton University*

Nineteenth-century British literature and culture have been a rich field for interdisciplinary studies. Since the turn of the twentieth century, scholars and critics have tracked the intersections between Victorian literature and the visual arts, politics, social organizations, economic life, technical innovations, scientific thought – in short, culture in its broadest sense. In recent years, theoretical challenges and historiographical shifts have unsettled the assumptions of previous scholarly syntheses and called into question the terms of older debates. Whereas the tendency in much past literary critical interpretation was to use the metaphor of culture as "background", feminist, Foucauldian, and other analyses have employed more dynamic models that raise questions of power and of circulation. Such developments have re-animated the field.

This new series aims to accommodate and promote the most interesting work being undertaken on the frontiers of the field of nineteenth-century literary studies: work which intersects fruitfully with other fields of study such as history, or literary theory, or the history of science. Comparative as well as interdisciplinary approaches are welcomed.

Titles published
The Sickroom in Victorian Fiction
The Art of Being Ill
by Miriam Bailin, *Washington University*

Muscular Christianity
Embodying the Victorian Age
edited by Donald E. Hall, *California State University, Northridge*

THE SICKROOM IN VICTORIAN FICTION

The Art of Being Ill

MIRIAM BAILIN

Department of English, Washington University

CAMBRIDGE
UNIVERSITY PRESS

CAMBRIDGE UNIVERSITY PRESS
Cambridge, New York, Melbourne, Madrid, Cape Town, Singapore, São Paulo

Cambridge University Press
The Edinburgh Building, Cambridge CB2 8RU, UK

Published in the United States of America by Cambridge University Press, New York

www.cambridge.org
Information on this title: www.cambridge.org/9780521445269

© Cambridge University Press 1994

First published 1994
This digitally printed version 2007

A catalogue record for this publication is available from the British Library

Library of Congress Cataloguing in Publication data
Bailin, Miriam
The sickroom in Victorian fiction / Miriam Bailin.
p.   cm.–(Cambridge studies in nineteenth-century literature; I)
Includes bibliographical references and index.
ISBN 0 521 44526 4 (hardback)
1. English fiction – 19th century – History and criticism.   2. Care of the sick in literature.
3. Medicine in literature.   4. Brontë, Charlotte, 1816–1855 – Characters – Sick.   5.
Dickens, Charles, 1812–1870 – Characters – Sick.   6. Eliot, George, 1819–1880 –
Characters – Sick.   I. Title.   II. Series.
PR878.S5B35   1994
5B35   1994
823′.809356–dc20   93-17721   CIP

ISBN 978-0-521-44526-9 hardback
ISBN 978-0-521-03640-5 paperback

Contents

Acknowledgments

I am much indebted to Catherine Gallagher for her generous help and encouragement during the composition and revision of this book. I also owe much to Alex Zwerdling for his early encouragement of my work and for his valuable comments on these chapters. Thomas Laqueur provided helpful advice in the early stages; and Garrett Stewart's thorough and exacting reading of the manuscript was of great assistance to me during the process of revision.

I am grateful to Washington University for a leave of absence and a faculty research grant which have enabled me to complete this project. A version of portions of this book appeared in *Modern Language Quarterly* 48 (1987): 254–278.

My deepest personal and intellectual debt is to Paul Rosenzweig. This book is dedicated to him.

A note on texts

Charlotte Brontë, *The Shakespeare Head Brontë*, 19 vols. Thomas J. Wise and J. A. Symington, eds. (Oxford: Shakespeare Head Press, 1931–1938). The following abbreviations are used for Brontë's novels: *JE* for *Jane Eyre*, *S* for *Shirley*, *V* for *Villette*.

Charles Dickens, *The New Oxford Illustrated Dickens*, 25 vols. (London: Oxford University Press, 1948–1958). The following abbreviations are used for Dickens's novels: *BH* for *Bleak House*, *DC* for *David Copperfield*, *ED* for *The Mystery of Edwin Drood*, *GE* for *Great Expectations*, *LD* for *Little Dorrit*, *MC* for *Martin Chuzzlewit*, *MHC* for *Master Humphrey's Clock*, *OCS* for *The Old Curiosity Shop*, *OMF* for *Our Mutual Friend*, *OT* for *Oliver Twist*.

George Eliot, *The Works of George Eliot*, Cabinet Edition, 24 vols. (Edinburgh: William Blackwood & Sons, n.d.). The following abbreviations are used for Eliot's novels: *AB* for *Adam Bede*, *DD* for *Daniel Deronda*, *FH* for *Felix Holt*, *LV* for "The Lifted Veil," *MF* for *Mill on the Floss*, *MM* for *Middlemarch*, *R* for *Romola*, *JR* for "Janet's Repentance," and *SM* for *Silas Marner*.

Only chapter numbers will be cited parenthetically within the text for novels, except in those cases in which book and chapter numbers are necessary. References to George Eliot's *Armgart*, "The Lifted Veil," and *The Impressions of Theophrastus Such* will be to the Cabinet Edition volumes and page numbers.

Introduction

The art of being ill is no easy one to learn, but is practised to
perfection by many of the greatest sufferers.
                                    Julia Duckworth Stephen

This study takes as its point of departure the pervasive presence of the
sickroom scene in Victorian fiction and claims for such scenes a
crucial therapeutic function within Victorian realist narrative and
within the society such narratives represent. At their most familiar,
scenes of illness are employed as registers of emotional tumult, as
crucial stages in self-development, and as rather high-handed plot
contrivances to bring events to their desired issue. I hope to
demonstrate that for all their predictability these scenes serve, in
themselves and in their relations to larger narrative structures, as an
adaptive strategy to encode and mediate competing personal, social,
and aesthetic imperatives. The sickroom scene, I argue, is staged to
call forth (in the breach) the conditions under which both the
intelligibility of realist aesthetics and the viability of realism's social
ethics of cohesion could be affirmed. It is an essential concern of my
study to explore the narrative effects and the cultural implications of
a cure for self and narrative incoherence that is repeatedly, often
obsessively, figured by the private intensities of a deviant state.

The first chapter suggests the range of meanings conveyed by
illness and ministration in early and mid-Victorian England and
situates the sickroom scene within the context of contemporary mores
and aesthetic preferences. The next three chapters concentrate on the
narrative effects of the sickroom strategy as they intersect with the
particular concerns and emphases of individual authors. And a final
chapter briefly traces the ways in which late Victorian fiction
reshapes the sickroom for its own purposes and in the process undoes
its recuperative compromise.

Although my discussion of illness addresses the complex and often

I

contradictory ways in which illness engages problems of power and gender, I have not identified a sole source of that power in a dominant ideology nor have I traced an exclusively gendered construction of illness. My difference in approach in this regard from many recent and compelling studies of illness and literature deserves some comment. There may indeed have been, as Sandra Gilbert and Susan Gubar contend in *The Madwoman in the Attic*, "a socially-conditioned epidemic of female illness" in nineteenth-century England and America.[1] As feminist historians, social scientists, and literary critics have demonstrated, there are significant relations between particular diseases (anorexia nervosa, agoraphobia) or classes of diseases (psychiatric, gynecological) and the cultural and historical conditions shaping women's social roles.[2] It is, however, also true that the long roll call of Victorian invalids includes many men as well as women, and that scenes of illness are as pivotal in works by Thackeray, Meredith, Kingsley, and Dickens as they are in the novels of Brontë, Gaskell, or Eliot. Charles Darwin, for instance, rivalled Florence Nightingale in working hours logged in the sickroom. George Lewes and George Eliot, Jane and Thomas Carlyle, Henrietta and T. H. Huxley are among the more famous couples who shared or competed with each other's bodily unease. Leonard Huxley writes in his memoirs of his father, the scientist and lifelong sufferer from dyspepsia: "He would come in thoroughly used up... and lie wearily on one sofa; while his wife, whose health was wretched, matched him on the other."[3] It is not my intention to reclaim debility and cultural incapacitation for men as if it were the prize in a critical or cultural sweepstake. Nor is it to "degender" invalidism. My aim is simply to concentrate on illness and sickroom sequestration as both a male and a female phenomenon of Victorian life and literature, taking into careful account significant differences as well as strategic similarities.

In general, I have chosen not to focus on the institutional constructions and deployments of sickness and health beliefs. I have concerned myself rather with what Roy and Dorothy Porter have referred to as "the manifest *personal* meanings such concepts conveyed within the *Lebenswelt* of those espousing them"[4] in particular as they are played out within contemporary literary conventions and imperatives. The scant reference to Michel Foucault's important and influential work on medical discourse in my account of the Victorian sickroom may be attributed in part to that emphasis, as well as to its underlying assumption that personal and collective meanings can be discerned apart from their institutional construction. But there is another reason for this omission as well. Although the steady rise in the medical profession's status and advances made in medical research in the nineteenth century have been usefully adduced as factors shaping the cultural meanings ascribed to illness, it is my view that such events had relatively little impact upon the representation of illness and recovery in early and mid-Victorian fiction. The marginalization of medical knowledge and discourse in such fiction (with the exception of satirical accounts of the inefficacy and commercial competitiveness of doctors) is evidence of their subsidiary importance in the construction of the social reality of the Victorian sick person.

The nineteenth-century sick were deeply concerned with their health and often obsessed with monitoring the body's vicissitudes, but this does not argue for an earlier date than the late nineteenth century for the ascendancy in England of scientific medicine based on a medical model of disease.[5] Large numbers of Victorian sufferers found alternative therapeutic methods to those offered by orthodox medicine, and the methods of the latter were themselves highly subjective and erratic.[6] And, although by mid-century changes in medical theory and professional organization were beginning to have an effect on the bedside practitioner, English doctors were highly resistant to specialization, diagnostic technology, and the application of the discoveries of the laboratory sciences to their practice.[7] According to Christopher Lawrence, prior to World War I "English medicine was pervaded by the ethos of the gentleman, and the experimental disciplines had a hard time gaining a foothold in the pre-clinical curriculum at the bedside."[8] Moreover, these changes at the professional and theoretical level only gradually had an effect on the collective representation or traditional views of the body and self which were being reinforced or altered by other discourses, such as Evangelical Christianity. This is not to say that British authors of the period failed to incorporate scientific theories of knowledge into their representations of reality, but rather to suggest that such theories did not dominate the figuration of sickness or its structural presence in Victorian fiction.[9]

In my consideration of the overlapping of social and aesthetic concerns in the figure of the sickroom I rely heavily if uneasily on the much-contested term "realism" to make good my assertions. I am guided by what, despite the contestation, I take to be a rough consensus about many of the central premises and objectives of mid-Victorian literary realism.[10] Most important for my argument is the realist commitment to the mediation of private and public spheres, of inner psychological complexity and external circumstance, of "disparities between observed social realities and an ideal of communal wholeness."[11] In a painful paradox which is itself testimony to the extent of those disparities, invalidism provided just such a mediational function – in effect serving as the antidote for the very disorders it signified. "As the child does not know how to be cured," Rousseau writes in *Emile*, "let him know how to be ill. The one art takes the place of the other and is often more successful."[12]

CHAPTER I

Life in the sickroom

There is scarcely a Victorian fictional narrative without its ailing protagonist, its depiction of a sojourn in the sickroom. Although the twelve pivotal illnesses that traverse the length of Elizabeth Gaskell's *Ruth* may mark the upper limit, multiple sufferers are the rule rather than the exception. The Victorian sickroom scene, at its most typical, serves as a kind of forcing ground of the self – a conventional rite of passage issuing in personal, moral, or social recuperation. The scenes are precipitated by or fortuitously linked to moments of crisis during which the sufferers, or those who are called upon to minister to them, have become separated from the social roles and norms by which they previously defined themselves: Lucy Snowe in *Villette*, for instance, left alone during the long vacation without work or colleagues, without friends or family ("the insufferable thought of being no more loved, nor more owned" [*V* 15]); Pip, alone in his room, with Magwitch dying in prison, Estella married, Herbert in Cairo, and Joe and Biddy estranged ("I had no home anywhere" [*GE* 55]); Romola, in flight from Florence and her faithless husband Tito, her father and godfather dead, Savonorola, her spiritual mentor, compromised and about to be executed ("the bonds of all affection were snapped" [*R* 61]); Alton Locke wandering through the streets of London following the ignominious collapse of the Chartist rebellion and the loss of his friend and protector, Sandy Mackay ("Sullen, disappointed, desperate...careless whither I went"[1]). Isolated and incapacitated by their loss of socially determined status and in retreat from what they experience as disabling psychological conflict, these characters fall ill themselves or are urgently summoned to the sickbed of another.

The transposition of social pathologies into bodily ailment serves to reclaim these characters in crisis by initiating them into the consoling community of the sickroom. The mute, imperative claims of the body become the means of substantiating a stable, unified self and a reassuring relation to others – a relation which explicitly evokes the attachment of parent and child. Pip comes to consciousness under the loving care of Joe Gargery who makes him fancy himself "little Pip again" (*GE* 57). The convalescent Alton Locke observes Lady Ellerton's "lavish kindness" with "a sort of sleepy, passive wonder, like a new-born babe" (36). Pendennis, recovering from fever in his chambers, "felt himself environed by [his mother's] love, and thought himself almost as grateful for it as he had been when weak and helpless in childhood."[2] Although these characters are on their way to a form, however attenuated, of social reintegration there is something about that "lavish kindness," something sufficiently compelling in general about the manifest pleasures and rewards of what Thackeray called "the joys of convalescence" (*P* 52) that resists the forward energies of the recuperating self. The conventional pattern of ordeal and recovery takes on its particularly Victorian emphasis in the location of the desired condition of restored order and stability not in regained health but in a sustained condition of disability and quarantine. "I died and came to life again as a patient" as Oscar Wilde put it in an evocative tribute to the advantages of illness and to its peculiar status as the terminal rather than the transitional stage in Victorian transformations of self.[3]

The sickroom in Victorian fiction is a haven of comfort, order, and natural affection. Romola lies on her "delicious bed," accepting the choice offerings of the villagers who attend her (68). Oliver Twist is "comfortably deposited" in a bed at Mr. Brownlow's and "tended with a kindness and solicitude that knew no bounds" (*OT* 12). The invalid's diet consists of what are invariably called "dainties," such as "delicate drinks / And rare white bread."[4] Even the hospital where Maggy in *Little Dorrit* was treated for fever is able to provide its impoverished patients with lemonade and oranges, "d'licious broth and wine," and of course, "Chicking!" (*LD* i. 9). So desirable are the conditions within the sickroom walls that characters are wont to express a desire to be or to remain sick in order to have access to its benefits. Marion Erle in *Aurora Leigh* longs to "be sicker yet, if sickness made / The world so marvellous kind" (iii, 1127–1128); and Jemima in Elizabeth Gaskell's novel *Ruth* remarks wistfully to the heroine: "I almost wish I were ill, that I might make you come at once."[5] This transformation of suffering into balm is particularly striking at a time when medical science had little capacity to heal or even to alleviate the symptoms of the multitude of disorders to which people were then subject – when in many cases the treatment was far more painful and more dangerous than the disease. Moreover, despite an increasingly specific terminology for bodily ailments available to laypersons and medical professionals alike, as well as a decided preference for empirical detail in fictional representation, the diseases from which the patients suffer remain for the most part unspecified. Although there is mention of bodily wasting and delirium, of fever and contagion, the conditions of illness remain reassuringly vague, merely the occasion for the benefits they elicit and the desires they legitimate. There is, perhaps, no more notable example of the disjunction between the experience of disease and its positive representation than that provided by the fiction of Charlotte Brontë. Herself the nurse and grieving witness to the sickness and death of five of her siblings, illness in each of her novels nonetheless provides the sole access to a hallowed space of connection, of repletion, and of liberty. Although such diseases as the nervous disorders in Brontë's novels or the contagions in Dickens's register the devastations of illness upon personal and communal stability, the narrative cure for disorder is more often than not illness itself and the therapeutic situation constructed around it.

The double status of illness as both scourge and boon was not solely a convention or desideratum of fictional narrative but rather a shared cultural experience. While the pervasive concern about bodily health recorded in the memoirs and correspondence of the period often takes the form of etiological speculation, description of symptoms, advice on treatment, commiseration and complaint, there is also ample testimony to the therapeutic effects of "life in the sickroom" – to borrow the title of Harriet Martineau's popular book on the subject. "I have not been so happy or so thankful in a long time," Florence Nightingale wrote from her ailing grandmother's bedside, a remark predictive of her future life in the sickroom as an invalid of fifty years duration.[6] Writing from her father's sickroom George Eliot commented: "These will ever be the happiest days of life for me."[7] Charles Lamb extolled the privileges of the sick man in his essay "The Convalescent," declaring "that from the bed of sickness (throne let me rather call it) to the elbow chair of convalescence, is a fall from dignity, amounting to a deposition."[8] Upon her recovery from a long illness in 1843, Maria Edgeworth remarked: "I thank God not only for my recovery but for my illness... my illness was a source of more pleasure than pain to me, and that I would willingly go through all the fever and weakness to have the delight of the feelings of warm affection and the consequent unspeakable sensations of gratitude. "[9] Charles Darwin's granddaughter Gwen Raverat recalled, "[I]n my grandparents' house it was a distinction and a mournful pleasure to be ill... At Down, ill health was considered normal. "[10]

Illness has always provided compelling images and sometimes plausible explanations for conditions of the spirit, the mind, the social body, and the body politic. Although it can be defined in sociological terms as a deviation from a functional optimum,[11] illness can also register such desirable and diverse deviations as the Christian grace of affliction or the distinctiveness of a refined sensibility. Jean Comaroff writes that "illness touches upon universal paradoxes of human existence, which are mediated by particular cultural concepts and values. These paradoxes centre upon the unity, and at the same time, the duality of body and mind, the ambiguity of self as subject and object, and the opposition of natural and social being."[12] Moreover, as Roy Porter points out, illness as the object of health care provides a major focus "of social interaction, communal ritual, rites of passage, objects of consumption, calls on services, junction-points between private and public worlds,"[13] all of which could be incorporated into its range of reference. These figurative possibilities of illness necessarily shift in accordance with changes in social and cultural arrangements, as do the actual definition, recognition, treatment, and experience of disease. Medical practice and research in turn reinforce and often shape cultural norms. There is, in short, a complex interplay between cultural patterns that shape behavior within the larger society, the professional patterns and disease concepts that shape medical procedure, and the individual experience of illness – an interplay which nineteenth-century fiction drew upon and subjected to its own imperatives in its representation of illness and ministration. With this in mind and with a keen awareness of the fact that historical boundaries are often as slippery as literary categories, I would like to suggest some of the specific factors which have contributed to what I take to be the particular emphasis and significance given to the sickroom during the period with which I am concerned. I should add that some of the factors I mention below are by no means exclusive to the nineteenth century. It is their conjunction with other culturally specific concerns and social forms that led to a dominant representation of illness in the literary imagination of Victorian England.

The location of the sickroom in relation to the society for which it served as corrective example has much to do with its appositeness to pressing Victorian concerns. In contrast to the impersonal, formal, and universalizing treatment practices of twentieth-century Westernized medicine, based upon scientific knowledge and technological innovation, expressed in a language apart from everyday speech, and performed in segregated settings such as hospitals and clinics, the nineteenth-century upper and middle classes were treated at home, sometimes, though not always, by a doctor whose professional qualifications resided as much in his relations to the family, standing in the community, and personal charm as in his technical skill and knowledge.[14] According to M. Jeanne Peterson, "among laymen and medical men alike, the practitioner was judged more by who he was than by what he did."[15] A servant or member of the family was usually in constant attendance, supplemented on occasion by the presence of a hired nurse. The principal nosological methods had to do with the observation of external and subjective manifestations rather than on hidden causes and thus diagnosis was founded on the patient's own subjective account of himself and his illness. Because the causes and cure of disease were still largely unknown, treatment was idiosyncratic and highly individualized, tailored to the individual for whom it was devised as well as to the image the doctor wished to project of himself in contrast to his professional rivals.[16] Relations between sickroom attendants and patients were thus in general characterized by intimacy, informality, and shared meaning, and the experience and treatment of illness were deeply bound up with community norms and values, with the complexities of moral valuation, and with one's sense of identity, self-worth, and placement within the social order – all of these, of course, central concerns of nineteenth-century fiction. The fact that people tended to think of disease as systemic rather than localized, as well as having to do with one's body's relations to the whole environment, contributed to the increasing association of illness with issues of identity and relationship in the eighteenth and nineteenth centuries. This "holism" also dictated treatments that required comprehensive 'regimens' which sought to regulate all aspects of one's way of life[17] and thus made the literary sickroom a legitimized site for the representation of an alternative society and mode of existence.

Some scholars have argued that the very notion of the "sick person" was a development of the eighteenth and nineteenth centuries. Claudine Herzlich and Janine Pierret contend that "in the nineteenth century, and particularly with the advent of tuberculosis, the figure of the sick person crystallized existentially and socially, assuming its modern form. This figure emerged as an individual yet also, and by the same token, as a social phenomenon. Henceforth the sick person was to be defined by his or her place in society."[18] Susan Sontag has argued similarly that "it is with TB that the idea of individual illness was articulated ... and in the images that collected around the disease one can see emerging a modern idea of individuality."[19] The concept of sickness as an identity, or, as Talcott Parsons puts it, a social role,[20] found its concrete expression in the many diaries by invalids during the period, including the previously mentioned *Life in the Sick-room* by Martineau.

The rise of a new corporeal language during these two centuries also contributed to the equation between illness and the self. The emphasis on the nervous system in eighteenth-century medical science provided a vocabulary for the embodiment of an ethical consciousness, a morality based on personal sensibilities which, more often than not, issued in and was certified by physical symptoms. Illness thus became linked to desirable states of delicacy, sensibility, and personal distinction. Tuberculosis in particular was viewed as a sign of specialness, of consuming passion, genius, or beauty.[21] The explicit linking of physical condition to states of mind did much to instill or at least to corroborate the notion so amply represented in eighteenth- and nineteenth-century novels that emotional crises articulate themselves with great lucidity and promptitude on the bodies of those who experience them.

The positive cultural valuations of physical responsiveness which were derived from Enlightenment philosophy and empirical science intersected in the Victorian period with the enormously influential Evangelical idealization of morbidity. It would, I think, be difficult to overestimate the sway that the Evangelical reading of pain had over the Victorian representation of illness. Like the sentimentalists and romantics who linked disability to superiority, the Evangelicals located privilege in a condition of suffering and frailty. According to Boyd Hilton, moderate Evangelicals "regarded pain as part of God's joyous plan for the moral redemption of mankind, while pre-millenarian extremists saw it as a sign that the thousand-year reign of felicity could not be long delayed."[22] Harriet Martineau asserted during her own long illness (while still a Unitarian) that "the supposition – indispensable and, I believe, almost universal, that pain is in some way or other, ordained for, or instrumental to good – the experience of men leaves this belief uncontested, and incontestable."[23] Evangelical tract stories for children, depicting illness and death, were "interwoven into the fabric of Victorian nursery and cottage life."[24] And in popular fiction heavily imbued with the religious temper of the times, the notion of the spiritual eminence conferred by debility is represented by such characters as George Arthur in Thomas Hughes's *Tom Brown's Schooldays* or Margaret May in Charlotte Yonge's *The Daisy Chain*. Delicate, sensitive, sickly, these characters preside over the events of the novel with a moral authority and saintliness of manner for which pain is both the origin and the sign.

The Evangelical valorization of suffering coincided with the mid-Victorian domestic ideal – the care of the sick being one of the primary duties and supposedly instinctive capacities of the angel in the house. Illness thus became one of the principal objects of sentimental pieties about family life and female nurturance. Sir James Paget, distinguished Victorian doctor and surgeon-extraordinaire to Queen Victoria, exemplified this attitude, and its familiar figuration in nursing and being nursed, in a letter to a colleague: "Among Darbies and Joans, I have just heard of the chief instance: our friend John Simon's father is 97, and at last seems dying, and his wife, who is 92, cannot be persuaded to have a nurse, for she is sure that she can herself do everything for him."[25]

Nursing the sick was, for both men and women, as sanctified an act as suffering itself. As long as it was not for hire, nursing was repeatedly invoked to verify in a way no other activity apparently could the genuineness of one's affections, the essential goodness of one's character. In a characteristically Victorian adaptation of the moral assumptions underlying the previous century's cult of sensibility, the shedding of tears over human distress was not in itself sufficient to attest to one's benevolence but required instead the practical demonstration of compassion that nursing affords. In *Tom Brown's Schooldays* the virtue of George's parents, and their fidelity to each other, is put beyond dispute by their refusal to flee a town ravaged by typhus-fever in order that they could nurse the afflicted. "Arthur and his wife both caught the fever, of which he died in a few days, and she recovered, having been able to nurse him to the end, and store up his last words."[26] In Thackeray's *The Newcomes*, the bond of fellowship that unites Clive's little band of artists in Rome is confirmed by their willingness to nurse each other back to health: "If one or the other was ill, how nobly and generously his companions flocked to comfort him, took turns to nurse the sick man through nights of fever, contributed out of their slender means to help him through his difficulty."[27]

"The cult of ill-health" that Gwen Raverat describes among the elder Darwins and their many descendants was common among the middle classes despite the coexistent imperatives of self-discipline, will-power, and industriousness.[28] It is most likely that they were related phenomena. Illness authorized the relaxation of the rigidly conceived behavioral codes which governed both work and play within the public realm. And as many memoirs of the time suggest, illness suspended the often draconian measures taken to instill "character" in Victorian middle-class children.[29] The positive associations adhering to both the pleasure and the pain of illness contributed to a strong social sanction for invalidism in Victorian England. As late as the 1880s Alice James noted how much easier and more pleasant it was to be ill in England than it was in a more disapproving America.[30]

The steady expansion of empirical method into all areas of knowledge and the assignment of almost everything to an organic or material base subject to natural law (including the imitative faculty itself)[31] combined with sentimental associations to expand the pertinence and significance of illness in fictional narrative and to link it specifically to the aims and assumptions as well as the customary subject-matter of a developing realist tradition. Realism, like illness, had to do with the material conditions of character and event, with causality, with organicist models of social order, and the accumulation of significant facts subjected to reasoned observation.[32] Realistic fiction, too, posed questions about the relation of mind to body, the individual to the collective, and sought to address itself to the crucial experiences of ordinary life. The language of realism also aspired to the conditions of illness insofar as its referential capacities resided in the most immediate and demonstrable way in the material world. The notion that a sick person's gestures are immediately apprehensible to the nurse frequently provided Victorian novelists with an enviable contrast to the failures of language outside the sickroom context. Moreover, the prescriptions realism provided in relation to the regulation of personal conduct were similar to the sanctions imposed by ill-health or seen as requisite to good health – the moderation of appetites, self-denial, patience, and quiet endurance. The link between realism and illness, specifically between the realist author and the medical man, is made explicit in George Eliot's description of Lydgate in *Middlemarch* who, "enamoured of that arduous invention which is the very eye of research...wanted to pierce the obscurity of those minute processes which prepare human misery and joy" (ii, 16): or Dickens's Physician in *Little Dorrit* who "really has an acquaintance with us as we are, who is admitted to some of us every day with our wigs and paint off, who hears the wanderings of our minds, and sees the undisguised expression of our faces" (ii, 25). These equations of the doctor and author also point up the intersection between the procedures of scientific analysis and the fundamental truths of experience and identity that characterized both the aims of realism and the ambitions if not the actuality of Victorian medical practice.

As I have attempted briefly to suggest here, despite the manifest emphasis of the Victorian sickroom on the simple gratifications of infancy, its recuperative power in fact rests upon the extraordinary inclusiveness of its significations and upon its consequent ability both to register and to appear to reconcile contemporary social conflicts and formal disjunctions within the "natural" domain of bodily process and exigent circumstance. If, in my portrayal of the sickroom as a kind of utopian order, I seem to ignore the real terrors of illness, it should be stressed that the positive connotations I outline cannot be separated from the pervasiveness of sickness and death in the lives of most Victorians. The widespread ravages of disease, particularly before the advent of bacteriology, provided the context for imagining crucial life events and forms of self-perception so persistently within the idiom of illness. In a way, the representation of the sickroom as haven provided remedial therapy for pain itself – a strategy for presenting and containing the awful and ever-present fear of physical vulnerability. In general, however, the sickroom registers the powerful desire for coherence at a time when economic, political, and social relations were undergoing profound reorganization and differentiation. Illness in the predominantly realistic fiction of the era enjoined a therapeutics of self that mediated what seemed at least to be the increasingly acute gap between inner and outer experience, between self and other, or, in terms appropriate to realist fiction, between experience and language.

There is a scene in Robert Louis Stevenson's *Dr. Jekyll and Mr. Hyde*, that reputed compendium of all things Victorian, which neatly exemplifies the invocation of malady to ensure the cohesiveness of realist narrative in the face of its own disintegrative tendencies. Jekyll's butler, Poole, has summoned Mr. Utterson, his master's lawyer and old friend, because Jekyll has been sequestered in his laboratory for weeks but for an occasional masked excursion to the anatomical theater to rummage through old crates from the chemist. His voice has altered and the only communication he has had with his domestic staff is the urgent issuing of prescriptions for a drug which on arrival never seems to satisfy. Jekyll, as we know, has been experimenting with the possibility of separating the two sides of man's nature in order to end what he calls "the perennial war among the members"[33] – those conflicts between self-denial and self-indulgence which so thoroughly pervaded, even constituted the Victorian notion of selfhood. Jekyll attributes his concentration on dual rather than multiple consciousness to the early stage of scientific research on the matter. "I hazard the guess," he writes to Utterson, "that man will be ultimately known for a mere polity of multifarious, incongruous and independent denizens" (70). At the point in the story to which I am referring, Jekyll is unable, for pharmaceutical reasons among others, to recover his Jekyll self – the self-denying professional – and in the form of Hyde seeks desperately for the compound which will restore him to his former condition. Utterson, confronted with a set of bizarre circumstances indicating a confusion of identities for which there seems to be no reasonable explanation, evinces a theory that he finds acceptable. Jekyll is ill, he contends, with some obscure malady. Such an ailment could conceivably alter the voice, require the use of a mask to conceal deformity, dictate Jekyll's sequestration, and explain the desperate search for a miracle drug. He concludes: "There is my explanation; it is sad enough, Poole, ay, and appalling to consider; but it is plain and natural, hangs well together and delivers us from all exorbitant alarms" (52).

As Stevenson (I like to think) must have been aware, Utterson's desiderata for an acceptable explanation are among the principal attributes of nineteenth-century realist narrative whose primary subject-matter, like Utterson's, is the problem of identity. It should be plain and natural; that is, it should eschew the supernatural, the fantastic, and the mysterious, associated with romance and gothic forms in favor of the plausible, the normative, or, as George Eliot famously put it in *Adam Bede*, "the faithful representing of commonplace things" (17); it should, moreover, "hang well together," that is, it should have a coherent structure, a causal sequence of events, and conform to notions of psychological unity and intelligibility; and finally, it should deliver us from all exorbitant alarms. It should, in other words, avoid excess and extremity, that which cannot be incorporated within a cohesive and totalizable system. Most important, the reassuring explanation that sustains these attributes is organic illness. It is precisely the function of illness, paradoxically, to ensure the cogency and coherence, the explanatory force and naturalness of realistic narrative as it confronts "the polity of multifarious, incongruous and independent denizens" of the supposedly single self – to call a truce, in other words, in "the perennial war among [its] members." If *Jekyll and Hyde* were a realist novel, not only would Utterson be right in his diagnosis, but he would become Jekyll's nurse rather than the precipitating cause of his death.

Scenes of illness intervene when narratives reach an impasse which cannot be overcome without the violation of accepted social and formal codes, and offer their particular solace, their plain and natural account of what would otherwise belie the progressive developmental theories of the Victorian social organism, and the concomitant aesthetics of continuity and closure. Elizabeth Ermarth has designated as "the important constant in realistic fiction" the maintenance of a tension between "the centrifugal forces of multiplicity, variety, disparity, ambiguity" with "centripetal forces of centering, rationalizing, synchronizing motive. Concordable differences always exist to be overcome."[34] Leo Bersani presents a slightly different perspective on the same tension: "The realistic novelist desperately tries to hold together what he recognizes quite well is falling apart."[35] The experience of a loss of inner and outer forms of self-definition which always precedes the Victorian hero or heroine's collapse into bodily crisis registers the incoherence at the heart of the narrative's ordering enterprise, its attempt to give shape to the dispersal of meaning and possibility it has engendered through its own particularizing, exploratory method as well as to the competing personal imperatives which register themselves in formal terms as problems of character formation and causality. Illness inserts itself as a form of absolute obligation – the usurpation on somatic and sentimental grounds of the moral and aesthetic issues which are both figured and elided by the narrative enclave of the sickroom. The protagonist's reemergence within the sickroom's privileged confines, with its alternative but congruent set of circumstances, gestures, and relationships, its rich contextual and figural allusiveness, and its ability to refer to other episodes within the main narrative, restores the desired coherence, or, at least, finds a place for it in narrative, but always, it needs to be emphasized, at the expense of those principles it attempts to shore up. The concept of a significantly structured identity developing in progressive stages within an established social order is represented by the violation of that concept and the narrative principles that underwrite it – through separation, suspension, and discontinuity.

The sickroom scene of necessity recalls or directly leads to that more famous Victorian *mise-en-scène* of high drama and ultimate meanings – the deathbed. It is from the perilous proximity to death that illness gains much of its affective force. But though it borrows heavily upon the awesome prospect of death, the scene of illness derives as much of its significance from the prospect of eventual recovery. John Kucich has noted that deathbed scenes are themselves part of "a larger movement toward recovery and completion." Death in Dickens, for instance, is represented as a passage to a "superior kind of integration."[36] The sickroom scene seeks instead to establish an earthly paradigm of such integration in the consolations of a known world. As such it fits more comfortably within the anti-metaphysical thrust of the realist mode, providing on the very boundaries of a possible transcendence a communal sanction for realism's moral affirmations. It better suits the concomitant mimetic bias of realism as well. If, as Garrett Stewart contends, "death in fiction aspires beyond mimesis,"[37] illness in fiction might be said to aspire to its restitution, the location of a redemptive form and content in the certainties of the organic.

This is not to say that the sickroom always stops short of death's solicitations or that it necessarily shuts down the otherworldly yearnings that the deathbed scenes so openly display. In its suggestive proximity to death and its frequent juxtaposition with deathbed scenes within one narrative, the sickroom rewrites for the human and the secular death's (uncertain) promise of wholeness and redress. Dick Swiveller's illness recapitulates Little Nell's suffering and death and retrieves its promise of fulfillment in a convalescent abundance of nourishment and love. *Ruth* reverses the sequence by presenting a narrative pattern of successive sickroom scenes which sustains the conditions under which the fallen heroine can find solace and indemnity until she is beatified at last by death. The unacknowledged pressure of a personal loss, a desire to stage the resuscitation of the beloved dead, may also be discerned in many of these scenes.[38] Preeminently a strategy for survival, the sickroom combines a reassuring sense of closure with the sustained possibility of sequence continually deferred.

THE CONSOLATIONS OF DEBILITY

Harriet Martineau calls the sickroom "a separate region of human experience" (125) and any investigation of the solace it provides must begin with that separate status. Separation is the basis of its function as a structural principle in the narratives in which it figures and of the set of oppositional categories or imperatives that it integrates, formally if not experientially. At the most general level the psychic and narrative space that the sickroom provides affords redress from the struggles exacted by the largely, but not solely, middle-class Victorian insistence on the primacy of duty over personal inclination. No matter how ambivalent the Victorians may have been about the community in whose interest they were called upon to subordinate their own ambitions and desires, and no matter what the evident personal cost of such subordination, the connection must be affirmed, an accommodation made. Literary and visual artists were expected to, and for the most part did, endorse the official ethic and thus, perforce, participated in its rigors by virtue of the check on their own imaginative range and inclinations. The tensions revealed so often in their relation to their own material and audience reflect the more personal struggles involved in such a task, struggles often movingly documented in their correspondence. The emphasis on consensus and community and the corresponding strain of asserting connections in the face of what seemed to be increasing fragmentation, made separation and connection the principal structural elements and thematic issues in Victorian narrative – issues that the sickroom and the therapeutic state were particularly suited to address.

First, the separation and seclusion of the patient within the sickroom and the sickroom from the household at large constitutes an accommodation of private and public claims. It offers a form of protection from the discontinuities of experience and frustrations of communal life which is nonetheless sanctioned by the accepted customs and treatment procedures of the community. Physical debility is itself a form of deviation from group norms, which instead of incurring opprobrium entitles the sufferer to sympathy, tenderness, and even respect.[39] It also calls into being an alternative community within the sickroom confines. It is, as Talcott Parsons has written, "a very strategic expression of deviance."[40] While on the one hand sickness elicits the reinscription of cultural norms and conceptual orders through the process of healing, at the same time it can implicitly challenge their validity or normative status.[41] The Victorian sickroom offers a critique of the status quo, in part, by offering an ideal social and personal order within a condition of affliction and marginality. In a sense this inverts Parsons's notion that illness constitutes an assertion of the self over the collective by representing the sickroom as the arena for the performance of the values and obligations that institutionalized roles and social expectations obscure or distort. In the narratives of the period, both fictional and non-fictional, to enter the sickroom is to gain entrance to a privileged sanctuary where one participates in a natural social order, a condition of spontaneous being and moral grace. "The invalid's room had an atmosphere of peace and encouragement which affected all who entered it," Gaskell writes of one of the many sickrooms in *Ruth* (36). Noting the attenuations of rank and intellect in the sickroom, Martineau comments, "in our retreat, moral considerations are all in all" (*LSR* 100). "Untruth, double-dealing, and selfish policy – assume so disgusting an aspect when tested by the trying light and amidst the solemn leisure of the sick-room" (*LSR* 186). "Within the four walls where the stir and glare of the world are shut out," writes George Eliot in "Janet's Repentance," "where a human being lies prostrate, thrown on the tender mercies of his fellow, the moral relation of man to man is reduced to its utmost clearness and simplicity...As we bend over the sick-bed, all the forces of our nature rush towards the channels of pity, of patience, and of love" (24). It is not the least of the appeals of the sickroom that what is exacted from one outside its walls – "patience," "pity," and "love," for instance – becomes not only possible, but irresistible in response to the unsolicited urgencies of illness, even, as is the case in Eliot's story, towards an abusive husband. In her *Notes from Sick Rooms*, Julia (Mrs.

Leslie) Stephen remarks that "the ordinary relations between the sick and the well are far easier and pleasanter than between the well and the well."[42]

The rhetoric of "inside" versus "outside" that structures these and other testimonials to the privileged nature of sickroom relations is reminiscent of the mid-Victorian endorsement of separate spheres – the sanctity, peace, and moral rectitude of home life versus the competitive struggles and ethical ambiguities of the public world. The family was presented by social theorists as a central conceptual model of social order and reform, whose exemplary status was predicated paradoxically on its incommensurability, its absolute separation from the competitive principles and rough justice of the marketplace.[43] The novelists incorporated this already problematic model into their representation of social conflict, but with the added complication of having to ground their closing affirmations in a familial harmony which they show to be implausible. As Janet Dempster's relations with her abusive, alcoholic husband in "Janet's Repentance" show, domestic life could be every bit as brutal, every bit as subject to antagonistic interests as the public sphere. The harmonious, benign, and mutually cooperative sphere of the sickroom intervenes upon the structural tensions this social and familial dissonance produces to negotiate the rifts both within and between the public and private arenas. "Within the four walls where the stir and glare of the world are shut out" Janet is able to reestablish (in the brief space before her husband dies) her marriage ties and affections.

Often, rather than reuniting kin, illness summons a society suited to one's own specifications and substitutes for the coercions of blood and marriage a physical tie as voluntary as friendship and as essential as survival. This ability to invent a new family for oneself through illness, to replace the betrayals of the old, is sometimes literalized when the ideal community which arises in response to the illness of the protagonist turns out to be family after all. Mary and Diana Rivers, who nurse Jane Eyre back to health, turn out to be long-lost cousins and replace the loathsome Reed sisters as her next of kin. A character's illness sometimes effects a more congenial alignment of familial allegiances. In Charlotte Yonge's *The Daisy Chain*, for instance, Margaret, the eldest sister who has lapsed into a lingering illness after the carriage accident that killed her mother, is reluctant to be moved from her sickroom to the "family-room," for she would be "giving up that monopoly of her father in his evenings, which had been her great privilege. "[44] (Access to fathers is a frequent incentive to invalidism in the Victorian novel.) Actual sufferers often found the creation of small, select societies around their bedsides to be one of the greatest advantages of illness. Florence Nightingale replaced the mother and sister with whom she had such a stormy relationship with the troops she called her children, and by a series of loyal friends who cared for her in her invalid state. One of Martineau's biographers notes that "she created for herself the perfect hospice, managed by her nieces and devoted maidservants, who wrote letters at her dictation, and filtered the flow of sometimes unwanted visitors."[45] Although the demarcation of public and private realms worked to confine women within the home, it is a little-noted irony that domiciliary privacy was, for many women, not private enough. Home was, in fact, something of a public thoroughfare requiring constant attendance upon visitors and family. The sickroom was often the only available room of one's own. Florence Nightingale reports in *Cassandra* that "A married woman was heard to wish that she could break a limb that she might have a little time to herself."[46]

Despite its separation from the more taxing demands of fellowship, the sickroom is still located in the domestic center of Victorian life and is thus intimately related to the social processes and expectations from which its own customs and rules of association and conduct deviate. As such it is set squarely within the domain of domestic realism and yet legitimizes a departure from the characteristic emphases associated with that mode of representation. Julia Stephen mentions with approval the absence in the sickroom of "the details that make familiar intercourse difficult."[47] George Eliot notes in "Janet's Repentance" that "here in the sickroom there are no self-questionings, no weighing of consequences"; and Harriet Martineau cites among the "gains and sweets of invalidism" the "extinction of concern" about "the ordinary objects of life" and "the abolition of the future, of our own future in this life" (*LSR* 197). The sickroom marginalizes, in other words, the requisite attributes of mimetic realism – the significance of details (in particular the details that make familiar intercourse difficult), of causal relations, of ordinary life, and of temporal sequence, while still invoking them by its very nature. It is a metonymic substitution which effectively eliminates that which it purportedly represents. The conditions of illness invoke, for instance, the issue of causality so crucial to the development of character and event in realist fiction and at the same time suspend it as a meaningful way of sorting out experience. The strong link in mid-Victorian medical understanding between mind and body and the repeated association of bodily process with organicist theories of social and self-development permits the etiology of disease to substitute for the chains of causation, of circumstance, and motivation that, as we have seen in *Jekyll and Hyde*, threaten to deliver even more undesirable effects than the sad, but plain and natural, conditions of bodily infirmity – to deliver, for instance, such exorbitant alarms as the uncontrolled eruption of sexual desire, an irremediable break with family or community, or an inassimilable division in self-perception. Sickness signifies the disablement such alarms presage, but forestalls their narrative consequences by displacing rupture to bodily process.

Illness not only substitutes the sick body for the troubled self, but becomes a way of accommodating desires which are not legitimated in the society at large. Alienation, as we have seen, can be redrawn as solidarity, and the antithetical forces of desire and repression can be brought into accord, the disintegrative potential inherent in each term made benign. Dr. Jekyll's project to separate once and for all the appetitive, dispersive self from the self-denying productive self is obviated by the natural restraint and legitimated hungers of the sick body. The disciplining of desire through institutional and internal-ized systems of constraint can thus be suspended in the sickroom without leaving its inhabitants vulnerable to the disruptive effects of their unbounded appetites. In an ironic reversal of Victorian mores and the anxieties they are meant to dispel, appetitive energies are limited only by organic capacity. The body thus becomes the regulatory mechanism of its own impulses, its requirements and limitations determining the extent of its gratifications. Florence Nightingale's dictum that "a patient wants according to his wants,"[48] must have seemed an exhilarating license to people who were repeatedly abjured to want according to the wants of others, or, in some cases, not to want at all. In Mr. Tryan's sickroom in "Janet's Repentance" for instance, Janet's "dark watchful eyes detected every want...and supplied the want with ready hand" (27); in *Great Expectations*, Pip notes that Joe's tenderness is "beautifully appor-tioned to my needs" (57).

Sickroom wants are not necessarily meager. Pendennis's illicit appetite for the lower-class Fanny Bolton is transposed to a convalescent hunger applauded by his own mother: "His appetite

was something frightful... He was like an ogre in devouring" (53);
and Dick Swiveller in *The Old Curiosity Shop*, made feverish by the
abuse of his appetites, now finds in his convalescence an almost
magical gratification of those appetites under the rubric of "delicate
restoratives:" "Behold! There stood a strong man, with a mighty
hamper, which... disgorged such treasures of tea, and coffee, and
wine, and rusks, and oranges, and grapes, and fowls ready trussed for
boiling, and calves-foot jelly, and arrow-root, and sago... Mr.
Swiveller... was fain to lie down and fall asleep again from sheer
inability to entertain such wonders in his mind" (64). Illness, it would
seem, is the sole medium through which fulfillment can keep pace
with desire.

The rigid inhibition of physical and emotional exposure in the
Victorian era is also suspended in the sickroom, which thus becomes
a privileged site of untroubled intimacy while staying within the
moderating decorum of social propriety and realist convention. If
private practices were far more various and indulgent than the
popular image of Victorianism has always led us to believe,[49] there is
no doubt that social and moral codes were strictly enforced in public,
and even more strictly so in fiction. Discourses of sexuality may have
been more widely dispersed and diversified during this period, but for
the average member of respectable middle-class society, "mum" was
the word. Gwen Raverat writes, "For nearly seventy years the
English middle classes were locked up in a great fortress of unreality
and pretence; and no one who has not been brought up inside the
fortress can guess how thick the walls were, or how little of the sky
outside could be seen through the loopholes."[50] Within the sickroom,
however, intimacy of expression, like the appetites it threatens to
unleash, is kept in check by the natural restraint of debility and at the
same time made obligatory by it. The sickroom, writes Martineau, "is
a natural confessional, where the spontaneous revelations are perhaps
as ample as any enforced disclosures from disciple to priest, and
without any of the mischiefs of enforcement... [I]t is scarcely possible
that in any other circumstances we could have known so much" (*LSR*
211). (Martineau's connection [and distinction] between the sickroom and the Catholic confessional is dramatized in *Villette* when the
inadequacy of confessing to a priest gives way to Lucy Snowe's
remedial revelations on her sickbed at La Terrasse.)

In the sickroom confidences are exchanged, clothes removed or
readjusted, soothing caresses administered to aching limbs, and basic

wants given utterance – all of this within the bedroom turned sickroom, a site suggestive of the intimacies which these activities both disguise and express. The confluence of Evangelical and sentimental associations with illness comes most fully into play in the complex negotiation of physical and emotional needs with the strict propriety governing their expression. Sexual passion is transformed into what Charlotte Brontë calls in *Villette* "the passion of solicitude" (23) and to the bodily intensities of convalescence, while still retaining its erotic suggestiveness. As Kingsley's Alton Locke says of his convalescence from fever, "the fury of passion had been replaced by the most delicious weakness" (36). In a phrase that captures the balance these scenes attempt to achieve, Trollope describes Lily Dale as "seated in that half-dignified and half-luxurious state which belongs to the first getting up of an invalid."[51] The association of conventions of female beauty and sensuality with the symptoms of ill-health allowed the latter to refer surreptitiously to the former. As Jean Strouse notes in her biography of Alice James: "a graceful languor, pallor, and vulnerability – even to the point of illness – were seen as enhancing the female form. 'Refinement' drew attention away from the base, ordinary body; illness delicately drew it back."[52] The erotic possibilities of the female invalid were more overtly promoted in the latter years of the century by George Du Maurier's hugely successful *Trilby*, for instance, or by Eliza Linton's suggestion in *The Girl of the Period* that ill-health properly manifested in "fragility" and "the long, loose folds of falling drapery" can revive marital passion: "Many a drifting husband has been brought back to his first enthusiasm by the illness of a wife who knew how to turn evil things into good, and to extract a charm even out of suffering."[53]

The patient and nurse in Victorian fiction are sometimes would-be lovers whose union outside the sickroom has been prevented or troubled by the instabilities of undisciplined or misdirected passion. Amy Dorrit and Arthur Clenham, Jane Eyre and Rochester, Lizzie and Eugene Wrayburn, Aurora and Romney Leigh are just a few of the couples who are permitted the intimacy of sickroom relations. The union established under the secluded and prescriptive conditions of the sickroom is offered as a model of exchange upon which a compatible marriage or a resumption of relations might be founded, and, significantly enough, the terms on which it might be sustained. Ruth says of the man who abandoned her, "I don't think I should love him, if he were well and happy, but you said he was ill – and alone –" (4). And Dickens, writing to John Forster about his impending separation from his wife Catherine, avowed that "if I were sick or disabled tomorrow, I know how sorry she would be, and how deeply grieved myself, to think how we had lost each other. But exactly the same incompatibility would arise, the moment I was well again."[54] The nurse–patient bond effectively supplants marriage as the preferred means to formal closure and societal consolidation. Nurses and patients may be parents and children, masters and servants, husbands and wives, lover and friends, but these particularized forms of relationship are subsumed under the generic roles and functions which illness prescribes. The nurse–patient relation preserves and intensifies the significance of familial and communal ties, but refigures them as immune to the economic, political, or sexual considerations that complicate and distort those ties outside of the sickroom enclave. Essentially the sickroom registers an image of social relations which requires forms of withdrawal as the principle mode of accommodation.[55] Sickness provides a position from which one can disinvest oneself from what are perceived as constraining or inauthentic roles and express feelings and essential truths about the undisfigured self. The physician "really has an acquaintance with us as we are," Dickens wrote; he "sees the undisguised expression of our faces." This is a form of romanticism as well as a dictum, as I suggested earlier, about the power of realism to lay us bare. The sick people of Victorian fiction are a bit like the rustics of Wordsworth's *Preface* with their "simple and unelaborated expressions." In a manner that discloses a central problem with which realism sought to contend, natural being takes over from social being as that which is most fully, if mutely, expressive of the self.

Despite such figures of compassion, decency, and romantic interest as Dr. Woodcourt in *Bleak House*, Dr. Crofts in *Small House at Allington*, and Lydgate in *Middlemarch* the nurse (the voluntary not the hired nurse) rather than the doctor is the primary caregiver in the sickroom scenes and an equal beneficiary with the patient of their salutary effects. The doctor was an intermittent visitor at the patient's bedside and his interest in his patients is most frequently shown to be determined by material considerations of profit, reputation, or the assertion of professional authority. He is, in any case, too firmly entrenched in the often divisive class and communal relations of his practice to serve as a socially cohesive force. Purportedly come to heal, the doctor brings to bear upon this most intimate and emotionally charged area of human experience the same contaminating aspects which are seen as infecting society as a whole. "The doctor's estimate, even of a confiding patient," George Eliot notes in "Janet's Repentance," "was apt to rise and fall with the entries in the day-book; and I have known Mr. Pilgrim to discover the most unexpected virtues in a patient seized with a promising illness" (2). If the eye for gain subverts the healing process of the sickroom, "the eye of research," for which Eliot commends Lydgate, is at once too penetrating and too remote to serve its reconciliatory purpose. The exclusion of the doctor's gaze from the sickroom signifies an attempt to place the body outside of the power and knowledge relations that, as Foucault puts it, "invest human bodies and subjugate them by turning them into objects of knowledge."[56] In *Jane Eyre* St. John Rivers looks on at the sobbing Jane "like a physician watching with the eye of science an expected and fully understood crisis in a patient's malady" (34). Dr. John in *Villette* is stigmatized for his "dry, materialist views" and for his purely scientific interest in disease. Perhaps the doctor is, in the main, an inappropriate participant in the sickroom exchange precisely because his area of expertise too accurately mirrors the Victorian novelists' own methods, whose disintegrative effects the sickroom is called upon to heal.

The relations between nurse and patient, on the other hand, are portrayed as tender, reciprocal, and mutually constitutive. Unlike the doctor who diagnoses and prescribes, the function of the nurse is to comfort and to serve. In Western culture nursing has long been associated with the maternal role – with affection, intimacy, compassion, and tendance.[57] The interaction between the nurse and patient in Victorian fiction is characterized by a combination of submission and authority, self-abnegation, and self-assertion, with the sick body providing the mediating term by which these apparent opposites can be simultaneously expressed and reconciled, and their destructive aspects neutralized. The patient asserts the fact of self through her physical debility, asserts her claim to attention and recognition, and to a degree of command – without incurring the guilt or risking the dangers inherent in self-promotion. Lily Dale, a social nonentity as a jilted lover, may "say whatever she likes till she gets well" (44:163). "To be sick," writes Charles Lamb, "is to enjoy monarchical prerogatives."[58] At the same time, the patient can relinquish the responsibility for determining his own action and allegiances without falling victim, as is so often the case in these novels, to false or oppressive authorities. Alton Locke, whose fever has drawn about him a little society of "tender and careful nurses" surrenders to feelings of "infinite submission" (36). The same dynamic holds true for the nurse who subordinates herself to the patient's needs and at the same time guides both his conduct and the disposition of his person. Both of these aspects of the nurse's role are exemplified in *Ruth*. One nursing figure's "senses seemed to have passed into the invalid and to feel only as he felt" (7), while another "reigned sole power and potentate in Ruth's little chamber" (11). The nurse both serves and authorizes the patient's assertion of being, and in so doing, her own. It is a fundamental assertion of this study that the nurse and patient are two sides of the same self, that, in effect, the subjectivity of illness and the psychology of nursing are one in their accommodation of conflicting allegiances within the secluded intimacies of sickroom relations. The identity between these roles in Victorian fiction is evidenced by the exchange (sometimes the repeated exchange) of nurse–patient roles between one pair of characters (Diana Warwick and Emma Dunstane in Meredith's *Diana of the Crossways*, Charley and Esther Summerson in *Bleak House*, Shirley Keeldar and Louis Moore in Brontë's *Shirley*, Janet Dempster and the Reverend Tryan in "Janet's Repentance"), or the constant shifting from one role to another by a single character (Caroline Helstone, Ruth Hilton, and Romola.)

Despite my studied attempt to assign gender randomly to the nurses and patients of my discussion above, these roles and the nature of the conflicts they adjudicate are inescapably related to the social roles and modes of self-presentation that are primarily associated with women. "Every woman is a nurse," wrote Florence Nightingale at the beginning of her enormously popular how-to book *Notes on Nursing*.[59] She could as easily have stated as her cultural given that every woman is a patient. It is by now a familiar paradox that women were expected to be capable, efficient caretakers of children and home, and yet were considered to be inherently dependent, weak, unstable, even childlike – captive to the tyrannical delicacy of their reproductive systems.[60] "[N]ineteenth-century culture seems to have actually admonished women to *be* ill," Susan Gubar and Sandra Gilbert have contended.[61]

M. Jeanne Peterson has argued that endemic physical and mental illness was far from the Victorian female norm,[62] but as Caroline Helstone in *Shirley* and Janet Dempster both discover, sickness or the nursing of sickness, in the home or among the neighboring poor, were two primary modes of self-expression and activity available to women of the middle and upper classes. Henrietta Litchfield, daughter of Charles Darwin, emulated both her father and her mother by being respectively patient and nurse. Because she was a lady, "she had nothing on which to spend her unbounded affection and energy, except the management of her house and husband; as it was, ill-health became her profession and absorbing interest."[63] "Professional work," Ann Douglas explains, "was hardly a socially acceptable escape from a lady's situation, but sickness, that very nervous condition brought on by the frustrations of her life was."[64] Carroll Smith-Rosenberg has described how hysteria functioned as a "socially accepted sick role" which provided middle-class women with relief from discontinuities in the ideal of womanhood.[65] In her discussion of women of the landed gentry in the nineteenth century, Jessica Gerard takes note of the other means of escape "from the isolation, self-abnegation, and conformity of domestic roles... the traditional duty of tending to the sick, elderly, and destitute on a personal basis."[66] Caring for the sick was not always an escape, however. The duty of unmarried women to nurse their ailing relatives at the expense of other aspirations or desires was frequently a source of great unhappiness and privation.[67] However different they may have seemed on the face of it, both nurse and patient roles confined women within the same restricted sphere and evinced in their different ways the disabling of the potentialities of the self to which their sex so often condemned them.

Women, nonetheless, repeatedly pressed the roles of patient and nurse into the service of contending against the very limitations they signified. It is precisely this paradox that makes the sickroom possible as an arena for representing a social order more amenable to female desires, and in general to mediate opposing cultural and personal imperatives. As a realm of freedom fashioned from the materials of restriction, it mediates what are essentially conflicting desires – to go beyond one's designated and restrictive social role and the largely internalized injunction to renounce that desire, to give voice to aggressive impulses and to stifle those impulses in the name of the society that elicited them. Again and again in works by women of the period, illness occurs when the desire to reject the characteristics and narrow range of functions considered appropriate for women threatens a profound loss of identity, whereas to accept them as conventionally defined would result in a return to frustration and self-attenuation. The miming of the customary constraints on women's lives in order to secure some power over them is a particularly disturbing version of the compromises that characterize the sickroom cure and the combination of complicity and resistance, subjugation and subversion by which people in general contend with conflict.

The sickroom in Victorian fiction does not extend the range of possibilities made available to women, but rather figures an expansion of the significance of nurses' and patients' roles in the construction of a just society and in the determination of their own fate, while still remaining within the codes of conduct deemed suitable to them.[68] This coincides with the essentialist feminism of the period which, in the words of Nancy Cott, articulated "a social power based on [women's] special female qualities rather than on general human rights."[69] In Elizabeth Barrett Browning's *Aurora Leigh*, Aurora nurses the once autocratic, now blind and wasted Romney, and with him, his campaign for a better, more equitable world. Lady Ellerton's larger healing ministry in *Alton Locke* is represented in the narrative by her nursing of the shattered hero. The heroic nurse was a common figure in novels by mid-Victorian women both before and after the Crimean War brought Florence Nightingale such celebrity. The reasons for the imaginative appeal of such figures are not hard to find. The nurse's duties outside the home corresponded to the male middle-class ideal of public service and yet could be seen as an extension of a woman's household tasks. The nurse embodies feminine ideals of compassion and self-abnegation, "doing" for others at the expense of her own vital powers but, at the same time, nursing puts her in a position of authority which may be openly exercised under the aegis of a uniquely feminine power. "Nursing," Nightingale wrote, "is the only case, queens not excepted, where a woman is really in charge of men."[70] Eliza Linton noted that nursing "pleasantly reverses the usual order of things, and gives into [women's] hands Hercules twirling a distaff the wrong way, and fettered by the length of his skirts."[71] And, at some level, even more appealing perhaps for women of the leisure classes was the overt, even publicly acknowledged sense in which lives, specifically male lives, depended on the execution of female duties which in the ordinary course of events were, according to Nightingale, mere "conventional frivolities" if not "bad habits."[72]

The plots of these novels follow a similar pattern of development. A woman leaves home often explicitly having broken communal and kinship ties and ends up ministering to multitudes, very often in a foreign land. Eliot's Romola, for instance, who flees the various men in her life who have negated her being and stifled her capacities for knowledge and achievement (or, for that matter, for pleasure) ends up in a plague-ridden village whose inhabitants she nurses back to health before falling ill herself. The "right to resist" that she finally claims for herself when she flees is immediately recuperated as self-sacrifice in an emotional economy that allows no surplus of self-delighting energy or release other than "the joys of convalescence." When she falls ill as a result of her exertions on behalf of others a loving and grateful community gathers about to nurse and comfort her. In Elizabeth Gaskell's *Ruth*, the seamstress seduced, impregnated, and abandoned by her upper-class lover expiates her sin by single-handedly nursing a hospital full of typhus patients, and becomes in the process a saintly figure who helps to heal social divisions. Harriet Martineau's *The Sickness and Health of the People of Blaeburn* recounts in fictional form the story of Mary Pickard, an American women, who nursed the population of an English village stricken with fever. She is referred to by the villagers as "The Good Lady" and leaves behind a legacy of moral and hygienic probity.[73] Each of these heroines, having exhausted herself in the service of others, becomes a patient in turn, thus assuring her return to the dependency and incapacity that mark her as female and initiating her return to private life and familial obligation. The reversion from nursing to being nursed has, however, its own compensations and in imaginative form at least achieves the reconciliation of the opposed desires to command and submit, to withdraw and connect, to authorize self-promotion and exact self-denial more effectively. The assertion of the materiality of the body through organic illness also had the power to negate the social body and its often punitive, always constricting cultural and customary dispositions – among them marriage and child-rearing.

Florence Nightingale is in many ways an exemplary figure both as the legendary Lady of the Lamp in Scutari and as the woman struggling to free herself from social, familial, and self- antagonism by nursing and being nursed. The convergence of roles in her life underscores their equivalence and the nature of the conflicts they seek to reconcile. In briefly tracing her career my intention is to demonstrate my earlier assertion that the use of illness to transform the given and to heal self-division continually crosses the boundary between the literary and the actual, and that those who incorporated the consolations of debility into their narrative structures as a principle of coherence were drawing upon the available symbolic structures at work in the social life around them. Furthermore, Florence Nightingale's experience, and its public representation, palpably contributed for good and ill to the shaping of those structures. Recent interest in Nightingale's life and writings among contemporary feminists suggests that "the Immortal Florence" continues to offer a compelling image of the vicissitudes of female ambition and desire.

FLORENCE NIGHTINGALE AND THE NEGATION OF THE BODY

On the opening page of her biography of Nightingale, Cecil Woodham-Smith writes, "It would have been better if Florence had been a boy."[74] Woodham-Smith's remark, in context, relates to the complications attached to the property of Nightingale's father, which, if Florence had been male, would have remained in the family rather than passing to her aunt and then to her aunt's eldest son. The comment, of course, is true in a more significant way than this, although the descent of property through the male line and with it the power such property confers is centrally at issue. Nightingale possessed, from an early age, a conviction of her own greatness, but, as a woman, she had no appropriate sphere within which to exercise her powers. Bound by laws excluding women from political and economic life, by conventions limiting them to the performance of social duties and the fulfillment of family obligations, and by the moral rigor with which she judged her own motives and actions, she suffered through long years of frustration attempting to discover a vocation that would free her from these checks on her ambition while still satisfying their claims upon her conscience. She wrote from her ailing grandmother's bedside: "Only think of the happiness of working, and working successfully too, and with no doubts as to his path, and no alloy of vanity or love of display or glory, but with the ecstasy of single-heartedness."[75] As the site of this remark indicates, she found a temporary respite from her conflicts in the nursing of illness – an overriding duty to which she could gratefully submit without incurring the guilt of self-initiated action. Like Romola, who longs to "be freed from the burden of choice" by "new necessities" (61), Nightingale longed "for some strong thing to sweep this loathsome life into the past" (W-S, 49). Nightingale ultimately translated this refuge from her hunger for accomplishment and her family's resistance to it into a clear sense of vocation sanctioned, according to Nightingale, by God Himself. After a protracted struggle with her mother and her sister Parthenope, during which illness was employed liberally by all parties in the advancement of their own interests, she began at the age of thirty-two the career that would send her to Scutari and the embrace of legend.

In becoming a nurse Nightingale was defying not only her family but also societal conventions and expectations. The wealthy and well-connected Nightingale was expected to make a brilliant social success, to marry well, and to bear children, not to immure herself in the sordid world of hospitals for the destitute or in the battlefields of Empire. What was considered the highest role a woman could perform within the home – an act of tenderness, sympathy, and tact – was, outside of the home and for hire, considered to be menial, degrading, and improper. Nurses belonged to the servant class and, as F. F. Cartwright notes, "when employed in private houses, were regarded as equals of the scullery maid rather than of the upper servants."[76] Although the paid nurse was not always such a reprobate as the popular image of her would have it,[77] nursing, even at the administrative level, was no job for a lady. Drunkenness and promiscuity were common, especially among those who worked in hospitals where "large supplies of alcohol were available in the wards and the presence of a number of young apprentices and house pupils encouraged prostitution."[78] For the most part nurses were untrained and uneducated and were required to work long hours under deplorable conditions without supervision and in difficult or even dangerous circumstances. Nightingale had to win the confidence of those who doubted that a "lady" could operate under such wretched conditions.

A combination of privilege, ruling-class connections, and fortuitous historical circumstances permitted her ultimately to overwhelm the opposition and to become nothing less than nurse-in-chief to the British Army at war. The spectacular nature of her accomplishments, her social rank, the drama of wartime, and the voluntary status of her work were more than sufficient to overcome the opprobrium attached to nursing and to the exercise of female authority in the public domain. Like Joan of Arc, to whom she was repeatedly compared, Nightingale became a heroine rather than a model who might provide a precedent for reexamining the capacities of women to work in fields from which they had been excluded. She could be conveniently considered *sui generis*. Still, Nightingale, in the popular representation of her as ministering angel to the troops, enduring incalculable hardship in a wholly masculine terrain to the acclaim of her nation and government, incarnated the shared fantasies and concrete aspirations of millions of women, who, like Dorothea Brooke in *Middlemarch*, wished for more than to have "lived faithfully a hidden life and [to] rest in unvisited tombs" (86).

Like her fictional counterparts, Nightingale came home from her triumphs a patient. She returned from the Crimea in shattered health and within two years had settled into the life of the confirmed valetudinarian surrounded by a chosen few who ministered to her wants – both professional and companionate. It is generally supposed that Nightingale had no organic disease. Though from time to time her doctors concurred that she was on the very brink of death she not only lived until the age of ninety, but continued to work indefatigably for, among other things, the reformation of the Royal Army Medical Services in England and then in India. Whatever the actual nature of her physiological condition might have been, and that she felt herself to be suffering is clear, she managed to work for her reformist aims more effectively through her status as perpetual patient than she ever did as physically active nurse and administrator. After a brief period of public celebrity, then, she imposed upon herself an obscurity made all the more hermetic by the exemptions and prescriptions of ill-health. To be the icon of public piety borne through the streets and presented at innumerable dinners and social occasions would have essentially returned her to the life she had struggled so hard to extricate herself from, to have her energies dissipated, a prey to constant interruption. As she put it in a private note, "there are hundreds of human beings always crying after ladies" (W-S 28). In Nightingale's view of it, the role of the leisured middle- and upper-class woman was to circulate continuously, to be occupied endlessly, doing nothing in particular. Invalidism permitted the inversion of this sentence imposed by her gender and class by permitting her to sequester and immobilize herself while laboring prodigiously on projects of both national and imperial importance. "Our bodies," she wrote of the common view of women, "are the only things of any consequence."[79] As nurse and then as patient, Nightingale used this cultural assumption to reverse what were for her its more onerous consequences. Just as her divine calling to nurse had superseded the authority of family by asserting a more exalted form of filial subordination and locating ambition in self-sacrifice, so the claims of her own sick body provided a set of emotional and physical imperatives which overrode more mundane familial and social obligations and left her free to pursue her own aims. Those aims, however, were still cast in the acceptable form of commitment to others at the expense of her own well-being.

In the place of conjugal and filial relations the soldiers became her family, her children, her beloved, and through a process of identification which seems to me at the heart of the figurative reversibility of nurse–patient roles, they became, quite simply, herself – the self whose needs she could not directly serve. In a letter to Sidney Herbert she wrote, "'Us' means in my language the troops and me."[80] Their suffering, their victimization were hers; the neglect of their needs by the authorities whom they loyally served and upon whom they were dependent was the neglect she suffered at the hands of a family and a society which thwarted her at every step. She never relented in her disdain for the notion of the prior or superior claims of kinship. In a private note of 1857 she wrote:

The real fathers and mothers of the human race are not the fathers and mothers according to the flesh... What is "Motherhood in the Flesh"? A pretty girl meets a man and they are married... The children come without their consent even having been asked because it can't be helped... For every one of my 18,000 children, for every one of these poor tiresome Harley Street creatures [her patients in her first administrative post] I have expended more motherly feeling and action in a week than my mother has expended for me in 37 years. (W-S 212)

It was only, in fact, when her mother, Fanny, became enfeebled by age and illness, a patient whom Florence could nurse, that she began to relent in this sweeping condemnation: "I don't think my dear mother was ever more touching and interesting to me than she is now in her state of dilapidation" (W-S 289).

On her return from the Crimea she replaced her mother and sister with devoted attendants, most notably Arthur Clough and his mother-in-law, Nightingale's Aunt Mai, who left her own husband and children to become Nightingale's nurse-companion. An intense affection grew up between Nightingale and her aunt, who referred to

her as "my child, my friend, my guide… my dearest one on earth or
in heaven." Nightingale wrote later, "We were like two lovers" (W-S
212). In addition to those who cared for her were the men who
submitted to be guided by her zeal for sanitary reform (the "band of
brothers" as they called themselves), who visited her daily and wrote
to her as often and whose widow she claimed to be at each of their
deaths. Most notable among them was Sidney Herbert, whose high
governmental positions (including Secretary of State for War)
assured her influence in the administration of the Army Medical
Services.

Her invalidism paradoxically enabled a life of almost uninterrupted exertion. The impression given by all the various sources –
memoirs, correspondence, biography – is of almost superhuman
activity, days and nights of urgent work amassing, analyzing, and
presenting immense collections of data, thousands of pages of notes,
millions upon millions of words. And along with this ceaseless effort
of marshaling and organizing facts and coaching her representatives
there was the immensity of the task itself – each hospital with its
supplies, its uniforms, its furniture, its personnel, its bodies, to be
itemized, cleaned, and arranged. The entire subcontinent of India to
be put in order, to be ventilated, to be drained.[81] Woodham-Smith
confesses to be wearied by the mere contemplation of the work
Nightingale performed from her sickbed. "Work always loomed
ahead of her, mountains of it, endless labor, endless toil which
somehow must be struggled through" (225). All this frantic activity
– urgent, momentous, unlimited in scope, incalculable in effect –
kept her as insulated from the common concerns of life, the dreadful
pull of the mundane chores and sapped energies that she associated
with the life of the idle and ornamental woman of her class, as did the
invalid life in which she immured herself. It is commonly conceded
that she became ill in order to work, but there is something to be said
for the notion that both the interminable work and the ever-present
threat of terminal illness were expressive of a supervening desire for
absolute control over the disposition of her own time and body.

While bodily suffering exempted her from the intrusions of female
duties it also testified to the enormity of the sacrifice her more
"masculine" work entailed, thus clearly distinguishing it from such
proscribed motives as self-fulfillment or professional ambition. Her
prostration and self-imposed obscurity called more attention to the
burden than the glory of such work, as did her frequent invocation of

God as her personal supervisor: "For His sake I bear it willingly, but not for the sake of Praise."[82] In her letters she referred to her sufferings most often in conjunction with her overwork, and insisted as each of her fellows failed in health that her sufferings were greater, her sacrifices more severe. There is something almost savage in her repeated insistence on the primacy of her own exertions and the suffering they caused her. Though she made obscurity a requisite of those exertions, among her co-workers and well-wishers there was to be no mistake that this work of hers was imperative and that it was costing her her life.

Finally, like her nursing, her disability mandated her confinement, thus keeping her well within the sphere where women could legitimately hold sway while still officially dependent on the power and mobility of men. The importance of this assertion of dependency in the very teeth of its defiance can, perhaps, be most vividly seen in her peremptory, even dictatorial demands on the time and dedication of Sidney Herbert and her continual reference to him after his death as her "Master." More concretely it can be traced in her continuing resistance to the enfranchisement of women, and to the certification of nurses. These changes would declare on the one hand the possibility of direct participation in government rather than the oblique "influence" that she practiced with such skill and determination, and on the other, the professionalization of the work which she continued to wish to be considered "a calling" – a matter of character, not of knowledge. What made a good nurse, as she delineated the qualifications, were honesty, truthfulness, quietness, cheerfulness, cleanliness, calm, and chastity. Again, she, herself, was the model from which she drew the likeness and only strong character and grueling experience had made her what she was. Medical knowledge and certifiable standards of performance would make nurses merely inferior doctors unable to claim, at whatever price in nominal subordination, the uniqueness of nursing and its particularly feminine character.

The doubleness of her self-image – indomitable yet frail, leader of men and loving disciple – and her image of nursing – autonomous yet subordinate, authoritative yet obedient – had its counterpart in her ambivalent attitude toward her own sex. *Cassandra*, her moving protest against the oppression and enforced idleness of women, gave way to diatribes against agitators for women's rights and contempt for women in general: "Women crave *for being loved*, not for loving.

They scream at you for sympathy all day long, they are incapable of giving *any* in return ... They cannot state a fact accurately to another, nor can that other attend to it accurately enough for it to become information" (W-S 260). At the same time, she insisted that women were uniquely suited for nursing and she delighted in the company of the young nurses from the Nightingale Training School. She condemned women who wished to be doctors on the grounds that they had "only tried to be 'men' and they have succeeded only in being third rate men" (W-S, 311). Yet she referred to herself as a man and wrote of her relations to Herbert and Clough: "Sidney Herbert and I were together exactly like two men – exactly like him and Gladstone. And as for Clough, oh Jonathan, my brother Jonathan, my love for thee was very great, Passing the love of women" (W-S, 260). Nightingale's complex and often punitive relation to her own sex is revelatory of the contradictory needs that the sickroom negotiates through its apparent combination of compliance and resistance to social norms and its simultaneous assertion and negation of the body.

Nightingale's obsession with dirt, foul air, and disease-bearing emanations from the body, a striking attribute of her writings even given the fact that she was a sanitary reformer and necessarily concerned with hygiene, may also be linked both to the sequestration that characterized her life and to the tyranny of gender roles. Even a cursory glance over her voluminous notes reveals an attention to the danger of infection from the environment that goes far beyond the conclusions of the zymotic theory of disease to which she stubbornly clung long after the germ theory was generally accepted.[83] Indeed, her resistance to germ theory may be understood not only as a resistance to its implicit undermining of the moral, social, and environmental causalities which provided the larger rationale for her devotion to nursing and sanitation but for the careful and elaborate management of her own well-being as well.[84] Nightingale wrote endless accounts of the poisonous odors and noxious exhalations which pervade the average household, breeding in the carpets, clinging to the curtains, stored up in porous brick walls and wood flooring. "A dirty carpet literally infects the room," she wrote in *Notes on Nursing*; mattresses are "saturated with organic matter" and cupboards "were always reservoirs of foul air" (50, 45, 18). But the real danger arose from the body. In her paper on sick-nursing and health-nursing she designated "the body the main source of defilement of the air. "[85] It should be noted in this connection that for six years of her invalidism she remained in one room only and on frequent occasions had her visitors (among them her personal physician) send notes to her from an adjoining room. She believed moreover, apropos of such extreme seclusion, that the interruption of other thoughts upon one's own mental activity decomposed nervous matter and could do positive injury to the brain.

Nightingale's profound sense of the invasiveness of bodies, their intrusion on time, on health, on the very air she breathed, may, I am suggesting, have been the primary determinant of her decision to be, as both nurse and patient, one who controls and limits that invasiveness. Although her preoccupation with contamination from without more than hints at personal pathologies, it refers on the most general level to a peculiarly female experience – the feeling of exposure (without sanctioned recourse) to the demands and constructions of others, the painful awareness that a woman's body (I quote Nightingale again) "is the only thing of consequence." Mary Poovey has asserted that Nightingale's hygienic concerns and principles helped underwrite the ethos of Empire.[86] Yet by interring her own body in a series of secluded sickrooms, declaring it, in effect, to be no body insofar as its customary functions were concerned, and by dedicating her life to the institution of hygienic procedures on a global scale, Nightingale enacted a familiar narrative of subjection as well. Her resistance to the disabling conditions of gender merely reconstituted those conditions under her own very efficient, very exacting, auspices.

If we can credit the report of her biographer, however, Nightingale's arduous career, her long years of largely self-imposed invalidism, and her, for the most part, anonymous efforts on behalf of the army, were well compensated by an old age blessed by all she had sacrificed. Indeed, even if we cannot fully consent to Woodham-Smith's summation of those blessings given, among other things, Nightingale's gradual decline into obesity and senility, it remains of interest, for it was in the imagination of others that Florence Nightingale's life so thoroughly satisfied conflicting needs:

If life had used her hardly, she was compensated now. Few human beings have enjoyed a fuller, happier old age. She was treated with an almost religious deference...and her utterances were paid the respect due to an oracle. To millions of women all over the world she was the symbol of a new hope, the sign of a new age. Nor was she separated from the common joys of life. Though she had never married, she enjoyed the pleasures of matriarchy. In the lives of a large circle of young people...she held the place of a powerful generous grandmother. (W-S 416)

Although Nightingale and the idealized nurses of Victorian women's fiction did much to improve the status of the nurse, it was Sairey Gamp who, with her mercenary pieties and comic violence against the ill, for most of the century epitomized the popular view. Licentious, avaricious, and abusive, these "hired handmaidens of death" as Hawthorne calls them in "The Minister's Black Veil," seem to be reviled and mocked in proportion to the value placed upon the cherished notion of natural female benevolence and nurturing propensities as antidotes to social ills. The successive presence of both kinds of nurse in the sickrooms of many novels of the period, or the explicitly stated exclusion of one by the other, serves, on the one hand, to emphasize the kinds of values which the sickroom relation between patient and nurse opposes to those outside of it. But opposites that are embodied in the same figure have a way of merging with or invading each other with unintended or ironic effects. The attributes and tendencies of the hired nurse both qualify nursing as redemptive act and make manifest the reductive terms upon which such redemption is achieved.

Sairey Gamp, for instance, represents all the earthiness, the familiarity with the gritty and the elemental that is excluded from the image of women and their tasks as nurses, mothers, and housekeepers in order to enshrine them as angels in the house. She reminds us that nursing is emptying bedpans as well as arranging bedclothes and that there are harsh and unpleasant realities of the sick body that cannot be cared for by mere watchfulness and a soothing presence. She also demonstrates that the selfless compassion of the nursing ideal can be based on a crippling attenuation of self as well as serving as a means to self-fulfillment. Sairey comes closest to the idealized nurse when Mrs. Harris, the other self she invents in order, according to Steven Marcus, "to define and celebrate herself"[87] has been exposed as illusory by her colleague Betsey Prig. A timid and deflated Sairey, her creative vitality and considerable narrative energies expended, tenderly nurses Chuffey, the nearly imbecile Chuzzlewit clerk, toward whom she had once directed the sharpest of her reproaches: "'Poor sweet dear!' cried Mrs. Gamp, with uncommon tenderness. 'He's all of a tremble...There's my blessed old chick!...Now come up to your own room and lay down on your bed a bit; for you're ashakin' all over...Come with Sairey!'" (*MC* 46). Herself "all of a tremble" on the verge of a public exposure of her imposture, Sairey has become the unlikely double of a man who, following the decease of his employer, comes close to having no identity at all ("Take him from me, and what remains?" [18]). The kind of ebullient inventiveness that Sairey possesses before the downfall of Mrs. Harris is one of the conspicuous casualties of the harmony the sickroom affords.

If the self-mutilations of selflessness are hinted at in Sairey's collapse into compassion, so, too, her aggressive bullying of patients ("Don't try no impogician with the Nuss, for she will not abear it" [40]) manifests the implicit aggression that the feminine authority in the sickroom usually disguises. The policing function which Grace Poole exercises in *Jane Eyre* over her patient Bertha Mason, for instance, exposes what is implicit in the later relation between Jane and Rochester – that the authority necessary to caretaking can easily slide over into enforcement and that the enclosure of the sickroom can serve as a disguised form of incarceration.

DISABLED MEN – NURSING WOMEN

The policing aspect of nurse–patient relations is especially evident in the recurring configuration in narratives of this period of women nursing disabled men. Another instantiation of the desire to readjust gender traits without endangering the fixed limits of the self, these couplings tread the line between enforcement and enablement. Sally Mitchell, reviewing women's recreational reading of the 1860s, quotes one contemporary male novelist's complaint that the "possibilities for a hero were, at present, limited to the consumptive, the insane, the hunchbacked, the lame, and the blind."[88] The reduction of the male to a condition of debility and dependence on the protective care of the woman he loves clearly has as part of its purpose the equalizing of an asymmetrical power structure and even the temporary ascendancy of the female.[89] The recurrence of this configuration in fiction by both men and women suggests as well that the Victorian male was often ambivalent or uneasy about passion and aggression and about restrictive definitions of the masculine. As Carol Christ points out in her essay on Victorian masculinity:

The historical tensions of the age placed male writers in a unique position: faced with a society that valued and rewarded male aggressiveness, yet ambivalent about its value, they idealized certain feminine qualities to which they themselves were deeply attracted as an escape from their dilemma.[90]

The disabled male under the care of a woman permits imaginative, if not actual, access to traits that were associated with femininity and allowed a retreat from those associated with manliness. For men and women the configuration seems to be an expression of longing for a less prescriptive assignment of gender attributes and a less punitive prescription in general of the nature of the self's desires. It is, moreover, a longing which, given these authors' own internal assent to the prevailing constraints, could only be represented (and often experienced) as a form of violence against the self – through, that is, the debility and restraint of the sickroom.

Tennyson's narrative poem, *The Princess: A Medley* will serve here as an instance of the significance of the configuration I describe above as well as of the general narrative dynamic which I have been outlining in this chapter. In *The Princess* Tennyson attempts to represent a more flexible view of gender types (to make "the man be more of woman, she of man")[91] without diminishing the distinctiveness of either sex. Several critics have noted the attraction Tennyson expresses in his poetry toward traits and powers ascribed to women and the concomitant attempt to ward off the dangers such an attraction presents.[92] The danger seems to be the possible collapse of those gender distinctions which preserve the female attributes he is attracted to and insure the continued empowerment of the male. Linked to the danger attendant upon such a loss of definitive distinctions, and perhaps underlying its terror, is the threat of a thoroughly ontological crisis – a frightening indeterminacy of being most graphically presented in *The Princess* by the "weird seizures" of the prince: "On a sudden in the midst of men and day," the prince recounts,

> And while I walk'd and talk'd as heretofore,
> I seemed to move among a world of ghosts
> And feel myself the shadow of a dream.   (1: 15–18)

What is of particular interest to me here is that these dangers are represented by an image of the monstrous inversion of the female nurse–disabled male configuration, and the avoidance of such dangers by its conclusive reinstatement as an ideal mode of interaction. Women engaged in the vivisection of a male body ("a living hound") are invoked briefly and suggestively as the repressed opposite of the scene of women nursing wounded men with which the poem attempts to contain the fluidity of forms it has put into play. The order that nursing women restore in the conclusion of the inner narrative, moreover, implicitly restores order to the poem's narrative and generic confusions – to what one contemporary reviewer called the "incoherency of its characteristics."[93]

"But thou have turned to something strange." This line addressed to Hallam's spirit in *In Memoriam* registers the recurrent anxiety in Tennyson's poetry about altered or indeterminate states of being. Nothing, it seems, holds more menace or fascination for him than the departure from fixed forms.[94] Even though such departures are often presented as the grounds for hope in the evolution of a higher form, a more perfect order, or as an enabling condition of poetic creativity, their presence is generally accompanied by an ominous sense of estrangement from the grounds of one's own being. What continually haunts Tennyson in his repeated musings about Hallam's form-lessness, for instance, is the fear that Tennyson will not know, or more importantly, be known by Hallam if their spirits should in some manner conjoin – the possibility that *he*, not Hallam, may have turned to something strange. It is this potential loss of a guarantee of the existence of a present more than a future self that seems most urgently at issue in these speculations and in the "strange experiments" (Prologue: 228) with sexual role reversal in the inner narrative of *The Princess*. It is moreover expressive of a general cultural anxiety about change and the loss of fixed forms for which the Victorian sickroom offers its succor. And just as it does for the female sufferers in narratives that express a yearning for and a dread of deviations from the norm, the nurse–patient scene to which Tennyson resorts at the end of that inner narrative both allows those experiments to take place while at the same time providing the necessary reassurance about the stable nature and boundaries of the self. Like those other narratives, stability is reasserted through the coercions of the body and its limitations.

In contrast to the social and ontological confusions of the inner tale, the opening of the frame narrative of the poem provides a detailed and substantial evocation of a progressive and enlightened social order rooted in tradition and consolidated by paternal benevolence. Sir Walter Vivian has opened his estate grounds to "the people" for a summer's day (Prologue: 3). The pupils of a mechanics'

institute, "of which he was the patron" (Prologue 6) conduct
"strange experiments" on the grounds "so that sport / Went hand in
hand with Science" (Prologue: 79, 80). The house and grounds
present a graceful and harmonious combination of past eras and
styles, and the objects on display there reach back to the "first bones
of Time" (Prologue: 15) and extend to the rich spoils of present-day
imperialism.

The only dissonant note in this otherwise happy medley of diverse
people and objects is the indignant protest voiced by Lilia, the
daughter of the house, against her brother's assertion that no women
of courage and nobility exist in the present era. "There are thousands
now / Such women, but convention beats them down," she contends,

> It is but bringing up; no more than that:
> You men have done it: how I hate you all!
> Ah, were I something great! I wish I were
> Some mighty poetess, I would shame you then,
> That love to keep us children!   (Prologue: 127–133)

The accuracy of her last assertion is attested to and its force
undermined by the fact that Lilia is herself described as "half child /
half woman," and her protest punctuated by the tapping of her "tiny
silken-sandaled foot" (Prologue: 101, 149). Inconsistencies of this
kind occur throughout the poem as Tennyson continually draws
back from the difficulties of imagining alterations in conventional
representations of gender, which, however desirable, would appear
to hazard the stability he describes in the opening.[95]

In the inner tale, such inconsistencies take over the narrative far
more fully as the unity shaped from distinct and disparate elements
with which the poem begins gives way to images of fragmentation,
dissolution, and indeterminacy of form. A young prince and his two
companions disguise themselves "in maiden plumes" in order to
infiltrate the women's college founded by the prince's betrothed,
Princess Ida. Ida has broken the marriage compact, concluded by
proxy when the prince was eight years old, in order to "live alone /
Among her women" (I: 48–49) and to educate them from "the habits
of the slave" (II: 77). The women have, with this end in mind, taken
a vow not to correspond with home or speak to any man for three
years. The prince's decision to infiltrate the college disguised as a
woman, his preference for "gentleness" rather than war, is in direct
opposition to his father's desire to take Ida by force. His implied

effeminacy (he has, in addition to pacific principles, "lengths of yellow ringlet, like a girl" [1: 3]) is also in contrast to the Amazon-like Ida who hails "those two crowned twins, / Commerce and conquest" (v: 410–11). Extraordinarily tall, Ida has tamed leopards, maintains a "monstrous woman-guard" (iv: 540) and eschews "love, children, happiness" in the pursuit of her feminist aims (iii: 159). "No doubt we seem a kind of monster to you," she tells the disguised prince who presses her to acknowledge children as a woman's due (iii: 190, 158).

The most "monstrous" image of unnatural or ambiguous forms, however (or, in this case, of the intermixture of incompatible elements) is Ida's evocation of women studying anatomy.[96]

> in truth
> We shudder but to dream our maids should ape
> Those monstrous males that carve the living hound,
> And cram him with the fragments of the grave,
> Or in the dark dissolving human heart,
> And holy secrets of this microcosm,
> Dabbling a shameless hand with shameful jest,
> Encarnalize their spirits. (iii: 291–298)

Science, which in the frame narrative went "hand in hand" with sport under the beneficent aegis of aristocratic patronage, is here linked to bestiality. Doctors studying their craft are "monstrous males" engaged in a hideous rite which requires the defilement of a living body with "fragments of the grave" and the desecration of the "holy secrets" of the human heart. Science – both the terrible knowledge it brings and the spiritual assurances to which it threatens to put an end – is at least one of the implied agents of that self-fragmentation so graphically suggested in these lines by the dis-memberment of the living body. The fragmented self is also represented by the self who dismembers, deranged by the savage energies which its own activities unleash when unrestrained by spirit and the secrets of the heart. Tennyson is here invoking the imagery and rhetoric of the anti-vivisection movement, which defended the compassion of the heart against the "mire of [scientific] materialism" by linking such materialism with unrestrained aggression. Propo-nents argued that "the practice of vivisection hardens the sensibility of the operator and begets indifference to the infliction of pain, corrupting medical students with a love of cruelty that they then indulge in their homes."[97] The public and professional thus intrudes itself upon the private sphere in a particularly brutal way; medical research leads inexorably to domestic savagery. But the intermixture of identities and categories that seems most threatening to the integrity and intelligibility of the self derives from the incursion of the private into the public arena figured in *The Princess* by "maids" who "ape" (the implication of the verb is unmistakable) "those monstrous males" by studying medicine. In the inner tale of the poem a mock-heroic fantasy is played out in which unsuspecting virgins are beset in their intimate spaces by beastly men intent on despoliation. Titillation tinged with anxiety about unrestrained appetite is briefly haunted by the terrifying possibility of a reversal of roles – of the cohabitation of virgin and beast in one body intent on the violation of male perquisites. The full emancipation of women, so this passage suggests, would entail the encarnalization of the guardians of the spirit and the irretrievable immersion of man into "the sensual mire" (v: 181) – it would entail no less than a devolution of the species into formlessness and incoherence.

Eve Kosofsky Sedgwick refers to this passage as a "critique of the specular rationalism of Western medical science," and includes it among the instances of Ida's "radical feminism."[98] The feminine ideal being asserted here as incompatible with the practice of science is, however, that of the far-from-radical conservator of purity and social order – of the man over the beast. Furthermore, this idea is asserted in implicit opposition to the image of women as "irrational and destructive forces of nature," the image which it historically replaced.[99] If males who dissect the living hound seem to be engaged in unholy rites, then the maids who ape them are like maenads or bacchantes whose revels include the frenzied dismemberment of male bodies. The possibility that women might be so engaged is raised in order to suppress it as unnatural – a violation of female nature – which fundamentally threatens the integrity of the male self and ultimately of the social order. The uneasiness of men about their own disintegrative energies leads to the denial of the existence of such energies in women to whom they look to nurse the fragments of their world back to wholeness. Women, the prince intones, unlike "the piebald miscellany man," are "whole and one" (v: 190, 192).

The threat raised by this passage and by Ida's feminist experiment in general is, indeed, allayed only when the princess and her pupils nurse the shattered bodies of the men who, in fighting for possession of the women, become the victims of their own aggressive passions aroused, according to the logic of the poem, by the women's aspirations to the power and privilege of "piebald miscellany." From bacchantes who murder to dissect, the women have become nurses who, through their "Angel offices," heal divisions they themselves have precipitated – who, in other words, call a truce in the "perennial war among [the] members" by declaring themselves *hors de combat*. The crucial imaginative force of women nursing disabled men is used to repel the anarchy implicit in female as well as male desire. The function of nurses is to preserve and guard the depleted and thus dysfunctional bodies of their potential or actual violators and to remain themselves within the physical and emotional circumscriptions of the sickroom.

> So was their sanctuary violated,
> So their fair college turned to hospital;
> At first with all confusion: by and by
> Sweet order lived again with other laws:
> A kindlier influence reigned; and everywhere
> Low voices with the ministering hand
> Hung round the sick: the maidens came, they talked,
> They sang, they read: till she not fair began
> To gather light, and she that was, became
> Her former beauty treble; and to and fro
> With books, with flowers, with Angel offices,
> Like creatures native unto gracious act,
> And in their own clear element, they moved. (VII: 1–13).

The clear and unequivocal assignment of "native" roles, the enhancement of women's conventional duties, and the protective care of passive, dependent men within the site of healing, is the closest Tennyson can come to his vision of a more equal distribution of gender traits which would recuperate rather than endanger the social body. Violence must be directed against the self in order to preserve its communal incarnation. Although the inner tale ends with the prince (still in the sickroom under Ida's care) hopefully invoking a "crowning race of humankind" in which woman will "set herself to man, / Like perfect music unto noble words" (VII: 269–270), that race remains safely in a vague and distant future along with the conventional marriage that is meant both to promote and presage it.

Meanwhile, the stay against ungovernable change and against the encarnalized spirit is the blind determination of the body in distress. Herbert Tucker's remarks on Tennyson's poetic strategy are relevant:

Tennyson resorted to self-limitation as a means of self-definition, a way of making himself known not only to himself but to others, in part because he wrote in and of a century that witnessed the disintegration of traditional limits and goals – well aware that the great world around him was spinning down the ringing grooves of change but fearfully ignorant of its destination, Tennyson defended against his ignorance by imagining terminal situations in accomplished verse.[100]

The prince's seizures end; the limited needs of the body put an end to the crippling indeterminacies of the mind; his existence, which seemed a mere "shadow of a dream," is confirmed by the solicitude of his nurse: " ... my doubts are dead / My haunting sense of hollow shows: the change / The truthful change in thee has killed it" (VII: 327–329). The change in Ida which has confirmed the prince's selfhood in its limited but more substantial form is also a diminishment of her selfhood – indeed much more conspicuously so. The princess is put in the anomalous position of nursing one who has destroyed her dreams of a fuller female self. Her "sanctuary" has been "violated" to create a sanctuary for him. "So blackened all her world in secret, blank / And waste it seemed and vain; till down she came, / And found fair peace once more among the sick" (VII: 27–29). It has been pointed out by both Eve Sedgwick and James Kincaid that as a privileged dependant the prince can more fully subordinate Ida to his needs and consolidate his hold over her.[101] This is most certainly the case, but as the conditions that enable it forcefully indicate, this masculine victory is achieved through a mutual defeat, just as Jane Eyre's feminine victory – her ability to shape her own life and validate her own perceptions – requires not only the unmanning of Rochester but also her own permanent confinement within the sickroom as prop and guide. In both cases the sickroom expresses the longing for change and protects against the uncertainties change brings; and both cases demonstrate the debilitating price paid for such mediations. The "terminal situation" which the sickroom affords in narrative after narrative is a perpetual convalescence, a debiliating compromise between a past that is no longer viable and an indeterminate future. As Sarah Gilead notes, for instance, of Lily Dale in *The Small House at Allington*: "Lily's illness is permanently, not transitionally, liminal, and not regeneration but its opposite takes place."[102] The movement from a condition of inadequacy to one of empowerment that marks a "successful" conversion or transformation is effected by the reinstatement of the ills against which the sickroom offers itself as antidote: continuity is affirmed through discontinuity, self-fulfillment through self-limitation, and solidarity through isolation.

Moreover, "sweet order" is brought, at least temporarily, to the confusion of narrative impulses ("between the mockers and the realists" [Conclusion: 24]) that underlies the medley of storytelling voices in *The Princess*. In the final scene the narrative achieves the structural coherence and stable meaning of a tableau – a transitional state is made permanent, a set of relations and identities is fixed within narrow, functional limits, and the whole is arranged with immediate intelligibility as its aim. Tennyson's odd *mélange* of genres hardly qualifies it as "realism," but it exhibits the same impulse toward a heterogeneity both threatening and desirable which must be formally reconciled and integrated in the name of self and social cohesion. The *tableau vivant* of the sickroom scene achieves this ideal of narrative closure and, at the same time, manifests the terms upon which that achievement is based.

Marian Erle's wish to "be sicker yet, if sickness made / The world so marvellous kind," becomes, as demonstrated briefly here, a central shaping influence on the structure of Victorian narrative. In the following discussions of the fiction of George Eliot, Charlotte Brontë, and Charles Dickens, I will be examining in detail the various narrative effects engendered by the desire of these writers to perpetuate or continually to reenter the "sweet order" of the sickroom, in order to minister to their own personal and aesthetic conflicts. I have proceeded with canonical test cases in part because I was initially drawn to this subject through the representation of illness in the works of these authors, and because they represent most fully and diversely the various emphases and narrative possibilities of the scenes in question. In the works I examine, scenes of illness and convalescence serve as structural inversions of the larger narratives in which they are embedded, as closures imposed upon the open-ended and dangerous mobility of psychic and narrative structures, and as constituent elements of alternative narrative sequences called up in opposition to the discontinuities of the dominant narrative mode. Like the sickroom solace they extend, these narrative strategies of wholeness and integration are founded upon and therefore register the growing alienation which later representations of illness will more openly declare.

CHAPTER 2

Charlotte Brontë: "varieties of pain"

One need look no further than the grim facts of Charlotte Brontë's own life to account for the ubiquity in her novels of states of fever, debility, hypochondria, and morbid decline: the unremitting toll of disease upon her family, the melancholy effects of frustration and grief, her own chronic ill-health and that of the ailing father she dutifully nursed until her own early death. Illness, as Brontë herself defines and portrays it, can also be a register of deviance or alienation from social and personal norms, and in this respect, too, she was in a critical position to judge from her experience the painful effects of marginality and social aberration. As Terry Eagleton puts it: "A crisis of social identity...was endemic in this Tory, socially respectable but none too affluent family."[1] The Brontë sisters in particular, as Eagleton sums up their situation, were genteel in the "rough-and-ready environment" of the West Riding in Yorkshire, educated but without social or geographical access to the world which might gratify their tastes and interests, and female, "trapped ...between imaginative aspiration and...a society which could use them merely as 'higher' servants" (8). ("A private governess has no existence," wrote Charlotte in a letter to Emily.)[2] Even after the success of *Jane Eyre* brought fame to Charlotte, her extreme shyness, her "deep and exaggerated consciousness of her personal defects,"[3] made her shrink from the wider world she longed for.

To feel oneself a victim (or reluctant beneficiary) of forces beyond one's control, captive to one's physical being, estranged from one's essence, and at the same time continually at variance with "proper" social adaptation and functioning, are the conditions of illness and the experiential medium of Brontë's characters. In her fiction illness both signals dispossession and designates the range of what is possible in the way of accommodation and affective ties to this world. Thus in her novels somatic disorder becomes the primary form of self-assertion, convalescence the measure of comfort, and physical dependency the enabling condition for intimacy.

If her novels seem to trace the progress of the self-reliant individual bravely making her own way in the world, this impression is countered by the oppressive, even brutal weight of fatality in the disposition of events, by the heroine's passive submission to external circumstances, and by her dependence on the kindness of strangers. Here, for instance, is Lucy Snowe: "I know not that I was of a self-reliant or active nature; but self-reliance and exertion were forced upon me by circumstances... and when Miss Marchmont, a maiden lady of our neighborhood, sent for me, I obeyed her behest, in the hope that she might assign me some task I could undertake" (V 4). Lucy is "forced," "sent for"; she "obeys"; she is assigned a task. At the end of the novel, set up in her own school by Monsieur Paul and aided by an unexpected legacy from Miss Marchmont, Lucy concludes: "The secret of my success did not lie so much in myself, in any endowment, any power of mine, as in a new state of circumstances, a wonderfully changed life, a relieved heart" (42). If Lucy's scarcely voluntary progress through the novel serves in part to resolve Brontë's ambivalence about enterprising activism (Eagleton 64), it also expresses her very real experience of helplessness, vulnerability, and social and physical paralysis – an experience supported, or perhaps more accurately aggravated, by the Calvinism of her childhood. "She believed," reports Mrs. Gaskell, "some were appointed beforehand to sorrow and much disappointment; that it did not fall to the lot of all – as Scripture told us – to have our lives fall in pleasant places; that it was well for those who had rougher paths to perceive that such was God's will concerning them" (510). Accordingly, her heroines' fortunes seem to be subject to sudden, inexplicable accessions of grace, or sickening, often bewildering descents into suffering and privation: Lucy buoyed by her friendship with M. Paul, then suddenly, unaccountably, denied access to him; Jane placed "on a pedestal of infamy" (7) by Mr. Brocklehurst or summoned to Miss Temple's room for tea "to feast as on nectar and ambrosia" (8); Jane wandering starving and penniless through the moors, then swept up from the verge of death into the warmth and compassion of the Rivers's household.

Her status as victim or beneficiary of circumstances extends to her inner life as well. Her apparent insufficiencies, her social insignificance, and her own protective mask of inconspicuousness render her

subject to the constructions that others impose upon her as well as to
the qualities others elicit from her. "He was the kind of person with
whom I was likely ever to remain the neutral, passive thing he
thought me" (2) Lucy says of Dr. John. And of M. Paul's insistence
that she act in the school play she avers, "I had accepted a part to
please another; ere long... I acted to please myself" (14). Deprived of
the usual avenues of advancement and recognition – beauty, rank,
status, and wealth – those qualities that might entitle her to
recognition – her passion, her imagination, her intellect – remain
hidden or, to use Brontë's own familiar term, "buried." Unlike
most of Dickens's and George Eliot's protagonists, who must learn
to recognize the existence and substantiality of other centers of
self, Brontë's heroines need to *be recognized*, to emerge from a condition of latency and near invisibility through the intercession of
others.

In characteristically fatalistic fashion, the divination of their inner
worth comes not through a gradual revelation of character but rather
from sudden miracles of perception and intuition. Rochester tells
Jane on the first night of their acquaintance: "I see at intervals the
glance of a curious sort of bird through the close-set bars of a cage; a
vivid, restless, resolute captive is there; were it but free, it would soar
cloud-high" (14). Asked to read Lucy's countenance on the evening
of her arrival at the Pensionnat, M. Paul, "the diviner," as Lucy calls
him, replies, "I read it" (7), a certainty of divination that is borne out
in their future encounters. "I scrutinized your face once," he tells her
later, "and it sufficed" (15). While the full extent of Madame Beck's
surveillance fails in the end to pluck out the heart of Lucy's mystery,
M. Paul can read her at a glance.

The reading of countenances refers to physiognomy and phrenology, both of which Brontë frequently employs in the assessment of
character in her novels. The theory of phrenology, developed at the
end of the eighteenth century by the Viennese physician Franz
Joseph Gall and popularized in England by George Combe, held that
the brain was composed of mental organs which were the localized
sites of specific functions or attributes such as veneration, benevolence, and amativeness. Furthermore, each organ and its corresponding attribute was believed to be indicated by a protuberance
on the skull's surface whose size and contour was an index of the
power of the organ's manifestation in a given person's character. The
theory provided amateurs and professionals alike with a kind of

cephalic braille of the mind's inner workings. Here, for instance, is how Brontë "reads" Hiram Yorke in *Shirley*:

Mr. Yorke, in the first place, was without the organ of veneration – a great want, and which throws a man wrong on every point where veneration is required. Secondly, he was without the organ of Comparison – a deficiency which strips a man of sympathy; and, thirdly, he had too little of the organs of Benevolence and Ideality, which took the glory and softness from his nature. (4)

The appeal of phrenology for Brontë lay, as Karen Chase points out, in its offer of a more complex and extensive understanding of personality than had been available hitherto, as well as of a solution to the narrative dilemma of how a first-person narrator gains access to other minds.[4] But its appeal also lay, I think, in the fact that the determinism of the system corresponded to Brontë's own sense of fatalism in the workings of human destiny, while its physiological manifestation offered the possibility of a legible inwardness, a making visible of her inner, and thus fullest and most expressive self – the basis of her only claim to recognition and to love.

The emergence into visibility of the inner resources (and weaknesses) of the heart and mind through the arrangement and size of protrusions on the skull or the lines on the face constitutes a kind of "turning inside out" or inversion of inner to outer similar to the manner in which disease in the nineteenth century becomes a means of bodily manifesting or disclosing one's individuality, and thus providing, as Susan Sontag puts it, "an interior decor of the body."[5] As employed by Brontë and others, it is another expression of the romance of realism, of the hope that the material world (the body in this case) could provide a fully expressive, unmediated language of our inner nature. The connection between the languages of physiognomy and disease (and between diagnosis and close reading) is suggested when Lucy Snowe reads the "hieroglyphics" on the King of Labassecour's face and discovers the evidence of "Hypochondria," the particularly male variety of the long-recognized nervous disorder of melancholia or depression (*V* 290).[6]

Both phrenology and disease are part of a general narrative dynamic in Brontë's novels which I intend to trace in this chapter. Given the absence of choice in Brontë's fictional world, the experience of latent worth and public nonentity, and the brutal and inevitable repression of hope and desire, the heroine's advancement and accommodation are achieved not through a fundamental alteration of the established order but through its inversion. Thus, deprivation and dependency are portrayed as fulfillment, confinement as liberty, the latent as the manifest, the periphery as the center, and incapacitation as power. Furthermore, the dissonant aspects of male–female relations which reflect larger societal contradictions and tensions are at least temporarily translated into latently homoerotic unions in which those tensions are submerged, defused, or repressed. And finally, because the dynamic of inversion is largely accomplished through the relations and transactions engendered by illness and debility, illness, in a very real sense, becomes the measure of health.

Although this dynamic is characteristic of all of Brontë's narratives, I will be focusing here on her third novel, *Shirley*, in which she attempted to extend her fictional range beyond the single perspective of the isolated and displaced heroine, and to restrain her romantic flights with a cooling dose of realism. As Brontë puts it, "If you think ... that anything like a romance is preparing for you, reader, you never were more mistaken. Do you anticipate sentiment, and poetry, and reverie? Do you expect passion, and stimulus and melodrama? Calm your expectations; reduce them to a lowly standard. Something real, cool, and solid, lies before you" (1). Rather than achieving the complex social texture of traditional realism, however, Brontë seems instead to have merely multiplied the centers of isolated, alienated consciousnesses, each trying to write counterfictions of their own lives. *Shirley* was written in the fearful eleven-month period during which all three of Charlotte's surviving siblings died; her characteristic narrative pattern of alternating damnation and election in this case might more appropriately be said to inscribe the awful rhythm of consumptive decline with its false hopes and bitter setbacks. Written under these harrowing conditions, as well as under the further strain of writing against her natural bent (resorting to realism, as Carol Christ suggests, in order to restrain imaginative desire)[7] the novel presents in its most acute form the extreme disjunction in Brontë's work in general between subject and object, desire and experience (and in narrative terms, between romance and realism) that illness represents and for which it offers its cure. Although she initially addresses this disjunction in terms of labor unrest and domestic discord, she turns to physical illness when she seeks a cure and not merely a diagnosis. The realistic mode, as Brontë conceives of and employs it, finally obstructs rather than enables a solution or compromise to the problems of the desiring self and its proper relation to the life outside itself, thus exacerbating the pervasive social ills presented in the novel and necessitating the retreat to the sickroom. Brontë preserves the realism of the narrative by introducing within the familiar domestic terrain of the sickroom the lyric intensities and formal symmetry of romance. Whatever Brontë's intentions, social solutions are ultimately forced to take secondary and derivative status to the establishment of a personal "solution" or refuge for the suffering self. Brontë's own remark about the writing of *Shirley* seems to corroborate this underlying romantic impulse: "[T]he occupation of writing it has been a boon to me. It took me out of dark and desolate reality into an unreal but happier region."[8]

Set in Yorkshire during the final years of the Napoleonic Wars, against the background of the Luddite riots and the paralysis of trade brought on by the Orders in Council, the novel not only depicts a division between men and women, and among women, but a whole society in profound disorder, its various social units radically at odds – workers from employers, the state from the manufacturing classes, clergy from laymen, High Church from Low. Furthermore, individuals are forced by circumstances to deviate from their own inclinations or to oppose their own prescribed destiny or condition.

What the narrator says of "old maids" is true for all the major and many of the minor characters as well: to a greater or lesser extent they have "violated nature," thus "their natural likings and antipathies are reversed: they grow altogether morbid" (22). Robert Moore, the presumptive heir to a great Antwerp merchant firm, must, because of reversals in the family fortunes, content himself instead with a cottage and clothmill "in an out-of-the-way nook of an out-of-the-way district" in Yorkshire (2). Born and, for the most part, raised in Antwerp by his Belgian mother, he is viewed by natives of the district as, and indeed feels himself to be, "an outcast and an alien" (2). Shirley Keeldar, the titular heroine and heiress of Fieldhead Manor, should have been a man with a man's advantages and perquisites: "They gave me a man's name; I hold a man's position... they ought to make me a magistrate and a captain of yeomanry..." (11). The Reverend Matthewson Helstone "should have been a soldier, and circumstances made him a priest" (2). Louis Moore should have been master of a household and is instead a servant to one. His pupil, Henry Sympson, "burn[s] day and night...

to be – to do – to suffer" (26), but is trapped in a lame and sickly body. Mrs. Pryor, despite her maternal longings, abandons her only child. And Caroline Helstone, her daughter, destined to be a lovely and compliant wife, must face the purposeless life of a spinster in the absence of a sufficient dowry to attract the man she loves. One could add to this list of "struggles... with the strong native bent of the heart" (*V* 4) Brontë herself, the trance-writer and romantic, fighting her own aesthetic and temperamental inclinations to write a realistic novel.

Caroline Helstone's relations and position in society make her, in a sense, the vulnerable point of conjunction of all the embattled factions and displaced lives in the novel. Linked to foreignness and to the Whig manufacturing interest through her kinship to the Moores and her love for Robert, to the Established Church and high Toryism through her uncle, the Reverend Helstone, and to the landed gentry through Shirley, Caroline is both genteel and poor, a member of the middle class with access to the "best families" of the neighborhood and sympathetic to the plight of the unemployed laborers to whom she, as a single, portionless woman without a vocation, is compared throughout the novel. Most important, given the central conflict of the novel, as a woman Caroline is the reluctant ally of the novel's neglected old maids, abused wives, and resentful, rebellious girls, trapped by their sex in monotonous, restricted, and self-denying roles. If, as Sandra Gilbert and Susan Gubar contend, "*Shirley* is about impotence,"[9] then Caroline is the impotent center of this deadlocked world.[10] It is in the workings of her fate (rather than in the more defiant, if no more successful Shirley's), in her interaction with others, in her response to seemingly intractable circumstances, and in the fulfillment she is allowed to achieve, that we can trace the limits of accommodation and redress that can be wrested from what Brontë views as the necessary order of things.

As I have indicated, Brontë's protagonists are rarely portrayed as the willing agents of their own destinies. Without any of the levers of power or advancement at their disposal, often not even desirous of the ends toward which they direct, however passively, their energies, they only reluctantly exchange "the palsy of custom" for 'the passionate pain of change (*V* 21). Still, Lucy, Jane, and William Crimsworth have industry and self-reliance thrust upon them, while Caroline, although sharing their orphaned state and limited opportunities, lacks even the goad of destitution to propel her beyond "the barren stagnation" (10) of her life. She is entrenched in the society of the West Riding, provided with friends, relations, and the promise of a competency. Work, the Carlylean prescription against inanition and despair, seems to offer her only "varieties of pain" (12). Her search for some activity to fill the void of her life once Robert Moore withdraws, and with him her expectation of marriage, leads her to seek out Miss Ainley and Miss Mann, both of them subject to the derisive contempt and condescension of the community, wearing away their lives in the approved occupation of the spinster without family – the care of the sick and the poor.[11] Caroline's investigation into the lives of those she proposes to emulate culminates instead in her declaration that there is "a terrible hollowness, mockery, want, craving, in that existence which is given away to others, for want of something of your own to bestow it on" (10).

Although the plight of the single woman is an important focus of Brontë's social commentary in the novel, marriage, the refuge from which Caroline seems barred by her poverty, is portrayed as unsatisfactory at best, self-destructive and enslaving at worst. As her Uncle Helstone tells her: "Millions of marriages are unhappy: if everybody confessed the truth, perhaps all are more or less so" (7). In a characterization of marriage that, ironically, describes the terms upon which the "happy" marriage of Robert and Caroline will be transacted, he concludes, "A yokefellow is not a companion; he or she is a fellow-sufferer" (7). Later, Mrs. Pryor warns Caroline against the "false pictures" of marriage given in romances: "They are not like reality: they show you only the green tempting surface of the marsh, and give not one faithful or truthful hint of the slough underneath" (21). The actual and prospective domestic relations depicted in the novel bear out their grim testimony. The Reverend Helstone's own marriage to the silent Mary Cave, for instance, "was of no great importance to him in any shape"; he neglected her so utterly that he "scarcely noticed her decline" (4). And Mrs. Pryor, who escapes from her drunken and abusive husband, James Helstone, is left "galled, crushed, paralyzed, dying" (24).

In addition to these marriages (which were based, at least initially, on sentiment) are those proposed for economic and class consider-ations without regard to the affections or inclinations of either party. Robert, in an effort to insure the financial future of his mill and to release himself and his family from debt, forswears his love for Caroline in order to propose to Shirley, upon whose land his mill is

located. Shirley, meanwhile, who loves Robert's brother, Louis, has
a series of wealthy and aristocratic suitors pressed upon her by her
guardian, Mr. Sympson.

The primary transgressors in this dismal state of affairs are clearly
the men, who are described by Robert Moore as "a sort of scum" (6),
ruled almost exclusively by unstable competitive and appetitive
forces. Contentious, arrogant, and rapacious, the men of Brontë's
Yorkshire seem to embody Shirley's and Caroline's worst fears about
them[12] – fears about inconstancy, tyranny, or more generally, about
the possibility that behind a pleasing exterior lurks a dangerous
stranger. "It was my lot," Mrs. Pryor tells Caroline, "to witness a
transfiguration on the domestic hearth: to see the white mask lifted,
the bright disguise taken away, and opposite me sat down – Oh God!
I *have* suffered!" (411).

Imprisonment and deprivation, then, are shown to be the lot of
both the married and the unmarried woman. The conflict between a
desire for romantic fulfillment and for autonomy, often considered to
be the central opposition in Brontë's narratives,[13] is, in *Shirley*, a false
dilemma. Rather than equally attractive but incompatible alternatives, both desires are shown to be chimerical – the stuff of romance
hiding "the slough underneath."

The intimate conflicts between men and women in the novel
parallel the larger social conflicts between the powerful and the
powerless. The workers, like the women, are at the mercy of their
masters: their needs are ignored, their protests are unheeded, their
material well-being is urgently at stake. Elizabeth Rigby (later Lady
Eastlake) the most censorious – yet, in a way, one of the more
perceptive of contemporary critics of *Jane Eyre* in her quick (and
horrified) apprehension of that novel's more subversive elements –
declared in her review "that the tone of mind and thought which has
overthrown authority and violated every code human and divine
abroad, and fostered Chartism and rebellion at home, is the same
which has also written *Jane Eyre*."[14] The parallel between the
unemployed workers and the powerless and oppressed women,
however, stops short at their common dependency on masters for
material and emotional well-being and their privation in a society
ruled by unrestrained competition rather than justice and compassion. Parallel becomes contrast when modes of redress or resistance
are at issue. Whereas "misery generates hate" (2) among the workers,
who seek relief through direct action, the women invert their

resentment and, like Mary Cave, Mrs. Pryor, and Caroline, retreat into passivity and illness. The women's rebellion, if it manifests itself at all, does so in a socially acceptable way, registering the inadequacy of the existing social order without overtly challenging that order or risking the identity, however partial, which is confirmed by it. As Talcott Parsons pointed out in *The Social System*, "from the point of view of the social system the sick role may be less dangerous than some of the alternatives."[15] The rebellious force of Caroline's protest against Robert's treatment of his workers (6) and against male neglect of women's education (22), is diffused by her conflicting need for the love and acceptance of those who determine her deprivation. Direct demand, as Caroline herself implies, risks both a loss of love and permanent abandonment: "Obtrusiveness is a crime; forwardness is a crime; and both disgust: but love! – no purest angel need blush to love!" (17).

The narrator makes it clear early on that the suffering depicted in the novel is, to a large extent, the result of forces against which it would be useless to struggle. A bad harvest, the "progress of invention," the war on the Continent (2) all account for the distress of the workers, while the sexual and material destiny of women is dependency even if they are given "scope and work" (23). The most either can hope for, it would seem, is leniency. Even Robert's drive for success is halted, and his livelihood threatened, by the stagnation of trade resulting from the government's Orders in Council, which, by "forbidding neutral powers to trade with France, had, by offending America, cut off the principal market of the Yorkshire woollen trade, and brought it consequently to the verge of ruin" (2). What remains of human agency in the novel, and hence of narrative propulsion, is dedicated to the thorough suppression of the unavailing impulse or emotion.

The internal logic of Brontë's self-imposed "realism" seems inevitably to lead to narrative stalemate, so incommensurate in her view is the "true narrative of life" (7) with even the most modest expectations of fulfillment, so hopeless is the possibility of effective resistance to the prevailing power structure. Realism, with its emphasis on disenchantment, is put into sadistic relation to romance rather than serving as a chastening corrective to it. (This reductive view of realism is itself, of course, a romantic notion.) Wish, expectation, and desire, rather than being modified by the limitations imposed by the circumstantial density of "real life," are instead

"crush[ed]" by the "inexorable," the "resistless" authority of Experience, with her "frozen" face, and her "rod so heavy" (7). "The
school of Experience" is "humbling, crushing, grinding" (7).
"Reason," contends Lucy Snowe in *Villette*, is a "hag" who
commands obedience at the price of "savage, ceaseless blows" (21);
and "Truth," the sovereign of "the dread, the swift-footed, the all-
overtaking Fact," is a "Power whose errand is to march conquering
and to conquer" any "temporary evasion of the actual" (39).

The narrative consequences of this disabling relation between the
actual and the desired are exacerbated by Brontë's attempt in *Shirley*
to substitute "something unromantic as Monday morning" for
"sentiment, and poetry, and reverie" (1). The structure of the novel
itself is effectively bifurcated between "reality," the external
narrative of social facts and action, which is unresponsive to human
wish and agency, and "the life of thought" (*V* 8),[16] the interior life of
romantic imaginings. The expression of this inner life of thought is
almost wholly contained in a kind of textual substratum of the
"objective" narrative – in diaries, recitations from secondary texts,
impassioned reveries, and mythic excurses – only to regain full
narrative status within the sickroom.

Caroline expresses her affection for Robert, for instance, by reading
to him "the sweet verses of Chenier" (6) and reveals her view of his
character by giving him Shakespeare's *Coriolanus*: "Now, read, and
discover by the feelings the reading will give you at once how low and
how high you are" (6). She expresses her growing despair, though
without acknowledging it as her own, by reciting Cowper's "The
Castaway" which she murmurs to herself "at the farthest and darkest
end of the room" while Shirley listens (12). We learn of Louis Moore's
feelings for Shirley through his private meditations: even the scene of
their declaration of love for each other is not dramatized but rather
contained in a "reading" of his diary. And there are Shirley's own
mystical visions of female equality, of Titanic Eves, heroic struggles,
and mythic couplings, which are read aloud from her schoolroom
copybooks found hidden away in Louis's drawer.

These textual interpolations and the surrounding realism of the
narrative in which they are embedded correspond to Brontë's own
experience of the two worlds in which she and her siblings lived – the
actual world of denial, frustration, and nonentity – and the fictional
worlds of their own construction in which they could indulge their
fantasies of self-assertion and passionate fulfillment. They communi-

cated their feelings and desires to each other through the indirect
dialogue of textual exchange: Anne and Emily writing their "diary-
paper" and the Gondal tales to each other; Charlotte and Emily
lying in the nursery-bedroom at night jointly composing their "Bed
Plays"; and Charlotte and Branwell creating the extensive Glasstown
saga (Gérin 149).

In *Jane Eyre* and *Villette* the central characters' inner emotional
and creative lives, denied expression or appropriate object in the
external world, are revealed in subtexts – in letters, paintings, student
compositions – but in those novels the subjective dimension is also
with varying degrees of success incorporated into the "true narrative
of life." In *Shirley*, however, the inner life competes for precedence
with the outer in an almost complete inversion of its terms. It is only
through Caroline's domesticated counterfiction to Shirley's mystical
visions – her fantasy of union with her mother within the sickroom –
that this suppressed libidinal and romantic material is brought up to
the surface and represented as a part of the objective narrative:

> The longing of her childhood filled her soul again... that her mother might
> come some happy day, and send for her to her presence – look upon her
> fondly with loving eyes, and say to her tenderly, in a sweet voice: –
> "Caroline, my child. I have a home for you: you shall live with me. All the
> love you have needed, and not tasted, from infancy, I have saved for you
> carefully. Come! it shall cherish you now." (18)

It is through the mediation of the sickroom that Caroline's wish to
be claimed, to assert her being without committing the "crime" of
"forwardness," becomes fact. Unable to imagine a viable identity for
her character through political, marital, or occupational means,
Brontë secures Caroline within the protective enclave of the sickroom
where exemption from the entanglements and frustrations of the
actual is a duty – a prescription for recovery. Instead of substituting
a fictive world for ordinary reality, the sickroom subdues and
transforms reality while still retaining its essential features. Thus,
Caroline can be both separate from the world yet part of it in an
acquiescence to the inevitability of helplessness, the conditions of her
"real" life... isolation, incapacity, and passive submission to fate –
offered as comfort and connection. Caroline's unconditional surrender before the obduracy of the Real ("to wait and endure was her
only plan" [13]) calls into being its repressed opposite, a sanctuary of
perfect harmony and gratified wishes – a kind of intermediary realm

of fulfillment between the extremes of Shirley's blasphemous defiance of the existing order (which can only be imaged in mythic terms) and complete subjugation to "the dark, cold side" of "the world and circumstances" (4).

The central scene of Caroline's illness is meant to be a crucial episode in the rite of passage from "Elf-land" to "the shores of Reality," described below as the passage from a romance to a realistic narrative:

Caroline Helstone was just eighteen years old; and at eighteen the true narrative of life is yet to be commenced. Before that time, we sit listening to a tale, a marvellous fiction; delightful sometimes, and sad sometimes; almost always unreal. Before that time, our world is heroic; its inhabitants half-divine or semi-demon; its scenes are dream-scenes...

At that time – at eighteen, drawing near the confines of illusive void dreams, Elf-land lies behind us, the shores of Reality rise in front. (7)

Instead, her illness marks the point of transition from the "true narrative of life" which has run aground on the barren and forbidding "shores of Reality" to the surreptitious reemergence of romance (of "sentiment, and poetry, and reverie") as a fundamental structural principle governing the narrative. Just as protrusions on the skull provide tell-tale evidence in phrenology, illness figures the involuntary emergence into visibility of the inner self, which, if read aright, makes legible its secret longings. As I will be demonstrating shortly, Caroline's illness and convalescence, viewed in the context of a sequence of parallel scenes and images, suggests a realignment and reinterpretation of the novel's overt realist mode and ideology. But the fact that continued debility is the enabling circumstance of this encounter and conciliation between inner and outer testifies to the persistent incommensurability of these two realms of experience. "I shall hardly wish to get well, that I may keep you always" (24), Caroline tells Mrs. Pryor – a statement that proves prophetic of the terms upon which the relationships in this novel are transacted and sustained.

The proximate cause of Caroline's collapse into illness is the apparent loss of any hope of Robert's love and with that loss the closing off of any means of self-definition: "she returned from an enchanted region to the real world: for Nunnely wood in June, she saw her narrow chamber...for Moore's manly companionship, she had the thin illusion of her own dim shadow on the wall" (10). This illusion of another self is, more generally, a projection of Caroline's fading sense of relationship to the external world in the absence of any fulfilling ties to it. To return to the "real world" is to become unreal, a "pale phantom" (10) of oneself – a familiar enough phenomenon in Brontë's novels, in which the heroines seem for the most part to haunt rather than to inhabit their own lives and surroundings. Tony Tanner mentions, for instance, the "defamiliarized void... which in more muted forms is Lucy Snowe's daily experience."[17]

Caroline's decline into illness "resolves" this impasse (as it did for the prince in Tennyson's *The Princess*) by exchanging the experience of ontological indeterminacy for the determinacy of the ailing body. By making her loss of identity and relation concrete, illness not only renders that loss susceptible to a form of redress, attention, and concern, it also allows for a passive form of self-assertion. It makes the self palpably present to itself, a process made manifest by the appearance at her bedside of Mrs. Pryor – Caroline's nurse, her mother, and her likeness. Formerly suffering from deprivation, solitude, and physical and mental restriction in her "narrow chamber," Caroline now finds – in that bedroom turned sickroom – communion and ease of mind through an intimate reciprocal connection that is immune to the disruptive aspects of male desire and domination. "My own mamma," Caroline says, "who belongs to me, and to whom I belong! I am a rich girl now: I have something I can love well, and not be afraid of loving" (25). In accordance with the paradoxical fate of the socially marginal, Caroline – a mere shadow in the "real world" – becomes substantial again in the "enchanted region" of the sickroom.

A similar pattern of ontological decomposition and passive self-substantiation in the romance world of the sickroom takes place in *Villette*. Lucy, too, is seen by others and by herself as "a colourless shadow" (15). She, too, represses her hopes and desires fearing 'the sin and weakness of presumption' (15) just as Caroline fears the "crime" of "forwardness." And, like Caroline, Lucy gives way instead to "despairing resignation." Her "want of companionship" at the Pensionnat during the long vacation, without even "the prop of employment" to sustain her, except for her attendance on a "cretin" (herself significantly unwanted and abandoned), is merely an extreme paradigm of her ordinary life, her bleak future (15).

Lucy's care of the "cretin" provides one of the recurrent but muted negative images of nursing in Brontë's fiction which subtend the more idealized representations. If the latter provide a romantic vision of full reciprocity, the former underscore Brontë's resentment at a coercive status quo which offers drudgery in the name of duty to the dependent and the powerless. John Kucich's distinction between a repression which in certain social contexts is "at the mercy of external compulsions" and one that in private relations can be converted to an intense and potent form of passionate inwardness is relevant here.[18] Like Caroline Helstone, who rejects the volunteer sick-nursing that is the lot of "old maids" in favor of what proves to be the "libidinal equality"[19] of sickness itself, Lucy's lonely ordeal caring for the "cretin" ends in her own womb-like sickroom among restored kin. Like "Bedridden Hassan, transported in his sleep from Cairo to the gates of Damascus" (16), Lucy awakens to find herself in a "calm little room...like a cave in the sea" (16), from which cozy vantage, "the fiercest breakers" of the outside world sound "like murmurs and a lullaby" (17). Deprivation is transformed into solace; the "outside world" to the inwardness of romance.[20]

Under the care of the Brettons, Lucy is transferred, like Caroline, from the spectral, frozen world of real life to an enchanted region of recognition, identity, relation, and comfort. Lucy's experience also repeats in its essential features that of Jane Eyre who, wandering destitute and alone from Thornfield, is brought grievously ill into the protective circle of her cousins, the Rivers family. The sheer energy of longing for lost family brings its palpable rewards in Brontë's novels, but only in response to the claims of debility – her private language of the heart. Reversing the order of nature, the illnesses that took her family away from her in life bring them back in her fiction. In *Villette*, as in *Jane Eyre* and *Shirley*, the restored family that materializes around the heroine's sickbed is a significantly improved version of its former incarnation. Caroline's mother is wholly devoted to her rather than rejecting; Jane Eyre replaces the dreadful Reeds with the welcoming Rivers family, and at La Terrasse Lucy is no longer the poor relation but the center of the Bretton household.

Later Lucy will be enthralled by the actress Vashti's physical expressiveness: "To her, what hurts becomes immediately embodied" (23). Lucy's ambivalence about this power may tell us something about the use of physical illness as the primary register of certain kinds of excessive feeling in Victorian fiction. The fire that erupts following Vashti's performance suggests that her embodied hurt with its combination of vulgar self-display ("a spectacle low, horrible, immoral" [23]) and incendiary passion could literally bring down the house. Lucy's embodied hurt, on the other hand, solicits intimacy and divulges intense emotion but offers at the same time its own stabilizing repertoire of roles, gestures, and attitudes which order and domesticate the domain of treacherous feeling. Bertha Mason and Jane Eyre enact these same alternatives.

Despite the fairy-tale depiction of Lucy's illness and convalescence, physical disorder is directly identified with psychological distress in *Villette* through the use of the available diagnostic nomenclature of the day.[21] Dr. John sees in Lucy signs of nervous disease, of the dreaded "Hypochondria" which responds to neither "pill or potion" (17). Lucy's own account of what first led to her confession and then to her collapse draws upon medical analogy: "a feeling that would make its way, rush or kill me – like (and this you will understand, Dr. John) the current which passes through the heart, and which, if aneurism or any other morbid cause obstructs its natural channels, seeks abnormal outlet. I wanted companionship, I wanted friendship, I wanted counsel" (17). Dr. John's response ("the priest came to your succour, and the physician, as we have seen, supervened") identifies both the sequence of narrative events and the historical shift in the etiologies of despair. Unhappiness had become a product of the nervous system rather than the soul. Brontë, in effect, reclaims the sickroom enchantment for realism through her medical reference and returns it to "dreamland" by the same route.

The necessary corollary to this self-emergence in the sickroom, however, is that to become well is to return to the sickness of nonentity. Outside the sickroom Lucy becomes a shadow again. Relatedness, hope, and desire are relegated, as they are in *Shirley*, to the "life of thought" and to the written word – in Lucy's brief correspondence with Dr. John and her three years of "perfect happiness" corresponding with the absent Paul.

Caroline's illness brings more lasting rewards. Even before she and Mrs. Pryor are known to each other as parent and child, they form a wholly loving community of two. Caroline's vision of the ideal marriage in which "affection is reciprocal and sincere, and minds are harmonious" (21) is also realized in the sickroom to a degree that is inconceivable elsewhere. "[L]oneliness and gloom were now banished from her bedside; protection and solace sat there instead. She and her nurse coalesced in wondrous union." Mrs. Pryor lives with Caroline "day and night," touches her gently, encircles her in her arms, yields to her caresses (24). The privileged "proximity of a nurse to a patient" eulogized in *Villette* (17) allows for an intensity of interaction, of self-exposure, and physical intimacy, divested of the disturbing male erotic element which has made such direct relational interaction dangerous outside the sickroom. Passion, which according to Shirley, is "a mere fire of dry sticks, blazing up and vanishing," (12), is converted into the more enduring "passion of solicitude" (*V* 23). Accordingly, Robert, the former master, is placed in a subordinate position to Mrs. Pryor, a position from which he is only partially redeemed. This supplantation of the marital or sexual union by the female relationship of nurse to patient is suggested earlier in the novel in a mention of Caroline's aunt (and Mrs. Pryor's sister-in-law), Mrs. Matthewson Helstone, and "a female attendant who had waited upon her in her sickness; and who, perhaps, had had opportunities of learning more of the deceased lady's nature, of her capacity for feeling and loving than her husband knew ... "(4).

In contrast to the unequal distribution of power and of labor which characterizes the relations between masters and dependants in the novel, the "self-elected nurse" (as distinct from "the hireling" [24]) and her patient take turns caring for the other in a cycle of dependency that prevents the permanent ascendance of one over the other. At one point, grieving for the absent Robert, "the patient [Caroline] lay mute and passive in the trembling arms – on the throbbing bosom of the 'nurse'" (24); shortly thereafter Caroline bids Mrs. Pryor to come and be comforted: "She sat down on the edge of her patient's bed, and allowed the wasted arms to encircle her" (24). Still later, when Mrs. Pryor is shaken by her memories of her husband, "the child lulled the parent as the parent had erst lulled the child" (24). Their union dispels the disruptive "other" in a female bond of reciprocal solace.

The Victorian sickroom is frequently portrayed as the site of a special rapport and tenderness between members of the same sex in direct or implicit distinction from the confusions and betrayals of male–female relations. In *Great Expectations*, as we have seen, the tender intimacy between Joe and Pip contrasts with Pip's vexed attraction to Estella. Or in *Diana of the Crossways*, the enduring friendship of Diana Warwick and Emma Dunstane is consummated by their reciprocal debility at crucial moments in the plot. Diana replaces Emma's philandering and neglectful husband, and Emma,

Diana's inconstant lover Mr. Dacier. The contact between nurse and
patient in these scenes is, as in *Shirley*, physically and emotionally
ardent:

She kissed her cheek.
"It is Emmy."
"Kiss her."
"I have no strength."
Emma laid her face on the lips. They were cold; even the breath between
them cold.
"Has Emmy been long...?"
"Here dear? I think so. I am with my darling"...
"You are in Emmy's arms, my beloved."
Tony's [Diana's] eyes closed for forgetfulness under that sensation. A tear
ran down from her, but the pain was lax and neighboured sleep, like the
pleasure.[22]

In *Shirley* the sequestered female space of libidinal solace and
reciprocity opened up at the heart of the novel by Caroline's illness
has its geographical counterpart in Nunnwood, "the sole remnant of
antique British forest" (12). Caroline asks Shirley, "Can you see a
break in the forest, about the centre?... That break is a dell; a deep,
hollow cup, lined with turf as green and short as the sod of this
Common... in the bottom lie the ruins of a nunnery" (12).[23] Shirley
responds, "We will go – you and I alone, Caroline – to that wood"
(12). A secluded place of harmony, of romantic legend (it was one of
Robin Hood's haunts), of nature, and the celibate female, Nunnwood
is a kind of Eden in reverse; the presence of men, both Caroline and
Shirley agree, would spoil it: "If they are of the wrong sort...
irritation takes the place of serenity. If they are of the right sort, there
is still a change" (12). And, indeed, men do ultimately spoil it. First,
Robert Moore comes between Caroline and Shirley exciting rivalry
and mistrust. Finally, and more decisively, Moore's commercial and
industrial interests violate the wild natural area and expel its fairy
inhabitants (37) in the name of progress. "Elf-land" itself undergoes
the transition to "Reality" that Caroline must undergo. As if to
underscore the essentially celibate or pre-sexual nature of Nunnwood,
and its association with the female romance of the sickroom, the
marriage settlements that conclude the novel coincide with and
materially contribute to its destruction.

Thematically, then, the nurse–patient relationship represents a
preferable alternative to marriage and the workplace, to the

instabilities of passion and competition, domination and subjection, and to the stifling malady of the quotidian. But a much more specific and formally subtle process of substitution and inversion takes place in a series of structurally analogous sickroom scenes. The process represents a romantic replacement for the dominant narrative mode (which threatened to end in stalemate) and is, in a sense, the structural equivalent to the sickroom itself and to its quarantine on "dark and desolate reality." Unconstrained by the web of probable circumstance and motivation, stable characterization, and linear progression of traditional realism, these scenes effect a symbolic interchange of identity and relation in the process of which the negative qualities primarily associated with men are, at least temporarily, neutralized or expelled. At the same time, Caroline moves from her peripheral status as abused child and forsaken lover to nurturing wife and daughter, or, in the idiom of the scenes themselves, from patient to nurse. Moreover, this internal romance narrative of sickroom scenes with its private dreamlike intensities, its formal symmetries, its archetypal figures, and its capacity to grant a fulfillment equal to desire, restores formal consistency to a novel which is badly floundering in a welter of styles, points of view, and unassimilated plots in its attempt to reconcile its competing impulses. In these "dream-scenes," the determined pulse of desire, (the "strong, naive bent of the heart") dominates over "the check of Reason" (*V* 23). Thus, Brontë's own narrative is given the "contrary turn" that Caroline wishes to give to St. Paul's first Epistle to Timothy on the position of women (18) while still maintaining her claim to orthodoxy.

We begin with Caroline's "dark recollection" (7) of her father, James Helstone. Although he is only a posthumous presence in the novel, he haunts it as the primal figure of debased appetite and corrupt authority. His disruptive presence as seductive and punishing father, husband, and lover, is gradually feminized and transformed during the course of the sickroom scenes.[24] He first appears before Caroline as a figure of romance, "dim, sinister, scarcely earthly" (7), following her uncle's denunciation of marriage. The hallucination images her own fears about such a union: she sees "another figure standing beside her uncle's – a strange shape – the half-remembered image of her own father, James Helstone, Matthewson Helstone's brother" (7). Caroline then recalls being left alone and starving, "shut up, day and night, in a high garret-room" to which her father would return each night "like a madman, furious, terrible; or – still more painful – like an idiot, imbecile, senseless":

She knew she had fallen ill in this place, and that one night when she was very sick, he had come raving into the room, and said he would kill her, for she was a burden to him; her screams had brought aid, and from the moment she was then rescued from him she had never seen him... (7)

The second scene, Caroline's reunion in the sickroom with the mother she had never known, recapitulates the central elements of the earlier scene with her father. It, too, is precipitated by thoughts of marriage – in this instance, the collapse of Caroline's hope of marriage to Robert, the attenuated version of her demonic father, who, like that father, has "deserted cruelly, trifled wantonly, injured basely" (37). Haunted by Robert's memory, Caroline undergoes solitude, deprivation, confinement to her "narrow chamber," and illness. This time, however, the nurturing mother, herself a victim of male depredation, appears to Caroline in the place of the punishing father in an almost hallucinatory recuperation from the earlier pain, loss, and, perhaps, guilt ("for she was a burden to him"). Just as Mrs. Pryor replaces James Helstone, the father, in this scene, Caroline replaces, or becomes a feminine version of, James Helstone, the husband. (The husband also becomes the dependent child.) Mrs. Pryor refers to Caroline as his "fairy-like representative" (24), "his living likeness," "this thing with [his] perfect features... has nestled affectionately to my heart, and tenderly called me 'mother!'" (24).

In the third of these scenes and, at least ostensibly, their *terminus ad quem*, the elements of apparent abandonment, confinement, deprivation, illness, and sudden reprieve are again present, as is their precipitating occasion, the contemplation of marriage. Following his confession to Mr. Yorke of his mercenary proposal of marriage to Shirley and the betrayal of his true feelings for Caroline, Robert is shot and wounded by a madman, confined in an upstairs room in the Yorke household where he is isolated and almost killed by the incompetence of Mrs. Yorke and Hortense Moore, and later battered and starved by the ferocious Mrs. Horsfall, a member of that despised species, the "hireling" nurse (24). Just as Caroline was "shut up, day and night" by her father, these women "held the young millowner captive, and hardly let the sun shine on him" (32). In Martin Yorke's admittedly exaggerated, but narratively definitive account (he is our only access to the events), he describes Moore as "mewed up, kept in

solitary confinement. They mean to make an idiot or a maniac of
him" (32). His words link Robert's treatment to Caroline's at the
hands of her father, while Robert's impending fate as "an idiot or a
maniac" makes him a potential Helstone ("idiot, imbecile") as well.

This scene, like the others, is marked by the archetypal, dream-like
patterns of romance, complete with Caroline's storming of the
dungeon where her captive lover lies imprisoned, and the defeat of
"the dragon who guarded his chamber," Mrs. Horsfall (32). The
besieging of the Yorke household appropriately begins with Martin
Yorke sitting alone in a wintry wood under the moon, reading "not
the Latin grammar, but a contraband volume of Fairy Tales" (32),
thus underscoring the romantic, fabular nature of this episode as well
as its illicit, or at least guarded, presence in a "realistic" novel. "He
reads ... a green-robed lady, on a snow-white palfrey ... arrests him
with some mysterious question: he is spell-bound, and must follow
her into Fairy-land" (32). At this point, Caroline appears before him,
"like some enchanted lady in a fairy tale" (23), the fate that Rose
Yorke had urged upon her earlier in place of her "long, slow death ...
in Briarfield Rectory" (23). With Martin's help, Caroline manages to
penetrate the fastnesses of Moore's sickroom and to revive her broken
Coriolanus. The only difference between this and the fairy-tales
Martin reads is the sexual role reversal between the liberator and the
liberated.

In this final transposition of identities, Robert takes Caroline's
place as the patient, the helpless victim of aggression and neglect, "a
poor, pale, grim phantom" (35) of his former self, just as she was once
a "pale phantom" for want of his companionship. He also takes over
her provisional role in the second scene as a feminized James
Helstone. "Unmanned" (33) by his experience, and thus denuded of
his threatening otherness, Robert is kept from becoming "an idiot or
a maniac" or more probably, a faithless tyrant. Furthermore, just as
Mrs. Pryor (the good nurse) supplants James Helstone (the bad
nurse) in the first two scenes, Caroline, assuming her mother's role,
supplants Mrs. Horsfall, upon whom the disruptive forces of avarice,
appetite, and aggression have now been displaced and then fully
expelled (or, to be more exact, paid off [35]). Through the progressive
transposition of structural relation and symbolic identity within and
among these scenes, Caroline not only moves from abandoned child
and lover to beloved wife and daughter, but also becomes the
maternal rather than the "unnatural" (24) Mrs. Pryor to Robert's

pacified and domesticated James Helstone. Within the romantic space of successive sickrooms, Caroline's initial fearful image of her parents' marriage has been exorcised and transformed into a benign equivalent to itself. And, with a nod to *Jane Eyre*, imprisonment with a mad person in a "high garret-room" is refigured as voluntary seclusion with one's beloved. The sickroom in Brontë seems to be the available alternative to the attic.

The apparent closure afforded by this process is, however, by its very nature, unstable. Indeed, even the quarantine provided by the sickroom sub-narrative and enclave serves as a somewhat flimsy barricade for the problems it excludes. As an intermediary realm between a total withdrawal into fantasy and the "black trance" (23) of real life (between "Elf-land" and "the shores of Reàlity") the sickroom enclave neither achieves autonomy from the real, nor does it, in ritual fashion, inform or revitalize the world outside its walls. On the contrary, in its essential identity as sickroom, it is necessarily defined in subordinate and deviant relation to the conditions of ordinary life that it abjures; the unity and solace it offers is forged out of the very untoward conditions that made that solace necessary – isolation, passivity, powerlessness, marginality, alienation, and sexual antagonism. The nurse–patient idyll itself is thus contaminated by the conflicts it seeks to expunge and is, in some cases, underwritten by the same power structure that it formally represses.

With this in mind, I would like to return to the union of Caroline and Robert and the terms by which it is achieved. As we have seen, the frightening potential for unreliability, aggression, neglect, or domination in heterosexual relations has been excluded from the sickroom through the "unmanning" of Robert (itself, of course, achieved and sustained through acts of domination and aggression). In the solipsistic manner characteristic of Victorian sickroom scenes in general Caroline, in a sense, makes everyone over in her own image, becoming father, lover, mother, and child in the progressive transposition of identities in the three major sickroom scenes. Such a conflation of identities is also characteristic of the romance mode which, according to George Levine, embodies "the secret lust of the spirit to impose itself on the world."[25] In Brontë's case, such a secret lust is, however, at least in part a response to the imposition of the world upon the spirit, and of the spirit upon the body.

The relationship affirmed in the sickroom remains, in essence, a bond of femaleness, or more accurately still, an exclusive bond of like to like. Caroline's "wondrous union" with her mother provides the model – "no human shadow came between her and what she loved" (25). The continued primacy of this relationship, and of female unions in general, is, in part, signaled by Mrs. Pryor's inclusion in the final settlement[26] with Robert, and by the way in which female intimacy continues to be juxtaposed to male culpability. When, for instance, Caroline tells Moore of her gratitude and devotion to her mother, implicitly invoking his own failure to succor her, he responds: "You talk in such a way about 'mamma,' it is enough to make one jealous of the old lady" (558), to which her not very reassuring reply is, "She is not old, Robert" (35). Later, he questions Caroline about how she learned of his mercenary proposal of marriage to Shirley:

"Miss Keeldar spent a day at the Rectory about a week since...and we persuaded her to stay all night."
"And you and she curled your hair together?"
"How do you know that?"
"And then you chatted; and she told you –"
"It was not a curling-hair time; so you are not so wise as you think... "
"You slept together afterwards?"
"We occupied the same room and bed. We did not sleep much: we talked the whole night through."
"I'll be sworn you did! And then it all came out – tant pis." (558–559)

Robert's jealousy as well as the conditions under which he is ultimately included within these privileged spaces of intimate connection are expressed with astonishing directness by Martin Yorke, the strange, almost preternatural youth whose function in the novel seems to be to underscore what the rest of the narrative obscures. "I think you had better strike a bargain," he tells Caroline; "exchange me for Mrs. Pryor...Will you agree? Make over Mrs. Pryor to my mother, and put me in her skirts?" (34). The sexual *double entendre* in the phrase "put me in her skirts" epitomizes the "bargain" that the inversion of sex roles within the sickroom achieves. Martin's proposed female impersonation would permit him access to an acceptable intimacy with Caroline as well as a disguised reinclusion of sexual desire.

Robert's "unmanning" in the sickroom has a familiar parallel in Rochester's fate as perpetual patient at the end of *Jane Eyre*. In *Jane Eyre*, however, there is no need for a Mrs. Pryor to guarantee future domestic felicity; Rochester is more permanently secured by his continuing incapacity and sequestration with Jane at Ferndean.

Ferndean, like Nunnwood, is clearly a female location "deep buried in a wood" (*JE* 37).[27] Most critics have viewed Rochester's debility as a chastening or domestication of his power – mythical, sexual, or social.[28] What I wish to stress, however, is not so much the symbolic significance of his disability as its outcome – the "perfect concord" (*JE* 38) of the sickroom relation which here, as elsewhere, seems predicated on the exorcism of all potential sources of discord in a fusion of identity so complete and so secluded from others that it appears invulnerable to rival affections, breaches of trust, or even differences in perception. "To be together," Jane says of her relation to Rochester, "is for us to be at once as free as in solitude, as gay as in company. We talk, I believe, all day long: to talk to each other is but a more animated and audible thinking... we are precisely suited to each other in character – perfect concord is the result" (38). In other words, nurse and patient "coalesced in wondrous union" (*S* 24).

This state of identity seems to require either the utter incorporation of the other, or, in narrative terms, the invention of a romance in which one can pass for two. Rochester, in effect, *is* Jane, just as Robert, at least temporarily, becomes Caroline. Not only does Rochester's physical debility mark him as feminized, or, like Robert, "unmanned," but also, because he is blind, he must submit to Jane's imaginative recreation of the world, to see as she sees, to, perforce, participate in her world. "He saw nature – he saw books through me; and never did I weary of gazing for his behalf, and of putting into words the *effect* of field, tree, town, river, cloud, sunbeam – of the landscape before us; of the weather round us – and impressing by sound on his ear what light could no longer stamp on his eye" (38, my emphasis). In the ultimate inversion of inner and outer, her inwardness, her imaginative recreation of the world into words, becomes his sole reality and thus, in a sense, *the* sole reality.

The close identification of lovers is a common feature of Brontë's novels. (Her sister Emily's famous line, "I *am* Heathcliff!" suggests that it was a familial inclination.) In *Villette*, Monsieur Paul's "affinity with women" (29), his rebellious independence of mind, coupled with his dogged loyalty to loved ones and conformity to his faith, even his physical appearance, mark him as Lucy's likeness: "We are alike," he tells her. "Do you observe that your forehead is shaped like mine – that your eyes are cut like mine? Do you hear that you have some of my tones of voice? Do you know that you have many of my looks?" (33). Despite these similarities, however, at the end of this novel, too, Lucy requires imaginative domination over the possible disruptive reality of him: "I thought I loved him when he went away; I love him now in another degree; he is more my own" (42).[29]

One evident personal source for this regressive longing for perfect concord only imaginable as total identity in secluded enclaves can be found in the tightly knit, exclusive society and joint imaginative lives of the Brontë siblings, "their oneness as a family – in temperament, outlook, and sensibility" (Gerin 161). As Charlotte described it in a letter written while she was a governess for the Whites,

My home is humble and unattractive to strangers but to me it contains what I shall find nowhere else in the world – the profound, the intense affection which brothers and sisters feel for each other when their minds are cast in the same mould, their ideal drawn from the same source when they have clung to each other from childhood, and when disputes have never sprung up to divide them.[30]

To an extent, all of Charlotte's fictive couples commemorate that harmony before the family's enforced separation, before the harsh intervention of financial need and ambition directed their attention toward what they perceived to be a hostile and unresponsive external world, and before they directed their desires toward the real-life inhabitants of that world – Monsieur Heger, Mrs. Robinson, Willie Weightman – the loved ones who did not reciprocate their love. The inability of all the Brontës to adjust to a world wider but far less accommodating than Haworth Parsonage and the fictional worlds they created there condemned them to remain in it as a place of premature burial ("I feel as if we were all buried here" Charlotte wrote [Gaskell 275]) as well as a refuge of privileged intimacy. In the Parsonage the conditions of deprivation doubled as the available terms of fulfillment, just as the final scene of illness in *Shirley* recasts in positive terms the essential attributes of the first – or just as illness itself registers both the loss or diminution of self and its sole means of preservation. Even the typhus fever that killed the elder Brontë sisters, Maria and Elizabeth, at the school for clergymen's daughters could, according to this emotional and experiential logic, be represented in *Jane Eyre* as the occasion for liberation from the enforced deprivations of Lowood School: "But I, and the rest who continued well, enjoyed fully the beauties of the scene and season: they let us ramble in the wood like gipsies from morning till night; we did what we liked, went where we liked: we lived better too" (9).

The sickroom secures for its inhabitants what they started out with, albeit under the guise of protection and solace: it exempts them from an active role in their own affairs; it attains their willing acquiescence to dependency; it sequesters them from society in closed rooms under a carefully observed regimen, obedient to the authority of the figure in charge or, alternatively, in the position of nurse. Ferndean is, after all, "insalubrious" (*JE* 37) and isolated, and Jane, however willingly, a perpetual nurse to an aging, half-blind invalid. Moreover, if her possession of Rochester suggests domination, it is also a form of subjection. As the narrator of George Eliot's *Felix Holt* comments, "strength is often only another name for willing bondage to irremediable weakness" (6). In a sense, the inversion of the intolerable into the desirable circumstance occurs not only within the novel, but between the author's life and her recreation of her own life as well. It is, for example, not difficult to see in the ending of *Jane Eyre*, transmuted into "a happy, succeeding life" (*V* 42), the shape of Charlotte's life at Haworth – itself an insalubrious and isolated setting – caring for her half-blind father and obliged to recreate the world in words.

The sickroom idyll, then, seems inevitably to bear the impress of the real. Circumstances do not change, only the presentation or interpretation of them does. The famous apostrophe to the reader at the end of *Villette* alludes obliquely to this imaginative process:

Leave sunny imaginations hope. Let it be theirs to conceive the delight of joy born again fresh out of peril, the wondrous reprieve from dread, the fruition of return. Let them picture union and a happy, succeeding life. (42)

In *Jane Eyre* and *Shirley*, Brontë does the work of the sunny imagination for us. The darker view of the same events remains implicit in them, however, because the conditions of intimacy, of "profound, intense affection" can be found 'nowhere else in the world' but in the protective quarantine of mutual dependency and illness.

It remains to be seen how the sickroom relation not only bears within itself the imprint of the reality it wishes to transform but is also underwritten or perpetuated by the struggles for money and power which it seeks to exclude. Although Robert remarks to Mr. Yorke that with Caroline's love an "unselfish longing to protect and cherish" would replace "the sordid, cankering calculations of... trade" (30), it is the latter that makes the former not only possible, but necessary.

Comparing Caroline's fate to that of the workers reveals the complicitous relation between the sickroom and the ills it seeks to heal. Although their modes of resistance are divergent, the fates of women and workers converge once more in their joint return to powerlessness. Submission and defiance alike are shown to lead to debility and defeat. Yet that very debility, for the workers as well as for Caroline, becomes the avenue of redress. The defeated workers have their immediate physical needs tended by the women at Fieldhead Manor after their abortive revolt is put down by soldiers. Physical suffering is the means by which moral pressure is exerted on those with the power but not the will to alleviate economic and social ills. Once the power of the masters has been demonstrated and consolidated by the disabling of the workers and of their protest, the workers' condition can be recognized and improved through the intermediary agency of nursing women.[31] No longer invisible (either as superfluities in a machine age or as a faceless, mutinous mob), the workers suddenly are visible objects of compassion as patients and victims. (Eagleton observes, "at the point of its most significant presence in the novel, the working class is almost wholly invisible" [49].) This process of substantiation with a price, begun by the rout of the rebellious workers at the mill, is completed when the victorious Robert goes to London. Whereas before he had been impervious, indifferent, even contemptuous of the misery of the unemployed, he is suddenly able to see and be moved by it:

Unknown, I could go where I pleased, mix with whom I would. I went where there was want of food, of fuel, of clothing; where there was no occupation and no hope. I saw some, with naturally elevated tendencies and good feelings, kept down amongst sordid privations and harassing griefs. I saw many originally low, and to whom lack of education left scarcely anything but animal wants, disappointed in those wants, ahungered, athirst, and desperate as famished animals: I saw what taught my brain a new lesson, and filled my breast with fresh feelings. (30)

Although brutal exploitation and neglect has been replaced by compassion, the physical substantiation of both women and workers as impotent victims, has, in fact, secured their subjection to their masters more effectively. It is significant that what enables Robert to see his workers as sufferers is his own invisibility (as well as their substitution by the urban poor). The omniscience of the master, his ability to move about freely and to survey the needs and desires of his inferiors, resides in his own inaccessibility and their materiality as suffering bodies. As Elaine Scarry observes in *The Body in Pain*, "to have no body is to have no limits on one's extension out into the world; conversely, to have a body...is to have one's sphere of extension contracted down to the small circle of one's immediate physical presence...to be intensely embodied...is almost always the condition of those without power."[32] The example of the workers in *Shirley* – both invisible and embodied – would seem to indicate that Scarry's formula requires this emendation: invisibility is an instrument, not the origin, of power.

Moore's conversion to paternalism precludes the possibility of a more equitable relationship with his workers by making physical dependency the grounds and the condition for redress. This process is given succinct expression by the plain-speaking Hiram Yorke's response to Robert's own disabled condition following the attack on his life:

This utter dependence of this speechless, bleeding youth...on his benevolence secured that benevolence most effectually. Well did Mr. Yorke like to have power, and to use it: he had now between his hands power over a fellow-creature's life: it suited him. (32)

and even more succinctly by his wife's response:

Mrs. Yorke was just the woman who, while rendering miserable the drudging life of a simple maid-servant, would nurse like a heroine an hospital full of plague patients. (32)

Caroline herself connects such nurturing benevolence with power and control when she says of the Yorkes' baby, "I feel that I love that helpless thing quite peculiarly, though I am not its mother. I could do almost anything for it willingly, if it were delivered to my care – if it were quite dependent on me" (23). Indeed, the frenzied machinations of Caroline, and the Draconian measures of the Yorkes, along with their respective allies, Martin Yorke and Mrs. Horsfall, to gain and secure exclusive access to Robert, amounts to a struggle for power over the disposition of his helpless body.

If Robert's experience of powerlessness, when he is shot by a "half-crazed" weaver, put within Mr. Yorke's power, then bullied and starved by a woman, seems to avenge by proxy his earlier actions against the workers and against Caroline, it should be noted that the means through which this is achieved endorse by imitation the inescapability of the disabling process; only the relative positions of the participants have been reversed, only to be reversed again. An appropriate finale to this series of power plays between Robert and his workers restores Robert to his position as their master just as he will be restored as Caroline's. When the newly paternalistic Robert chooses not to pursue his attacker, sickness does his work for him, thus providing a further opportunity for him to display his benevolence even as he is avenged: "[T]he poor soul died of delirium tremens a year after the attempt on Moore, and Robert gave his wretched widow a guinea to bury him" (37).

Even the appearance of equality in the sickroom reunion between Caroline and Robert ("You speak my experience," he tells her in a phrase that recalls Jane's function for the blind Rochester [33]) is undercut by the fact that they have been brought together on terms that invoke the worst aspects of the marriage that their own union is meant to abjure. Again Martin Yorke is the demystifying agent. His services as guide and go-between are exchanged for sexual favors (a kiss) with a hint of sadism ("Wouldn't I have you in good discipline if I owned you!" [34]), and for the pleasure of exercising power: "I have power over her, and I want her to come that I may use that power" (33). Martin's double role here recalls Rochester's question, and his relation, to Jane Eyre: "By what instinct do you pretend to distinguish between...a guide and a seducer?" (14). Despite the apparent transformations of the horrors of the Pryor–Helstone marriage into the "ideal" union between Caroline and Robert, the terms upon which the earlier marriage was consummated and sustained still cast their shadow on its reformed counterpart.

The relations between Shirley and Robert's brother Louis more fully expose those terms, though still in a relatively benign form. Louis professes a desire for "ascendancy" (29) over an ever-erring, ever-resistant Shirley: "In managing the wild instincts of the scarce manageable 'bete fauve,' my powers would revel" (29). She, conveniently, longs to submit to a "master" but only after "rousing his whole deliberate but determined nature to revolt against her tyranny, at once so sweet and so intolerable" (37). The skirmishes that characterize their courtship resemble those that sustained the piquancy of Jane's and Rochester's pre-nuptial exchanges. They are punctuated by interludes of gentle affection elicited by the illness of one or the other of the combatants.[33] This erotic and relational preference reenacts the punishing terms of social relations as a game made pleasurable by the interchange of dominant roles. (Only ostensibly, of course; Louis is the acknowledged "sovereign" [37].) The concluding arrangement of Jane's and Rochester's life together and the primacy of Caroline's and Robert's relationship in *Shirley* would seem to suggest that the sickroom offers a more palatable version of pain experienced as pleasure than such apparently sado-masochistic games could afford. At the very least it establishes a companionable truce between sovereign and subject while assuaging conflicting desires to occupy both positions at once.

For Brontë, ultimately, there seems to be no available alternative to relations based upon the cruel opposition between domination and submission; there are only more or less consolatory variants – "varieties of pain." If *Shirley* registers a protest against such a state of affairs, it also raises it to the level of a cosmic principle. "I believe," Robert tells Mr. Yorke before he is shot down,

I daily find it proved – that we can get nothing in this world worth keeping, not so much as a principle or a conviction, except out of purifying flame, or through strengthening peril...we are sickened, degraded...our souls rise bitterly indignant against our bodies; there is a period of civil war; if the soul has strength, it conquers and rules thereafter. (30)

The way of the polity and the hearthside is the way of the soul as well.

Whereas Jane Eyre is permitted to secure her incapacitated lover – a perpetual convalescent from the "crushing, grinding" lessons of experience (14) – under her domination as his nurse and guide in a secluded and implicitly primal location, Caroline, in accordance with the dictates of Brontë's professed realism, must be returned to "the shores of Reality" outside the sickroom walls. It is a reality that belongs to Robert, as the subdivision of Nunnwood and the correspondent subduing of female harmony under male dominance demonstrate. With Robert's restored health, the repeal of the Orders in Council, the advantageous marriage of his brother, Louis, and the development of new markets, "the manufacturer's daydreams [were] embodied in substantial stone and brick and ashes – the cinder-black highway, the cottages, and the cottage-gardens...a mighty mill, and a chimney, ambitious as the tower of Babel" (37). Caroline's daydreams, meanwhile, and the Elf-land she has surrendered, have – after a brief fulfillment in the sickroom – reverted to tales told by women, to women.

"What was the Hollow like then, Martha?"

"Different to what it is now; but I can tell of it clean different again: when there was neither mill, nor cot, nor hall, except Fieldhead, within two miles of it. I can tell, one summer-evening, fifty years syne, my mother coming running in just at the edge of dark, almost fleyed out of her wits, saying, she had seen a fairish (fairy) in Fieldhead Hollow; and that was the last fairish that ever was seen on this country side...A lonesome spot it was – and a bonnie spot – full of oak trees. It is altered now." (37)

CHAPTER 3

Charles Dickens: "impossible existences"

"Wishin' you lots of sickness" (*MC* 29), Sairey Gamp's parting salute to her colleague, Betsey Prig, has a wider application and significance in Dickens's fiction as a whole than its immediate comic context would suggest. There *is* "lots of sickness" in his novels, and the profits to be gained by it are neither solely nor primarily confined to those for whom it provides a ready source of income. Sairey's mercenary reversal of the usual parting expectations of good health, however rich a source of humor, corresponds to the consistent reversal of illness from curse to blessing in the lives of most of the major and many of the minor characters who inhabit the Dickens world. Illness in Dickens's fiction is the *sine qua non* both of restored or reconstructed identity, and of narrative structure and closure.

Dickensian patients, like their counterparts in other Victorian fiction, move from the extremities of personal crisis in "the fevered world" to the protective sequestration of the "fevered room" (*LD* ii, 33) where a loving nurse or sequence of nurses[1] stands by with soothing remedies at hand and where the barriers between hitherto estranged loved ones, or between aspects of their own divided selves, collapse under the leveling power of physical distress. In just such a manner is Eugene Wrayburn united with Lizzie Hexam, Arthur Clenham with Little Dorrit, Dick Swiveller with the Marchioness, and Oliver Twist with, first, Mr. Brownlow, then the Maylies. It is thus that Pip is reconciled with Joe, Esther Summerson with Lady Dedlock, Martin Chuzzlewit with Mark Tapley, and, of course, all of them with themselves.

In addition to being the hallowed ground of matrimonial, filial, and self-unification, the Dickensian sickroom serves as a kind of provisional or preliminary heaven – a status underscored by its repeated association with the *locus amoenus* of the pastoral. Oliver Twist, for instance, convalesces at the Maylie cottage in the country:

"Who can describe the pleasure and delight, the peace of mind and soft tranquillity, the sickly boy felt in the balmy air, and among the green hills and rich woods of an inland village!" To "pain-worn dwellers in close and noisy places such 'sunny spots' are 'a foretaste of heaven itself" (30). Pip, slowly recovering from his fever, takes an excursion into the country with Joe "where the rich summer growth was already on the trees... and sweet summer scents filled all the air" with the sound of "Sunday bells" as an accompaniment (*GE* 57). Even in the midst of London, Dick Swiveller, in a convalescent "luxury of repose," finds himself "staring at some green stripes upon the bed-furniture, and associating them strangely with patches of fresh turf" (*OCS* 64), and the ailing Arthur Clenham, "dozing and dreaming" in the very heart of the Marshalsea prison, feels "some abiding impression of a garden [steal] over him – a garden of flowers, with a damp warm wind gently stirring their scents" (*LD* ii, 29). These convalescent intimations of immortality seem to lend a more general credence to the retarded Maggy's tribute to the hospital in *Little Dorrit*, as well as to the inverted norms of Sairey's earlier benediction. "Oh so nice it was," Maggy rhapsodizes, "such a Ev'nly place!" (i, 9).

Sweet-smelling, orderly, companionate, peaceful, and remote from worldly care and want, Dickens's sickrooms resemble those encountered in Victorian fiction generally, although at times surpassing them in the particularly Dickensian degree of their coziness and conviviality and in the extent of the contrast they provide to the manic restlessness and profusion of the narratives they conclude. The healing processes of the Dickens sickroom are, however, invariably preceded by an intermediate stage of feverish delirium, which give the sickroom scenes in his novels their particular and defining relations to the narratives in which they, and their suffering protagonists, are embedded.[2] Working, in a sense, backwards and forwards from these delirious episodes, I will be considering, in what follows, the implications of Dickens's own explicit linking of the narrator to "a sick man" dwelling "in narrow ways" and the narrative to the sick man's "restless dreams" (*OCS* i).

The feverish state of mind and body, which figures so prominently in the progression of Dickensian disease, varies little in its essential features whether the sufferer be the negligible and culpable Lewsome in *Martin Chuzzlewit*, the central and "pattern" Esther Summerson in *Bleak House*, the innocent Little Nell, or the worldly and cynical

Eugene Wrayburn in Dickens's last complete novel, *Our Mutual Friend*; all suffer alike; all are tormented by the same dread. In Dickens's fiction, to be feverish is to be overwhelmed by a sickening convergence of identities, places, and stages of life, and to be tortured by the concomitant and compulsive need to keep separate, to detach, or to reconcile the press of images that become confounded each with the other. This horror of indistinct or dissolving boundaries, and the urgency with which the sufferer seeks to reestablish order and distinction, is accompanied by a profound restlessness of mind and body – of wandering endlessly without progressing.

At the height of his fever, Pip's hallucinations depict the vertiginous terrors implicit in the loss of a distinct identity and the inability to distinguish among the identities of others. He recalls:

that I confounded impossible existences with my own identity; that I was a brick in the house wall, and yet entreating to be released from the giddy place where the builders had set me; that I was a steel beam of a vast engine, clashing and whirling over a gulf, and yet that I implored in my own person to have the engine stopped, and my part in it hammered off. (*GE* 57)

Similarly, in the midst of her feverish delusions, Esther Summerson imagines herself to be attached to a flaming necklace "strung together somewhere in great black space." Like Pip, she "prays to be taken off from the rest" (*BH* 35). During her delirium, the confounding of Esther's own past existences becomes the source of "painful unrest" during which "divisions of time became confused with one another... At once a child, an elder girl, and the little woman I had been so happy as, I was not only oppressed by cares and difficulties adapted to each station, but by the great perplexity of endlessly trying to reconcile them" (35). The same restless inability to distinguish among the stages of one's life and to separate the cares appropriate to each besets Lewsome, whose "haggard mind" gropes "darkly through the past, incapable of detaching itself from the miserable present... seeking but a moment's rest among the long-forgotten haunts of childhood and the resorts of yesterday, and dimly finding fear and horror everywhere!" (*MC* 25). For Little Emily in *David Copperfield* when she was, in Mr. Peggotty's words, "took bad with fever," there was "no to-day, nor yesterday, nor yet tomorrow; but everything in her life as ever had been, or as ever could be, and everything was as never had been, and as never could be, was a crowding on her all at once, and nothing clear nor welcome" (51).

And Dick Swiveller "ramble[s] ever through deserts of thought where there was no resting-place...with no change but the restless shifting of his body and the weary wanderings of his mind, constant still to one ever-present anxiety" (*OCS* 64).

As if in direct response to such feverish longings for detachment or separation, a total lapse in consciousness ushers in the ensuing stage of convalescent peace and plenty, of order and restored relation. Like the pastoral "heaven" it precedes, this period of unconsciousness hints at the final rest of death itself.[3] Esther, for instance, speaks of the "repose that succeeded, the long delicious sleep, the blissful rest, when in my weakness I was too calm to have any care for myself, and could have heard...that I was dying; with no other emotion than with a pitying love for those I left behind" (35). Dick Swiveller sinks into a deep, dreamless sleep, and awakens "with a sensation of most blissful rest, better than sleep itself" (64). And Oliver Twist, falling asleep in the protective custody of the Maylies after a night of pain, "felt calm and happy, and could have died without a murmur" (30).

Identity is clearly at issue in all of these delirious states, as are the separations and connections that inform and complicate its fashioning and that necessitate the sickroom's powers of reconciliation. The presentation of the dilemma of identity as both an endless restlessness and disorientation, and a painfully undesirable attachment or connection, suggests that a fixed identity with its potentially unassimilable implications and conjunctions is as threatening as an indeterminate identity with its equally undesirable uncertainties and insecurities – perhaps more so.[4] As the deliriums suggest, the search for sustaining and defining connections is also a flight from the convergences that such a search continually threatens to reveal: "the confounding of impossible existences with [one's] own identity" implicit in such pairings as Orlick with Pip, Bradley Headstone with Eugene Wrayburn, Quilp with Nell, or in such unholy alliances with violence, passion, or injustice as Arthur Clenham's and Esther Summerson's with the sordid facts of their own pasts and origins, or Pip's with his benefactor, Abel Magwitch; the confusion of "divisions of time" such as Esther's lonely and disgraced childhood casting its shadow upon her protected life at Bleak House; or, conversely, the ignominies of Little Emily's fall lending a retrospective taint to her uncorrupted youth in Yarmouth.

The dread of convergence which haunts these and other sufferers is posed against what is generally felt to be the great syncretic gift of

Dickens's imagination – his ability to link apparent differences or incongruities in ways that confirm the intelligibility and coherence of a world in danger of disintegration. John Forster notes that "few things moved [Dickens's] fancy so pleasantly" as "the coincidences, resemblances, and surprises of life," and that Dickens would often observe that "people supposed to be far apart were so constantly elbowing each other; and to-morrow bore so close a resemblance to nothing half so much as to yesterday."[5] Dickens's contemporaries saw in such patterns of congruence the affirmation of an order unseen but cohesive and ultimately benign in effect. One commentator, cited in Forster, asserted that Dickens's imagination "could call up at will those associations which, could we but summon them in full number, would bind together the human family, and make that expression no longer a name but a living reality" (Forster 727n.) But the constant elbowing of "people supposed to be far apart" and the resemblance of tomorrow to yesterday are the very attributes that torment the fever patients and engender their agonized desire to "be taken off from the rest." Unsuspected connections could clearly be as painful and disorienting as they could be the grounds of compassion and solidarity. Dickens himself once referred to his ability to "fancy or perceive relations in things that are not apparent generally" as an "infirmity" (Forster 721). The connections rise unbidden and unleash a correspondent effort to avoid, as Esther says of her own feverish delusions, "the great perplexity of endlessly trying to reconcile them."

The Victorian assertion of a "common humanity" in general had to negotiate the increasingly complex and fiercely defended divisions and stratifications of nineteenth-century society. Separations of every kind characterized the Victorian social structure – separations between work and home, women and the workplace, children and adults, men and women, class and class.[6] The multiple gradations of subclasses which constituted the Victorian middle class sought to confirm their social and economic progress and the growing perquisites pertaining to their status through subtle and not so subtle discriminations in every area of their lives. Who one was seemed increasingly to depend on who one wasn't and, more important, perhaps, who one no longer was. The rise and fall of reputations, of fortunes gained and lost, and class hurdles jumped, of respectability painstakingly acquired yet continually menaced, required the vigilant maintenance of distinctions not only between the high and the low, the reputable and the disreputable, but between yesterday and today. Richard Sennett writes: "respectability founded on chance: that is the economic fact of the 19th Century which was associated with a demography of expansion and isolation."[7] The compulsive need experienced during the delirious stage of fever to keep yesterday from encroaching on today or tomorrow, or to keep someone else's menacing attributes from encroaching upon one's own sense of self expresses with great acuity what the cultural mandate to make these distinctions exacted – the feverish restlessness required to stay ahead, or at least to hold one's place, and the continual sense of being haunted or pursued by the denials by which the social self is constructed.

The replication of career and class anxieties within the delirium had, in fact, a contemporary medical sanction. Victorian doctors were in general agreement that the fear of financial and professional reverses and of the resultant loss of social status were among the primary sources of nervous disease among men.[8] M. Jeanne Peterson notes that among the upper-class families she studied nervous disorders frequently appeared among professional men. "What is striking," she writes, "is that men suffered so often from depression, and descriptions of their illnesses sound very much like those usually attributed to Victorian women."[9] According to Janet Oppenheim, Victorian and Edwardian doctors generally focused on "the professional and commercial middle classes when considering male nervous exhaustion" because:

Unlike members of the aristocracy and gentry who had an assured position in society, and equally unlike the workers who had no claim to social standing at all, the middle-class husband and father was always negotiating a place for himself and his family on the social ladder. The need to secure a sufficient income, to keep competitors at bay, and to meet financial obligations all pressed the more ponderously on him, adding a weighty load of anxiety to the daily business of managing his affairs.[10]

There was, moreover, a general ambivalence toward the very enterprising energies which offered such palpable rewards. The self-estrangement figured in Dickens's depiction of delirious states could, in other words, derive from the necessity to disavow not only the past, but also the aspirations that demanded such a disavowal to begin with. Alexander Welsh suggests, for instance, that the "broader cultural motive" behind Dickens's reconstruction of the blacking warehouse incident as a pivotal childhood trauma was "the need to justify a rise in the world, so desired by the sons of the nineteenth century."[11] The discrediting of the drive for personal success was also corroborated by the medical establishment, which warned against the dangers of overwork and excessive ambition. "In striving to outstrip his rivals, a man could obviously destroy his own health" and prove himself "socially dangerous."[12] The usual prescription of extended rest for breakdowns in health resulting from overwork and anxiety has clear attractions. Charles Lamb writes of the sick man:

A little while ago he was greatly concerned in the event of a law-suit, which was to be the making or the marring of his dearest friend. He was to be seen trudging about upon this man's errand to fifty quarters of the town at once ... The cause was to come on yesterday. He is absolutely as indifferent to the decision, as if it were a question to be tried at Pekin. Peradventure from some such whispering, going on about the house, not intended for his hearing, he picks up enough to make him understand, that things went cross-grained in the Court yesterday, and his friend is ruined. But the word "friend," and the word "ruin," disturb him no more than so much jargon. He is not to think of any thing but how to get better.[13]

The anxiety of convergence that structures the deliriums is a principal source of the restless complexities of Dickens's narratives and of the partitioning of competing energies in his frequent doublings of plot and character. Narrative and delirium are explicitly linked in the pursuits, chases, and "feverish wandering journey[s]" that so often serve as analogues and central structuring elements of the Dickensian search for self. They are described in similar language, their propulsive energy derives from the same source, and in most cases the feverish journeys are transposed into the fevers of mind and body and are cured by the separations and connections of the sickroom community. Here, for instance, is Carker fleeing his pursuer and the collapse of his resolute social and professional advance:

It was a fevered vision of things past and present confounded together; of his life and journey blended into one. Of being madly hurried somewhere, whither he must go. Of old scenes starting up among novelties through which he travelled. Of musing and brooding over what was past and distant, and seeming to take no notice of the actual objects he encountered, but with a wearisome exhausting consciousness of being bewildered by them, and having their images all crowded in his hot brain after they were gone. (*D* 55)

What awaits Carker at journey's end is the terrifying fate that haunts both delirium and narrative and which the sickroom refuge intervenes to prevent – the collision of irreconcilable selves and the disintegration of identity and form: "he...was beaten down, caught up, and whirled away upon a jagged mill, that spun him round and round, and struck him limb from limb...and cast his mutilated fragments in the air" (*D* 55).

The bodily stasis of delirium in effect figures the disintegrative nightmare of Dickensian narratives of self-discovery – a nightmare continually averted in these narratives by spatial and temporal mobility. As Dickens asserted to Forster with reference to his own restless life, "it is better to go on and fret, than to stop and fret" (639). And again: "If I couldn't walk fast and far enough I should just explode and perish" (721). By permitting through displacement and deferral the contiguity of oppositional categories and discarded identities, the narrative constitutes a form of spatial quarantine sustained by constant motion and dislocation. Whether it is Quilp chasing Nell and Grandfather Trent, Esther pursuing her mother, or Eugene leading Bradley Headstone on what seems to be a wild-goose chase – instances I will be discussing in some detail – the more culpable figure in each set of doubles is kept at a distance, though always in dangerous and suggestive proximity.

The prolonging of these feverish journeys, or, more accurately, their compulsive continuation, provides a middle ground between full disclosure (or exposure) and total denial. Esther Summerson, for instance, can neither fully separate herself from, nor accept (and publicly proclaim) identification with Lady Dedlock once their relationship has been made known to her. To do the former would be to deny her own existence, and to do the latter would be to expose her mother's guilt to others and with it her own "inheritance of shame" (*BH* 44). Her "feverish, wandering journey" with Bucket in the always receding footsteps or planned diversions of Lady Dedlock's own flight-cum-journey dramatizes the dilemma of identity as Dickens posits it and serves as partial solution as well. By always approaching but never reaching her purported goal, Esther maintains both a crucial distance from, and a connection to, her own identity in all its aspects. In Patrick Creevy's characterization of her pursuit "Esther...will drive across her whole life in the dark night and, at the end, confront the question of her real worth and proper direction."[14] If so, it is an odd form of confrontation, for, although Esther is, in a sense, finally united at the end of her journey with both of her parents, and thus presumably with the full disclosure of her origins, the configuration of the meeting indicates the partially suppressed nature of its significance for her – her father is buried and her mother dies in disguise. Lady Dedlock, as I suggest above, is herself racing both toward and away from identities she can neither fully acknowledge nor utterly repudiate. She dies at the threshold of the cemetery. The separations among Esther, Lady Dedlock, and Captain Nemo (or "nobody") are thus maintained at the very moment of their reunion, a separation that is reinforced both by Esther's prior and subsequent illness.[15]

The attempt to shape an identity which keeps antithetical or undesirable elements separate holds out the prospect of a continual restless oscillation among the manifestations, both ghostly and substantial, of the "multifarious...denizens" of the single self.[16] Indeed, all of the restless attempts at segregation in *Bleak House*, (and, by implication, in Dickens's fiction generally) are linked through the vagrant Jo to the phenomenon of "moving on," a form of social quarantine of undesirable elements which simply spreads contagion rather than containing it. Esther's apparently purposeful pursuit of her mother back and forth over the same terrain is finally the same as Lady Dedlock's restless change of venue ("Lady Dedlock is restless, very restless...Today, she is at Chesney Wold, yesterday she was at her house in town; tomorrow, she may be abroad" [16], or even Esther's own increasingly frenetic busyness ("I shall be always coming backwards and forwards" [51], she assures Ada). Each has as its animating impulse the prevention of that terrifying possibility glimpsed in Esther's delirium that "divisions of time" might become "confused with one another" and with them the identities appropriate to each. Each is engendered by the same inability to reconcile past and present selves, the same desire to keep the disgraces of the past from infecting the loyalties and affections of the present. "How often had I considered within myself," Esther recalls, "that the deep traces of my illness, and the circumstances of my birth, were only new reasons why I should be busy, busy, busy" (44). And just as in her hallucinatory impression during her fever that she was laboring up "never-ending stairs" (an impression of non-progressive movement common to Dickensian fevers in general) none of these "feverish, wandering journey[s]" leads anywhere. The selves cannot be expunged or assimilated, they can only be out-distanced.

The internalization of the narrative wanderings into the feverish wanderings of bodily ailment both identifies narrative and life as diseased, and provides an antidote to the expenditure of nervous energy which continually threatens to run athwart the operative values of social stability and communal obligation. The desire to be "taken off from the rest" is finally accomplished by the narrative interregnum of the sickroom scene and its removal from the main narrative's causal and developmental sequences. The progress of disease and the body's healing processes substitute for what Dickens calls in *Edwin Drood* "the vast iron-works of time and circumstance" (13) and constructs (and sentimentalizes) a self and set of relations which are free from the anxieties of differentiation by virtue of being *hors de concours*. As Pip says of his convalescence from fever under Joe's care: "I would half believe that all my life since the days of the old kitchen was one of the mental troubles of the fever that was gone" (*GE* 57). Fever both makes and unmakes the world.

The recapitulative nature of Pip's delirium and the new life it ushers in goes far towards substantiating his "half"-belief that his previous life has effectively been eliminated as a determinant of character and destiny. Pip's feverish fantasies do, in specific and revelatory fashion, reenact his "life since the days of the old kitchen," and his recovery seems to constitute a recovery of his childhood at Joe's side. In his life, as in its feverish reenactment, he attempts to sever himself from the "impossible existences" which have become confounded with his own identity; he struggles with potential murderers; and he fails to distinguish among the people "who meant to do [him] good" and those who wish him ill (57).[17] Within the confined and clearly designated boundaries of the sickroom, the plurality of surrogate and repudiated selves with which Pip contended in the course of his career of expectancy settle into one innocent and childlike man: "I knew that there was an extraordinary tendency in all these people, sooner or later to settle into the likeness of Joe" (57). The exclusions of the sickroom permit the convergence of many into one to take place without danger by narrowing the possible existences to nurse and patient.

The competitive relations which characterize the struggle for economic advancement and acquisition are replaced by the simple exchanges of the therapeutic relationship. Pip, under the care of Joe, the step-brother of whom he was once so ashamed, is all "helpless passivity." He is now required by his condition to "submit...to all [Joe's] orders." His hopeless and excessive desire for Estella, the instigating motive for advancement, is exchanged for "the tenderness of Joe … so beautifully proportioned to my needs" (57). And his once vague and immoderate expectations, previously expressed in the form of superfluous valets, have become simply defined and thoroughly provided for by Joe, his far from superfluous nurse: "I was to be talked to in great moderation and … to take a little nourishment at stated frequent times… He did everything for me" (57). Pip, in short, feels himself to be "little Pip again" and notes with satisfaction that "there was no change whatever in Joe" (57). Not only has the intervening narrative been exorcised as one of the mental troubles of the fever that was gone, but "the days of the old kitchen" have been recreated in the sickroom as an idyll, purged of the violence and guilt that had oppressed Pip even then. As in Charlotte Brontë's novels, the powerful association of sickness with childhood and with protective succor operates to refigure the past within the present.[18] Dickens's uncertainty about how to end *Great Expectations* suggests that the sickroom was as far as he could go with confidence in the shaping of an appropriate terminus for his hero, once Pip had renounced his expectations of rising in the world. The disjunctive violence of sudden illness and enforced passivity imposes the moderating and affirmative side of the realist agenda by fiat. Depletion is presented as the consequence and the cure for the feverish energies of passion, ambition, and shame.

The fate of such characters as Maggy in *Little Dorrit*, Mr. Dick in *David Copperfield*, and Chuffey in *Martin Chuzzlewit* provides an ironic commentary on the permanent disability and cessation of story implicitly necessary to the sickroom cure. Maggy, whom we have already encountered extolling the "Ev'nly" virtues of the hospital where her fever was cured ("she had never been at peace before" [9]), gains her peace of mind at the expense of further growth and maturation. "She had a bad fever, sir," Little Dorrit explains, "and she has never grown any older ever since" (9). Chuffey, Anthony Chuzzlewit's aged clerk, another fever victim, is only half a self, drawing whatever of sentient being he possesses from the presence of his employer. The most revealing metaphor for the crippling division upon which closure or "rest" in Dickens's novels depends, however, is the severed head of King Charles the First, the reappearance of which continually disrupts Mr. Dick's Memorial in *David Copperfield*. In Mr. Dick's account of his own illness "the people about [King Charles] have made the mistake of putting some of the trouble out of *his* head … into *mine*" (14). The figure Mr. Dick uses is suggestive of the convergence of a repudiated or traitorous identity with one's own despite all attempts, literally and figuratively, to take it off from the rest. Mr. Dick's uncorrupted, childlike innocence is continually haunted by the self he wishes to expunge.

The novel that most fully exemplifies the dynamic I have been describing and the problems it addresses is *The Old Curiosity Shop*. The informing impulse of that novel – to keep Nell's "innocent face and pure intentions" surrounded, yet distinct, from "associates as strange and uncongenial as the grim objects that are about her bed" (*OCS* Preface) – is only a more mythic or (as Dickens's narrator Master Humphrey suggests) allegorical presentation of what I am designating as the central anxiety in Dickens's fiction. The effort to "imagine [Nell]...holding her solitary way among a crowd of wild grotesque companions; the only pure, fresh, youthful object in the throng" (1) takes the form of her feverish wandering journey, driven by her grandfather's restless desire to restore or surpass their lost fortunes and respectability, haunted and pursued by the past and its menacing representatives, across a countryside blighted by the race for gain:

How every circumstance of her short, eventful life, came thronging into her mind as they travelled on!...scenes of a year ago and those of yesterday mixing up and linking themselves together; familiar places shaping themselves out in the darkness from things which, when approached, were of all others the most remote and most unlike them; sometimes a strange confusion in her mind relative to the occasion of her being there, and the place to which she was going, and the people she was with. (43)

Restlessness, self-estrangement, and a sense of being haunted by past or alternative identities are the stuff of Nell's journey and her delirious response to it, but Dickens's conception of Nell's unassailable purity posits an ideal of such immaculate separateness that only death could suffice to insure it. In Dick Swiveller's sickroom scene, however, Dickens is able to provide an earthly equivalent to the asylum Nell seeks, "where...temptation would never enter, and her late sorrows and distress could have no place" (46). Dick's feverish delusions reenact Nell's journey as wasting illness and his blissful convalescence preserves for representation her ultimate destination.

Tossing to and fro upon his hot, uneasy bed; tormented by a fierce thirst which nothing could appease; unable to find, in any change of posture, a moment's peace or ease; and rambling ever through deserts of thought where there was no resting-place... with no change but the restless shiftings of his body and the weary wanderings of his mind, constant still to one ever-present anxiety... always shadowy and dim, but recognizable for the same phantom in every shape it took, darkening every vision like an evil conscience, and making slumber horrible; in these slow tortures of his dread disease, the unfortunate Richard lay wasting and consuming inch by inch, until at last, when he seemed to fight and struggle to rise up, and to be held down by devils, he sunk into a deep sleep and dreamed no more. (*OCS* 64)

Dick's physical and mental restlessness during his fever parallels Nell's own "restless change of place" on her journey toward a haven from her grandfather's sins and from the depredations of Quilp (43). The "weary wanderings of [Dick's] mind" reenact her "wandering up and down... " with a "strange confusion in her mind" (43), her "want of rest, and lack of any place to lay her aching head" (44). The same "phantom" of his "ever-present anxiety" (his King Charles's head), haunts Nell, too. "Shadowy and dim" figures seem continually to appear before her out of nowhere, arising suddenly from niches and recesses, from deep sleep or lonely speculation. Mrs. Jarley's waxworks of famous criminals are "dusky figures" haunting Nell's nights (29). Grandfather Trent, robbing her while she sleeps, emerges out of Nell's "deeper slumber" as a ghostly "figure in the room," "a dark form," "a dreadful shadow" (30). The fire-tender from the hellish steel mill first appears to Nell as "a black figure which came suddenly out of the dark recess" (44). And, while she wanders alone one night wondering "how many murders might have been done, upon that silent spot... there suddenly emerge from the black shade of the arch, a man... The street beyond was so narrow, and the shadow of the houses on the side of the way so deep, that he seemed to have risen out of the earth" (27). The man she sees is Quilp himself, the demonic prototype of all these specters "darkening every vision like an evil conscience" – the bad dream of innocence and "pure intentions." ("Quilp was a perpetual nightmare to the child, who was constantly haunted by a vision of his ugly face and stunted figure" [29].) Nell's pristine univocality is pitted against and continually menaced by Quilp's insouciant heterogeneity, his unabashed defiance – in his person, his dress, his diet, and in the company he keeps – of the distinctions that the others seek so desperately to maintain.

Dick's fever recapitulates not only Nell's restless motion, but that of all the novel's principal characters who, in Grandfather Trent's urgent words to Nell, are "too near to stop, and be at rest" (15). Restlessness is, quite simply, endemic to the world of the novel[19] (as it is to Dickens's narratives in general) from "the never-ending restlessness" of the crowds of London in the opening passage, to the "throngs of people intent upon their business" in the Northern manufacturing town hurrying by Nell and her grandfather "with no symptom of cessation or exhaustion" (44).

The "symptom" of cessation and exhaustion belongs rather to Dick's convalescence in the sickroom – a state of quiescence and quarantine which ends the strain of getting ahead and defuses the fear of stasis. The "restless shiftings" and "weary wanderings" of Dick's illness in its virulent stage give way to "a sensation of most blissful rest," and when he regains consciousness, the doctor's orders are, significantly enough, that he be "kept quite still" (64). That such a state is valued ambivalently by Dickens is suggested by, among other things, the remarks of the prison doctor in *Little Dorrit*, who praises the prison for the same reasons:

"We are quiet here; we don't get badgered here; there's no knocker here, sir, to be hammered at by creditors and bring a man's heart into his mouth... Elsewhere, people are restless, worried, hurried about, anxious respecting one thing, anxious respecting another. Nothing of the kind here, sir... Peace. That's the word for it. Peace." (i, 6)

In the sickroom, the fierce appetites that plague those outside its walls are moderated or made benign by the physical depletion of illness and appeased by the simple diet of the invalid. Characterized earlier as a "careless profligate" and a "brute... in the gratification of his appetites" (23), the now convalescent Dick is satisfied with "thin dry toast" and "a great basin of weak tea" taking "his poor meal with an appetite and relish, which the greatest dainties of the earth, under any other circumstances, would have failed to provoke" (66). The dreadful shadow of violation hovering about Nell throughout her sad journey, invoked perhaps most graphically by Quilp's occupancy of her bed, ("You're sure you're not going to use it, you're sure you're not coming back, Nelly?" [11]) is exorcised by proxy through the innocent cohabitation of Dick and the Marchioness, his little orphan nurse, during the weeks of Dick's illness. "I told 'em you was my brother, and they believed me, and I've been here ever since" (64). (The Marchioness also removes Dick's clothes in order to sell them "to get the things that was ordered for you" [64].) Dick's status as Quilp's "adopted son" and the Marchioness's hinted identity as the illegitimate offspring of Quilp and Sally Brass[20] make their healing relations as patient and nurse more than just a contrast to the illicit lusts of their progenitors, but an apparent transformation of the world they are heir to. Through the spontaneous generation peculiar to sickroom–bedroom confinements (as opposed to the more notorious Spontaneous Combustion) Dick and the Marchioness in a sense give birth to the other in a decisive separation from the guilty entanglements of the past.[21]

In the sickroom counterpart to Nell's feverish flight from self, redemption comes (insofar as it comes at all) in the form of an effacement of tainted origins. It is one of the telling ironies of Nell's story that her journey toward a safe abode keeps her out of reach of the single gentleman, Trent's younger brother, who, pursuing her with his wealth and good intentions, would seem to offer her just such an abode. She flies not only from Quilp and the diseased appetites he represents, but also from the knowledge that the single gentleman brings along with his blessings – the sad and sordid tale of Nell's mother's misery at her father's hands, of class transgression, and the decline of fortune and status. Her pursuers and the knowledge they bear are inseparable (a connection which is underscored by their common deformity).[22] The desire to keep Nell's "innocent face and pure intentions" distinct from "guilt and shame," the desire, in other words, to separate the inseparable, is a desire which could be fulfilled, and a journey which could end, only in death, or in the privileged space of the Victorian sickroom, where such separations occur under doctor's orders.

THE NARRATOR'S "RESTLESS DREAMS"

The Dickensian delirium, with its convergence of irreconcilable identities and divisions of time, its restless oscillations that bring "no change" (*OCS* 64), functions, as I have been arguing, as a compressed version of the narrative as well as of the life that narrative recounts. Through the various quarantines afforded by mobility and by partitioned selves, the narrative structure is, in turn, an attempt to dispel the nightmare of convergence and stasis which the delirium dramatizes. And just as the delirium is an analogue for the narrative, so the patient might be seen as a potential double or analogue for the narrator (and, ultimately, for the restless figure of the author himself) – a narrator tormented by his "infirmity to fancy or perceive relations in things that are not apparent generally," haunted by his own unapparent relations to the existences his imagination brings to life, and seeking a palliative for his infirmity in the mobility and indeterminate identity of omniscience.[23]

The opening passage of *The Old Curiosity Shop* provides an explicit paradigm of the equation between the narrator's mode of composition, the wandering journey of the narrative, and the patient's restless compulsions. The imagination is linked to an infirmity characterized by the uncontrollable perception of relations in things, as well as offered as a potential cure for that infirmity through the enforcement of saving distinctions. The connection Dickens makes so early in his career between the life of the imagination and the feverish dreams of the sick man suggests how deeply he felt its force. I will be examining the passage closely and, therefore, quote it in its entirety.

Night is generally my time for walking...I have fallen insensibly into this habit, both because it favours my infirmity and because it affords me greater opportunity of speculating on the characters and occupations of those who fill the streets. The glare and hurry of broad noon are not adapted to idle pursuits like mine; a glimpse of passing faces caught by the light of a street lamp or a shop window is often better for my purpose than their full revelation in the daylight, and, if I must add the truth, the night is kinder in this respect than day, which too often destroys an air-built castle at the moment of its completion, without the smallest ceremony or remorse.

That constant pacing to and fro, that never-ending restlessness, that incessant tread of feet wearing the rough stones smooth and glossy – is it not a wonder how the dwellers in narrow ways can bear to hear it! Think of a sick man in such a place as Saint Martin's Court, listening to the footsteps, and in the midst of pain and weariness obliged, despite himself (as though it were a task he must perform) to detect the child's step from the man's, the slipshod beggar from the booted exquisite, the lounging from the busy, the dull heel of the sauntering outcast from the quick tread of an expectant pleasure-seeker – think of the hum and noise being always present to his senses, and of the stream of life that will not stop, pouring on, on, on, through all his restless dreams, as if he were condemned to lie dead but conscious, in a noisy churchyard, and had no hope of rest for centuries to come. (*OCS* 1)

Although in each section of this passage there is restless movement, a preoccupation with identity – both obscured and revealed – and the construction of mental images (dreams and air-built castles) derived from the "stream of life," they nonetheless present two strikingly different images of the narrative impulse, the activity of the imagination, and the narrator's relation to his subject: the one external, controlled, detached; the other internal, hallucinatory, complicit. The relation between these two images of the narrator is similar to that between the narratives and their delirious recapitulation, and between the omniscient narrator and the characters themselves. In each case the difference between authority and victimization is a matter of controlled distance, of distinctions carefully maintained.

In the first paragraph, the narrator, Master Humphrey, describes himself as one who habitually walks the streets under the protective obscurity of the night, observing the half-lit faces of other pedestrians and speculating on their characters and occupations. Such speculations, and the "air-built castles" to which they give rise, are his "purpose," his "idle pursuit." In the second paragraph Master Humphrey's point of view of the streets and his own activity there gives way abruptly to that of a "sick man" who dwells in "narrow ways." Rather than a walker in the streets, his infirmity favored by darkness, in pursuit of others as a stimulus to his imagination, this narrator is confined within those streets, victimized by his infirmity, preyed upon by the sound of the crowd with its "incessant tread," its "never-ending restlessness." Far from a mere pastime with no consequences beyond his own aesthetic enjoyment, his speculations about the "characters and occupations of those who fill the streets" is a feverish, uncontrollable need. He feels himself "obliged" (as do the other patients in Dickens's fiction) "despite himself," to make distinctions among the people whose disembodied presence so haunts and oppresses him: "to detect the child's step from the man's," the "beggar" from the "booted exquisite," the "outcast" from the "pleasure-seeker."

Whereas Master Humphrey's effacement of his own identity and infirmity is an enabling condition of his pursuit, as is the partial view he obtains of his subjects ("it affords me a greater opportunity for speculating"), the crowd in the streets is an ineluctable part of the sick man's own infirmity. Despite his efforts at maintaining self-sustaining distinctions among them, they are an image of his own restless being, the material, not of ephemeral air-built castles, but the stuff of restless dreams which he is condemned to dream throughout eternity. This hallucinatory reversal of the narrator's distance and control over his material identifies the sick man as the incarnation of the latter's suppressed fear that his researches may lead him to confound his own identity with the restless lives of his subjects – that the infirmity he conceals, in other words, is not only his physical deformity, but his own implicit relation to the crowd he observes. As Audrey Jaffe notes in her discussion of Master Humphrey's replacement of painful autobiographical material with narrations about others: "An omniscience that makes itself felt is on the defensive, insisting on its outside stance because it is caught inside."[24] The sick man of Master Humphrey's imagination represents the narrator's own anxiety of convergence. From the former's vantage, immured in Saint Martin's Court, Master Humphrey is not the privileged observer of others, but rather one with the restless stream of life, which, in the ghoulish concluding simile, is implicitly compared to a kind of animated death in a "noisy churchyard."

Although the narrative pursuit and its enabling characteristics are shown here as incipient disease, it is important to note that the very mobility that links Master Humphrey to those he observes is what spares him the sick man's troubled awareness of that link. His capacity to hide from the knowledge of his own complicity and engagement with the stream of life and its earthly corruption depends upon his "moving on," preferably under cover. The restless journey of the narrative (or, in this instance, of the narrator) which Dickens diagnoses as symptomatic of disease is nonetheless a desirable, even necessary means of masking the anxiety that fuels its wanderings. Until the sickroom reestablishes a stability and control more exclusive than the separations and suspensions of the journey, and the distancing and anonymity of the observer's stance, it is better to move than to be immobilized, an easy prey to the shameful associations from which one is fleeing. It seems appropriate, therefore, that when Master Humphrey is not traveling incognito on his nocturnal excursions, he shuts himself away in closely guarded retirement, permitting only a few select friends, "men of secluded habits," to join him now and then (*MH* 1).

The relation I have drawn here between the narrative project as "idle pursuit" and its feverish inversion as a sick man's compulsory "task" – the one maintaining a self-exculpatory distance from its object, the other signaling a collapse of that distance and internalization of its object – has its closest narrative exposition in Bradley

Headstone's and Eugene Wrayburn's macabre "chase," and in Eugene's subsequent illness, in Dickens's last completed novel, *Our Mutual Friend*. As both character and "portrait of the artist,"[25] Eugene brings the thematic and structural implications of Dickensian infirmity into sharp focus. Like Master Humphrey, Eugene professes to choreograph his movements as well as his relative distance and position *vis à vis* the object of his "pursuit," but, in the illness that follows the collapse of that presumed control and distance, his carefully plotted designs are exposed as feverish wanderings and a profound loss of control. It is, in fact, Headstone, in his terrible restless obsession with both social rectitude and his passion for Lizzie Hexam, who answers Mortimer Lightwood's question about where Eugene is going and what he means by it.

Eugene, as is made apparent from the first encounter with him at the Veneerings' dinner party, "buried alive in the back of his chair" (*OMF* i, 2), cultivates a nonentity bordering on self-repression, disavowing through his studied nonchalance an air of bored lassitude any possible imputation of direction or purpose. By positing an identity for himself which is, in effect, no identity, he attempts to distance himself from both the limitations and strictures of his father's conventional social expectations for him, and from the unbounded desires and urges elicited from him by the lower-class Lizzie Hexam. "I am," he proclaims, "an embodied conundrum" (ii, 6). The deliberate assumption of a lack of identity *as* his identity permits Eugene, as it did Master Humphrey in his role as concealed observer–omniscient narrator, a certain mobility, an apparent freedom of movement among the avatars of the traits and emotions which he, himself, disclaims.

For instance, Eugene's participation as concealed observer in his midnight hunt with Mortimer after the accused murderer, Gaffer Hexam, and his subsequent voyeuristic observation of Lizzie through the windows of her dwelling permits him to engage vicariously in the passions and preoccupations of others while maintaining an at least nominal distance from the burden of emotional conflict and self-incrimination. Despite a sense of complicit relation to those he "pursues" on his night walks, Eugene can still make the crucial distinction between "the real man" and himself: "If the real man feels as guilty as I do," he tells Mortimer, "he is remarkably uncomfortable" (i, 13). Eugene's use of the phrase "the real man" here serves to emphasize his self-protective stance as a nonentity. Like

Master Humphrey, he is merely a recording consciousness rather than an active participant in the affairs of men. Furthermore, just as Master Humphrey's "idle pursuit" was facilitated by the partial obscuring of the faces of those he observes ("a glimpse...is often better for my purpose than their full revelation"), as well as of the obtrusive and self-revelatory aspects of his own identity, Eugene's nocturnal pursuits depend at least as much upon not fully seeing his subjects as upon not fully being seen by them. "'Eugene,'" Mortimer says after joining his friend one evening on his chase through the streets with Bradley at his heels, "'I cannot lose sight of that fellow's face.' 'Odd!' said Eugene with a light laugh, '*I* can'" (iii, 10).

By leading Bradley on in a manipulative manner, presumably for his own pleasure, Eugene manages to maintain his stance as neither the pursuer nor the pursued and thus to deny the kind of purposive direction or fixed relation to its opposite that each identity entails. He is able, thus, to control by intentional design the confusion of his own desiring relation to Lizzie Hexam. Through his role as voyeur–participant he manages to remain in constant proximity to the sources and manifestations of his own guilty desires. The chase, as designed, has no end in view beyond its own perpetuation.

In the careful contrivance of Eugene's chase with Bradley we can see in more overt form the same positioning that was at work in Esther's unfulfilled pursuit of her mother. No matter how contaminating such impulses or energies are, they are still, in a measure, life-sustaining. As the following quotation indicates, with its parallels to Master Humphrey's less troubling and ostensibly more detached pursuit, Eugene's (diseased) desire to sustain the titillating proximities of his endless chase serves as the wellspring, or germ, of his creative energy, a constant stimulus to his imagination:

I stroll out after dark, stroll a little way, look in at a window and furtively look out for the schoolmaster...Having made sure of his watching me, I tempt him on, all over London. One night I go east, another night north, in a few nights I go all round the compass...I study and get up abstruse No Thoroughfares in the course of the day. With Venetian mystery I seek those No Thoroughfares at night, glide into them by means of dark courts, tempt the schoolmaster to follow, turn suddenly, and catch him before he can retreat. Then we face one another, and I pass him as unaware of his existence, and he undergoes grinding torments. Similarly, I walk at a great pace down a short street, rapidly turn the corner, and, getting him out of view, as rapidly turn back...Thus I enjoy the pleasures of the chase, and derive great benefit from the healthful exercise. (iii, 10)

Dickens nonetheless makes clear through Eugene's subsequent illness that the intricate design of continuous deferral and displacement which Eugene traces in the process of his evening "diversions" with Bradley has its disturbing counterpart in the restless and guilt-ridden compulsions of the sick man–narrator of *The Old Curiosity Shop*.[26] Even before Eugene's collapse, it becomes increasingly evident that, despite his disclaimers, what he calls his "amiable occupation" (iii, 10) has become something of a pre-occupation, not only in the sense of an obsession, but also in the sense of an activity (here, implicitly perpetual) prior to the assumption of a professional and marital identity which would fix forever his now fluid and indeterminate nature. Moreover, marrying Lizzie would constitute, despite his disavowal of any desire for advancement, a sickening slide in social status and respectability. The sexual transgression implicit in his attraction to Lizzie is closely allied if not identical to the more serious transgression of social barriers.[27] Both Eugene and Bradley's desire for Lizzie is profoundly destabilizing – it is the mechanism by which each is forced to confront, and, in their nightly chase to enact, the self-estrangement imposed by class divisions and the categorization of experience that sustains them.[28] Eugene's genteel self-oblivion is a far less punitive form of repression than is Bradley's anguished disavowal of his impoverished beginnings: "[R]egarding that origin of his, he was proud, moody, and sullen, desiring it to be forgotten." Nevertheless, Eugene's full articulation of the problem Lizzie presents applies in equal measure to both men: "Out of the question to marry her...and out of the question to leave her" (iv, 6). Like Master Humphrey's sickly *alter ego*, the wary and painstaking Eugene glimpsed by Mortimer during an evening's chase seems "obliged as if it were a task he must perform" to prevent, through more and more ingenious exertions, the confounding of Bradley's "impossible existence" with his own identity – to prevent, in other words, a collision between his own conflicting appetites and allegiances. The moment of the dreaded collision arrives, however, in the displaced form of Bradley's homicidal attack upon him, which, aptly enough for an attack by an *alter ego*, fulfills, if only abortively, Eugene's suicidal desire for a self-oblivion more durable than his self-negating stance could afford him. "You don't know," he tells Lizzie just before the attack, "how the cursed carelessness that is over-officious in helping me at every other turning of my life, won't help me here. You have struck it dead, I think, and I sometimes almost wish you had struck me dead along with it" (iv, 6). Bradley, the fierce embodiment of his own reckless passion, tries to oblige him.

Bradley is himself the victim of a parallel collision with yet another *alter ego* – the utterly disreputable Rogue Riderhood, with whom Bradley drowns while locked in a deathly stranglehold. That homicide so often smacks of suicide in Dickens's novels merely reaffirms the identity of the impossible existences who chase each other through the pages of his novels. And as with so many of the doubled characters in his other novels – Blandois and Arthur Clenham, for instance, or Pip and Orlick, Esther and Lady Dedlock – one figure of each pair meets a violent end, and the other falls ill. In a manner that recalls the respective fates of Jane Eyre and Bertha Mason, the debility and restraint of the sickroom is the envisioned alternative to what amounts to self-destruction. Or, to put it in a slightly different way, the disavowed self is severed, leaving a depleted and ailing survivor.

In the delirium of Eugene's subsequent illness, his waywardness and self-negation and the evasive maneuverings of his mock wanderings with Bradley are, as they were for Master Humphrey's sick-man counterpart, internalized and exposed as periodic and frightening losses of self and as anxious uncontrollable wanderings through vast and unknown territory: "I begin to be sensible that I have just come back, and that I shall lose myself again…If you knew the harassing anxiety that gnaws and wears me when I am wandering in those places…They must be at an immense distance!" (iv, 10). If Bradley's attack and Eugene's own feverish fantasies seem to disclose the illusory and ultimately self-destructive nature of his attempt to deny or control aspects of himself he cannot acknowledge, they also, in the manner of such deliriums generally, set the stage for his final severance from those aspects within the sickroom quarantine and through his continuing debility. Eugene's withdrawal and self-negation are now diagnosed as symptoms of his illness rather than as a self-imposed means of evading a guilt-ridden identity. Having rejected his father's, then Bradley's, interpretations of his intentions and his destiny, and preferring his own "over-officious" self-presentation as an insoluble enigma, he submits at last, under penalty of death, to the identity imposed upon him by his nurse, Jenny Wren.

In a sense, Jenny combines in one person the two nurses of Victorian fiction – the one aggressive, knowing, mercenary, the occasional agent of revenge; the other nurturing, compassionate, chaste, the midwife of redemption. The self-estrangement that attends the bifurcation of rival attributes is expressed not in the haunting or pursuit of repudiated identities but in the cohabitation of two selves in one ailing body. Despite Dickens's urgent calls for sympathy on behalf of the "poor, poor little doll's dressmaker" (ii, 2), Jenny, with her luxuriant, golden hair and deformed body, seems a grotesque icon of the morality which insists upon a stark polarization of social and libidinal selves, which refuses, as Karen Chase says of Dickens in particular, "to countenance mixed moral and psychological conditions."[29] Jenny is either sadistic or "all softened compassion" (iv, 10), debased or exalted, the nurse who sprinkles pepper on the plasters she applies to the reprehensible Fledgeby's wounds and who delights in his pain, and the nurse who saves Eugene through the application of a healing word.

Still, although Jenny expresses in her strange, hybrid nature the continued attempt to segregate such apparent deformations or infirmities of the spirit as anger and aggression from the "healthy" personality – to cleave Fanny Cleaver from Jenny Wren – their joint occupancy of her own tormented body is shown to provide her with what proves to be valuable access to both. It is an access which, as we have seen in Eugene's designed proximity to Bradley, provides the germ of the imaginative life – a germ which is necessarily both enabling and disabling.

Garrett Stewart singles out as those gifts which make Jenny "the perfect nurse" Jenny's "lenitive and healing fancies" allied to her "practical dexterity" acquired in the exercise of her "imaginative craft."[30] Of Jenny's ministrative presence by the suffering Eugene's bedside, he has this to say: "She is...her transcendent fancies given flesh within the golden bower of her hair, a personification at Eugene's side of her own dream of heaven, the very vision of her vision."[31] It is for Jenny's vision of angelic children bringing "ease and rest" (*OMF* ii, 2) that Eugene presumably summons Jenny to his side, yet "the secret power" (iv, 10) she possesses which enables her to intuit his needs and interpret his ravings is as much a product of her "earthy" as of her "elevated" nature (ii, 2). What Dickens calls her "lower look of sharpness" – an aspect or component of her sadistic "Cleaver" side – often accompanies her most penetrating intuitions. Jenny's imaginative insight into the desires and motives of others – their "tricks" and their "manners" – may be "in com-

pensation for her losses," (ii, 2) but it has as its source the knowledge
her losses bring her of cruelty and debasement, of resentment, and
even of inspired revenge. As Robert Garis observes, "Jenny Wren's
speech has a vitality, a particularity of detail, a sharpness of idiom, a
fullness of spirit that makes her anger seem an act of life."[32]

Jenny ("a child – a dwarf – a girl – a something" [ii, 1]), takes her
place among the many artist figures in Dickens who suffer from a
visible infirmity (and whose art requires constant mobility).[33] Master
Humphrey is, he tells us, "a misshapen, deformed old man" (*MHC*
1). In *David Copperfield*, the itinerant cosmetician, Miss Mowcher, is a
dwarf whose artful intervention conceals the imperfections of her
clients while giving her a privileged view into their flaws of character.

The physical infirmity of these figures exempts them from the
standards of judgment Dickens applies to his able-bodied characters.
They are permitted their sharp knowingness, their otherwise dangerous mingling of personal innocence and unsavory experience, because
they are marginal figures, unfortunates, who do not threaten the
carefully maintained categories of the larger society of the novels in
which they appear. Their infirmity, however, serves not only to
exempt them from "the blame and the shame" (*BH* 36) as it does for
all of Dickens's characters, but also to mark their perception of
"relations in things that are not apparent generally" *as* infirmity – by
definition a condition requiring a cure. Yet, in the paradoxical terms
in which that infirmity is presented, a cure would entail the loss of
their artistry. The narrator *is* the sick man of the opening passage of
The Old Curiosity Shop, and the end of the invasive access of the stream
of life into his consciousness – the end of his chronic attempts to
distinguish among individual characters and traits within that stream
– would mean an end to his art. We are now, perhaps, in a better
position to see why Jenny is the appropriate figure to act as mediator
between the warring elements in Eugene's psyche and midwife at his
"rebirth" into a sanctified and narrowly defined domesticity, and
why the cure she effects ultimately spells the end of his designs, and,
in some respects, her own.

Jenny's intercession as nurse, before Lizzie assumes that crucial
and intimate role, is particularly mandated by the circumstances
surrounding Lizzie and Eugene's union. Lizzie has too long been the
designated object of Eugene's passion and too palpably in conflict
with her own desire for him to be permitted the more intimate duties
of the sickroom until their relations have been thoroughly purged of

threatening emotion – the disease that has infected Eugene with his tormenting restlessness. In their confusion and self-deception and in their promises to desist – broken even as they are made – in their exultation over the power each exerts over the other and their simultaneous decrial of their own weakness to resist the other's allure, one feels a palpable pressure against the restraints of the novelistic and societal decorum that asserts itself so strongly, for instance, in the courtship of their parallel lover-protagonists – in John Harmon's paternalism and Bella Wilfer's pert, euphemistic coyness.[34]

I have previously noted the equivocal status of the sickroom as both domestic refuge and privileged locale of bodily intimacy. Physical congress is made not only innocent but obligatory within the context of sickroom ministrations and through the transference of lover and beloved into nurse and patient. Dickens, however, has shown in other novels a certain cautious unwillingness to rely on context alone to effect the transference. The reunion of Little Dorrit with Arthur Clenham in his sickroom at the Marshalsea is a case in point:

As he embraced her, she said to him, "They never told me you were ill," and drawing an arm softly round his neck, laid his head upon her bosom, put a hand upon his head, and resting her cheek upon that hand, nursed him as lovingly, and GOD knows as innocently, as she had nursed her father in that room when she had been but a baby, needing all the care from others that she took of them. (ii, 29)

The emphatic inclusion of the phrase "and GOD knows as innocently," and the linking of the one act of nursing with the baby Little Dorrit's babying of her father, suggests an apprehension about possible suggestions of dalliance in this scene. This suffices for the saintly Little Dorrit, but, in order to defuse Lizzie and Eugene's passion and legitimate their union, Bradley dies violently, Eugene hovers close to death, and the already compromised Jenny assumes the nurse's role, while Lizzie remains almost unnoticed and unremarked in the background: "[Jenny] would keep her ear at the pillow...listening for any faint words that fell from him in his wanderings and she would change the dressing of a wound, or ease a ligature, or turn his face, or alter the pressure of the bedclothes on him, with an absolute certainty of doing right" (iv, 10). The "certainty of doing right" is contingent not only on Jenny's dexterity, but on the apparent limits set by her deformity on the sexual implications of her acts. Lizzie takes her place only after Jenny exercises one of her artistic functions as interpreter and translates Eugene's feverish, uncontrollable repetition of Lizzie's name as the single word "Wife." Jenny shapes, and in so doing contains, the incoherent and incessant expression of desire within the concrete and fixed referent of bourgeois domestic relation, just as the novelist contains the feverish repetition of narrative obsessions within the convalescent fixity of incapacity. In Lizzie and Eugene's future union, the roles of nurse and wife, patient and husband become tantamount, and the process by which desire is turned to need, aggression to dependence, and illicit union to sanctified domesticity is completed. A later glimpse of Lizzie and Eugene on a visit to the Harmons confirms the transformation and its consequences: "'But would you believe, Bella,' interposed his wife, coming to resume her nurse's place at his side, *for he never got on well without her,* 'that on our wedding day he told me he almost thought the best thing he could do, was to die?'" (iv, 16 [emphasis mine]).

Eugene, of course, does not die, but, in the logic of the sickroom cure, he does the next best thing. Eugene post-cure is a Eugene disfigured and depleted. The process has left him "wan and worn," led about by his wife ("nothing short of force" will make her leave his side), and blessed with the paternal approval he had once proudly spurned (iv, 16). The illness that originally signified his excessive, unformed, and thus "diseased" desire now becomes an illness that conversely functions to insure that such energies cannot reassert themselves. He is too wan and worn for excess. Eugene seems as aimless and defeated now as he was at the start, minus the élan that had once made him seem more the victim of privilege than of privation. The nonentity that gave him a certain insouciant freedom, an ability to play both domestic[35] and rebellious roles, has given way to a loss of particularity – nonentity as depletion. The paradoxical nature of his cure, as it reflects the larger problem of cure as closure, is brought home in a curiously revealing passage following Eugene's vow to "fight" for Lizzie "in the open field" (iv, 16). In it the glow of conviction is taken for the flush of fever, the temporary effacement of the signs of his mutilation for the recurrence of disease:

The glow that shone upon him as he spoke the words, so irradiated his features that he looked, for the time, *as though he had never been mutilated.* His friend responded as Eugene would have him respond, and they discoursed of the future until Lizzie came back. After resuming her place at his side, and tenderly touching his hands and his head, she said:

"Eugene, dear, you made me go out, but I ought to have stayed with you. You are more flushed than you have been for many days. What have you been doing?"

"Nothing," replied Eugene, "but looking forward to your coming back." (iv, 16)

Lizzie's diagnosis of Eugene's animation as ailment, besides ending any further discourse of the future, suggests that the reinvigoration of the wan, disfigured Eugene would merely reinstate the original illness from which he gradually recovers. That is, the very energy he requires to do battle "with and for" Lizzie is seen as dangerously allied to the reckless energy (i,13) his passion for her once inspired. The effacement of his mutilation by the glow of a recovered vitality would eradicate the sign of his separation from his former self and from the man whose "wild energy" (ii, 15) became associated with his own – Bradley Headstone.

It is worth recalling here that Esther Summerson's disfigurement – the product of illness – also functions as a mark of separation from the shame of her past, as well as being the symbolic trace of that shame. It serves as the visible sign of the separation between one stage of her life and the next (to being "something different from what I then was" [*BH* 31], and between her own person and that of her mother. Just before Esther succumbs to the illness that will make her "different from what [she] then was" the ailing Jo confuses her with Lady Dedlock ("ain't the lady t'other lady?" [*BH* 31]). Her scars prevent the full identification of herself with her mother, which in the larger metaphorical context of the novel would signify the perilous convergence of guilt and shame with respectability and restored status. Esther says of the moment of Lady Dedlock's revelation of their relationship to one another, "I felt, through all my tumult of emotion, a burst of gratitude to the providence of God that I was so changed as that I never could disgrace her by any trace of likeness; as that nobody could ever now look at me, and look at her, and remotely think of any near tie between us" (*BH* 36). Her disfigurement functions as a kind of corporeal quarantine from the threat of contamination both of and by others. It also signifies the scarring that such differentiation entails. She can no longer inadvertently shame her mother or be shamed by her, but she is also, in a crucial sense, no longer fully herself. It is only with the death of her mother, the fixing of her new identity as Mrs. Woodcourt, and the creation of a new

Bleak House that the "deep traces" of her illness are, as Dickens hints, permitted to disappear.

In Eugene's case, it has become Lizzie's implicit and ironic function to prevent the disappearance of his mutilation – the sign of his separation from Bradley and the passions he represents. Eugene's cure is ensured by continuing debility overseen by his lover, turned "guardian" (iv, 16) and nurse. Eve Kosofsky Sedgwick has pointed out the diminution in the capable, even heroic, Lizzie that such a transformation entails. "Lizzie stops being Lizzie, once she is Mrs. Eugene Wrayburn."[36] In keeping with Sedgwick's perception of Lizzie's diminished status, the new Mrs. Wrayburn has become, in effect, the sentinel standing guard over her husband's desire for her.

Lizzie's equation of animation and ailment returns us to the equation between narrator and sick man. Eugene's imaginative nocturnal designs in pursuit of and in flight from the embodiment of his own guilty passions are, like Master Humphrey's air-built castles, associated with the diseased fantasies of a sick man. The association invites the corollary, underscored by Eugene's enforced quiescence under Lizzie's care, that cure means an end to restless energy; and since that energy is generative, an end not only to desire but to creation. The imaginative impulse to design, rooted in passion and resistance to passion, in the confounding of impossible existences, and in the effort of disassociation, becomes simply "one of the mental troubles of the fever that was gone." Even Jenny, as I mentioned earlier, suffers a diminution of power through the cure for which she is so signally responsible. If her interpretation of what Eugene means has restored legibility at the expense of his designs, her affirmation of the domestic virtues to which she, herself, stands in such equivocal but creative relation, has put a limit to her own artistry as well. In the following passage, Lizzie, the prospective wife, displaces Jenny as Eugene's nurse with an implied decrease in the latter's visionary power:

"Is he conscious?" asked the little dressmaker, as the figure took its station by the pillow. For, Jenny had given place to it immediately, and could not see the sufferer's face in the dark room, from her new and removed position.

"He is conscious, Jenny," murmured Eugene for himself. "He knows his wife." (iv, 10)

It should not be surprising to find artistry linked to illness in the works of a man who is famous for his own febrile imagination, and who considered his own manic restlessness to be an unavoidable aspect of the artistic temperament. As he wrote to Forster: "The wayward and unsettled feeling...is part (I suppose) of the tenure on which one holds an imaginative life" (Forster 640). To Mrs. Watson he wrote "I am the modern Embodiment of the old Enchanters whose familiars tore them to pieces. I weary of rest, and have no satisfaction but in fatigue."[37]

Among the sources of Dickens's prodigious expenditures of productive energy was surely the fear, expressed in the many deliriums depicted in his novels, that "divisions of time" might become "confused with one another," that "everything...as ever had been, or as ever could be," might come crowding on him "all at once," that the shame and impoverishment of the little boy might, for instance, converge upon the grown, successful man, or the private sinner upon the philanthropist and family man. In recollecting for Forster the famous episode of his employment at Warren's blacking-warehouse, the anxiety about the convergence with past, present and future selves predominates. Dickens expresses his former "agony" at the superimposed image of the "learned and distinguished man" he had hoped to be with the neglected warehouse drudge he had become, of the "shame [he] felt in his position" with the esteem in which his gifts had once been held, and of the famous man he later became with the humiliated boy he never could forget. "[E]ven now, famous and caressed and happy, I often forget in my dreams that I have a dear wife and children; even that I am a man; and wander desolately back to that time of my life" (Forster 640).

Dickens's creative life could be seen as a chase like Eugene Wrayburn's after and away from the avatars of his own obsessive desires, a frantic busyness like Esther's to prove his worth, or a feverish journey like Nell's in flight from the ghosts of the past and in pursuit of an always receding sense of repletion and ease of mind. His exuberant inventiveness and almost ferocious will seems to have been fueled by the energy of disassociation and denial as much as by a profound knowledge of the impossible existences inhabiting the single self. He knew only too well the self-consuming resentment of the petty bourgeoisie for their "betters," the clenched fear of "wandering desolately back" to forgotten origins, the restless struggle to rise. In the great, and ultimately comforting, Manichean struggles staged in his novels between the simple and immutable categories of good and evil, passion and repression, one can discern the minute and fragile gradations by which failure and success, innocence and guilt, yesterday and today are measured and precariously, feverishly, maintained.

In his fiction, Dickens imagined "a foretaste of heaven itself" in the liminal exclusions of the sickroom and the enforced lassitude and diminished appetites of the sick body. Here at least was a place where vigilance could be suspended, desire and invention stilled, the feverish journey ended. His idealization of incapacity expresses the yearning of his aspiring and restless age for exemption and surcease as acutely as the convergence of the delirium expresses its feverish desire to "get on."

CHAPTER 4

George Eliot: "separateness and communication"

> I felt that there was a life of perfect love and purity...in which there would be no uneasy hunger after pleasure, no tormenting questions.
>
> Dino Bardi in *Romola*

When Fedalma, in George Eliot's *The Spanish Gypsy*, says, "I will take / this yearning self of mine and strangle it" (xxiv:163), it is preparatory to making the difficult choice of abandoning her lover, Don Silva, for her historical and racial destiny as a leader of the gypsy people in their search for a homeland. When Lucy Snowe in Charlotte Brontë's *Villette* says, "in catalepsy and a dead trance I studiously held the quick of my nature" (12), it is to steel herself against the pain of living in a society which could offer her neither satisfying love, stirring vocation, nor compelling identity. The promptings of the self for expression and fulfillment and the apparent necessity for their repression are at issue in both of these quotations and in the work of both Eliot and Brontë generally, but the differing circumstances and considerations involved in the adjudication of this dilemma indicate a central distinction in these writers' respective preoccupations and concerns. Brontë, as we have seen, is far more absorbed in wresting a personal settlement, however meager, from an intractable world ruled by fate, and brutally careless of the single life, than she is in "the growing good of the world" (*MM* 86) or any other of "the tempting range of relevancies" (*MM* 15) to which Eliot was so deeply committed. Eliot is more akin to Dickens in the scope of her concerns and commitments, as well as in her sense of the interdependence of human destinies. Unlike Dickens, however, whose lack of psychological depth she deprecated,[1] her social dramas are primarily played out in the complex inner lives of her characters, in their often debilitating struggles with their own egotism, their misguided motivations, and their destructive impulses. Moreover, for

Eliot, with her view of the real as a web of relations and of minute and interlocking processes of change, human life and history appeared far more responsive to the actions and choices of individual members of society than it did for either Dickens or Brontë. In Eliot's novels, even an unspoken wish can send shock waves through the whole delicate social organism. As one might expect, her depiction of the sickroom sanctuary is more inclusive in its healing powers and more precise about the nature of its exclusions. In addition to the secluded, inviolable, if limited intimacy and peace of mind which the sickroom affords in the fiction of Dickens and Brontë, the sickroom for Eliot offers, under the rubric of domestic realism, a vision of absolute moral clarity, of perfect integrity of motive and deed, and even of a kind of epistemological certainty. It is, in effect, the romance of her realism, the ideal toward which the social ethos of her realist program aspires.

The expressive vigor of Eliot's many tributes to the broader reconciliatory effects of relations within the sickroom has as its most immediate personal source her experience of nursing her father in his final illness. As I noted in my introductory remarks to this study, she referred to the time she spent tending him as "the happiest days of life to me."[2] Her often onerous and monotonous duties through the long years as her father's housekeeper and companion were, in the imminent shadow of death, charged with an immediately appre-hended and elevated significance, transfigured from mundane to blessed. Under the pressure of such heightened circumstances the recalcitrant particulars of the often difficult and strained relations between father and daughter were dissolved into a luminous whole of need expressed and answered: "My heart bleeds for dear Father's pains, but it is blessed to be at hand to give the soothing word and act when needed" (*GEL* 1:270). In return for these ministrations she received "a thousand little proofs that he understands my affection and responds to it" (*GEL* 1:270). ("Poor girl," wrote Cara Bray to her sister, Sara Hennell, "it shows how rare they are by the gratitude with which she repeats the commonest expressions of kindness" [*GEL* 1:272].)

The father who had once expelled her from his house for refusing to attend church during the so-called "Holy War," thus un-derscoring the extent of her dependency upon him for the necessities of life, was now dependent upon her in the extremity of his own need. Although his need gave her dominion of sorts over him and enhanced her worth in his eyes as well as her own, her nursing absolved her in her own mind from any imputation of gain or possible self-aggrandizement by the humble nature of her tasks and the clear limits on her ultimate efficacy: "I am enjoying repose, strength and ardour in a greater degree than I have ever known and yet I never felt my own insignificance and imperfection so completely" (*GEL* 1:269). Submission to the duty of nursing her father satisfied the exigent demands of her conscience as well as her desire for love and esteem.[3]

Although the approaching death of Robert Evans promised an imminent release from the constraints of his authority over her life, that life had provided her, in however diminished and precarious a fashion, with a home, a status, and a livelihood. "What will I be without my Father?" she wrote plaintively to Cara Bray. Moreover, those very constraints were to her a "purifying, restraining influence" which held in check the "earthly sensual and devilish" aspects of self which she feared would overtake her in his absence (*GEL* 1:284). While a life of self-suppression under the constant fear of estrangement and deprivation of affection lay behind her and an uncertain destiny and fear of self-dispersal lay ahead, Eliot found in the tender mercies of nursing a transcendent meaningfulness in the ordinary details of life and a simple and stable relation between love and duty. The temporary reprieve from her own dilemma that she found in the nursing of her father informed her subsequent search for some means by which all the variables of human satisfaction, attainment, and loyalty might be bound together naturally and indivisibly.

The most direct expression of the therapeutics of nursing can be found in her first book of fiction, *Scenes of Clerical Life*. The plot of "Janet's Repentance" traces in its broad outlines the struggle of Eliot with her father, and, like that earlier conflict, finds its resolution in the sickroom as the permanent site of restored relations and internal equanimity. Janet's story also concerns the withdrawal of her chief source of affection and social status, banishment for insubordination, and a "Holy War," this one between the followers of the recently arrived Evangelical minister, the Reverend Tryan, and the opponents of his social and doctrinal innovations led by Janet's husband, the abusive, alcoholic lawyer, Robert Dempster. Dempster epitomizes in its most extreme form the vanity, egoism, and gross sensuality of the town of Milby before "Evangelicalism brought into palpable existence... that idea of duty, that recognition of something to be lived for beyond the mere satisfaction of self" (JR 10). This effect of Evangelicalism is the humane essence which Eliot distills from the "narrow conduits of doctrine" (10) and whose penitential effects, prescribed for the whole community, she tests at the level of the individual, or as she puts it, in "the life and death struggles of separate human beings" (10). This narration of individual division and strife set against the background of its communal expression – political, social, and religious – links "Janet's Repentance" with such later fiction as *Felix Holt* and *Romola* and shares with those works the structures of coherence which are meant to encompass and unite part and whole, but which seem only to demonstrate their incommensurability. Moreover, like Brontë's *Shirley* and Gaskell's *Ruth*, "Janet's Repentance" presents a counter-narrative of sickroom scenes interwoven with the narrative of mixed conditions and punitive facts. Keen vision alternates with the "truth of feeling" and external circumstances with desiring subjectivity.

Janet is the first of Eliot's many protagonists who are trapped in loveless and degrading marriages, caught between their duty to observe the ties they have voluntarily chosen and publicly declared as binding, and their sense of the impoverishment of those connections, assailed by guilt and self-reproach for marrying blindly and to such disastrous effect, as well as for their rebellious urge to free themselves from the yoke they themselves have fashioned.[4] Hers is the first instance of what Romola comes to think of as the "insoluble problem" of "duty" (*R* 56). Janet has already suffered greatly from her precipitous marriage when the reader first meets her, and she bears the signs of her husband's physical abuse and her own alcoholic self-abuse. The relations between husband and wife reach a crisis when Janet is driven by an increase in her husband's brutality and drunkenness to a "fit of passion" and refuses to pick up the clothes Dempster has flung angrily onto the floor of the drawing-room. In his rage at her defiance he ejects her from the house in the middle of the night in her "thin night-dress" (JR 14).

The crisis Janet experiences at this point is indicative of the central dilemma of the self which is the prelude to scenes of illness in Victorian fiction, just as it was the background to the particular solace Eliot found in the nursing of her father. Until Dempster's fall from his horse and subsequent illness returns her to a secure place and defined role by his bedside, Janet is, as David Carroll puts it, in "a deathlike limbo in which the self, unrelated to the world, begins to disintegrate."[5]

Now, in her utmost loneliness, she shed no tear: she sat staring fixedly into the darkness, while inwardly she gazed at her own past, almost losing the sense that it was her own, or that she was anything more than a spectator at a strange and dreadful play. (*JR* 16)

Forced to define herself apart from her marital duties, Janet's life seems only "a dreary vacant flat, where there was nothing to strive after, nothing to long for" (16). She shrinks from "any active, public resistance" to her husband, for she has "no strength to sustain her in a course of self-defence and independence" (16). Consonant with the general function of illness in the story, the enfeeblement of her mother is raised at this point as a possible means of sustaining Janet's sense of self and purpose: "If her mother had been very feeble, aged, or sickly, Janet's deep pity and tenderness might have made a daughter's duties an interest and a solace; but Mrs. Raynor had never needed tendance" (16).

Janet's inability to assert herself on her own behalf derives not so much from the fear of her husband as from the fear of her husband in her: "She felt too crushed, too faulty, too liable to reproach ... even if she had had the wish to put herself openly in the position of a wronged woman seeking redress" (16). Dempster's exertion of his will over others, his drunken fits of passion, his triumphant egoism, are her own tendencies writ large, his cruel treatment of her the chastisement of her conscience for her own sense of guilt and unworthiness. "There was a demon in me," she tells Tryan, "always making me rush to do what I longed not to do" (18).

Although Janet is one of Eliot's idealized characters, like Romola and Daniel Deronda, whose defects seem "hardly distinguishable from ethical virtues,"[6] the picture of her as a young woman that emerges from Milby gossip and her own recollections is reminiscent of the young Gwendolyn Harleth. She is "spoiled" by her widowed mother, "a little too lifted up, perhaps... and too much given to satire" (3) but superior in beauty and attainment to those above her in rank, "proud in strength and beauty, dreaming that life is an easy thing" (15). The passionate nature of her early attachment to Dempster, when "he laid scarlet poppies on her black hair, and called her his gypsy queen" (24), further contributes to the submerged indications of Janet's culpability. In her later life these buried traces of willful egoism and sensual pride are expressed in her bitter reproaches to her mother, her "proud, angry resistance" (13) to her husband, and her equally proud denial to the world of his cruelties.

It is significant in this regard that the event which precipitates her separation from her husband is her own act of aggression against him, no matter what the provocation might have been.[7]

Janet's inability to resist Dempster's tyranny decisively is the product of her own sense of guilt, a guilt which is shown to be at least partially justified; but the narrator is careful at the same time to exculpate her as the determining cause or provocation for Dempster's abuse: "But do not believe that it was anything either present or wanting in poor Janet that formed the motive of her husband's cruelty. Cruelty, like every other vice, requires no motive outside itself – it only requires opportunity" (13). Janet's continual oscillation between guilt and a sense of victimization and her subsequent inability to determine a course of action ("to be good and to do right" [18] as she puts it) is characteristic of the inner life of Eliot's protagonists generally. Moreover, as the narrator's participation in the allocation of blame and exoneration in this story suggests, such oscillations are also characteristic of Eliot's moral aesthetic – her insistence upon the link between "seeing truly and feeling justly" (*GEL* II:423) and her uncompromising awareness of the difficulties involved in both activities. Her probing scrutiny into the intricate workings of motive and desire, her careful tracing of "unapparent relations," are meant to serve as a corrective for variances in individual and social angles of vision, but as the following sample of quotations from her works indicates, one's most strenuous efforts to see truly and feel justly are infected by subjectivity. One can never, it seems, get to the bottom of the unintentional duplicity of self and language:

Examine your words well and you will find that even when you have no motive to be false, it is a very hard thing to say the exact truth, even about your own immediate feelings. (*AB* 17)

For in the painful linking together of our waking thoughts we can never be sure that we have not mingled our own error with the light we have prayed for. (*R* 15)

Private prayer is inaudible speech, and speech is representative: who can represent himself just as he is, even in his own reflections? (*MM* 70)

As the quotation from *Romola* suggests, the process of active perception and discrimination can be "painful" as well as inconclusive. It requires the asking of "tormenting questions" and holds out the threat of even more tormenting discoveries about the self and its relation to other selves. For Eliot, as for Dickens, the acute awareness of "unapparent relations," could be experienced as an infirmity, "a disease of consciousness" rather than a cure for doubt and error (LV 1). Eliot's story "The Lifted Veil," from which the latter quotation is taken, is perhaps the most explicit evocation in her works of the act of perception as ailment. Latimer, the hero of the tale, is afflicted with the power to penetrate the minds of others whether he wishes to or not. He specifically identifies his preternatural insight as a "disease – a sort of intermittent delirium, concentrating the energy of brain into moments of unhealthy activity" (LV 1). Like the sick man in Dickens's *Old Curiosity Shop*, Latimer (a poet manqué) suffers from a feverish, involuntary version of the narrator's fine discernment of character and motivation. Moreover, Latimer's ability to hear the thoughts of others neither increases his sympathy nor enables him to act fitly, but rather diminishes his estimation of others and fuels his self-doubt. "Seeing truly," even if possible, in other words, has no necessary moral effect nor does it provide the grounds for determining right action and belief, innocence or guilt. On the contrary, it can cause a paralysis of the will. Noting the relation between Latimer's gift and realism as narrative mode, Sandra Gilbert and Susan Gubar point out that the insights of realism "can diminish the self, inundating it in the trivial pettiness of humankind, tainting it with the secret corruption of neighboring souls, and paralyzing it with the experience of contradictory needs and perspectives."[8] We should not be surprised, then, to find Eliot on occasion celebrating the radical reduction of consciousness rather than its expansion, and locating the empirical basis for right action and perception not in an exhaustive exploration into the nature of reality, but in the mute, imperative fact of physical need and the involuntary spasm of response. Nowhere does she do so more eloquently than in "Janet's Repentance" when Janet, wavering between a wish to return to her husband and her fear of the resumption of her marital troubles, is brought to the sickbed of her husband who lies suffering from "meningitis and delirium tremens together" (22):

Day after day, with only short intervals of rest, Janet kept her place in that sad chamber. No wonder the sick-room and the lazaretto have so often been a refuge from the tossing of intellectual doubt – a place of repose for the worn and wounded spirit. Here is a duty about which all creeds and all

philosophies are at one: here, at least, the conscience will not be dogged by
doubt, the benign impulse will not be checked by adverse theory: here you
may begin to act without settling one preliminary question. To moisten the
sufferer's parched lips through the long night-watches, to bear up the
drooping head, to lift the helpless limbs, to divine the want that can find no
utterance beyond the feeble motion of the hand or beseeching glance of the
eye – these are offices that demand no questionings, no casuistry, no assent
to propositions, no weighing of consequences. Within the four walls where
the stir and glare of the world are shut out, and every voice is subdued –
where a human being lies prostrate, thrown on the tender mercies of his
fellow, the moral relation of man to man is reduced to its utmost clearness
and simplicity: bigotry cannot confuse it, theory cannot pervert, passion,
awed into quiescence, can neither pollute nor perturb it. As we bend over
the sick-bed, all the forces of our nature rush towards the channels of pity,
of patience, and of love, and sweep down the miserable choking drift of our
quarrels, our debates, our would-be wisdom, and our clamorous selfish
desires. This blessing of serene freedom from the importunities of opinion ...
is one source of that sweet calm which is often felt by the watcher in the
sickroom, even when the duties there are of a hard and terrible kind.

Something of that benign result was felt by Janet during her tendance in
her husband's chamber. (24)

I have quoted this passage at length in order to draw attention
both to its fervor and to the exhaustiveness of its claims for the act of
nursing. George Eliot's own poignant experience can certainly
account for some of this intensity, but it can be ascribed as well, as I
have indicated above, to the tormenting and insistent pressure of
those aspects of consciousness which are so specifically itemized in the
process of banishing them from the sickroom: passion, doubt,
opinion, self-questioning, the weighing of consequences, the probings
of conscience, the clamor of desire. These are no less than the
circumstances and conditions from which the narrative of the town of
Milby's social and religious strife and Janet's private marital agonies
have been generated, no less than the exploratory and inductive
methods of the realism which Eliot, more than anyone, proffered as
curative, not merely diagnostic. The expressive structure of this
passage itself seems to be partly in response to the conflict between
Eliot's chosen mode of representation with its claims to inclusiveness,
to confronting "things as ... they are" (*GEL* II:362) and her desire for
"a life of perfect love and purity" (*R* 15). The cumulative force of its
steady concatenation of parallel phrases runs counter to the fact that
it is more remarkable for what it excludes than for what it contains.

In other words, the passage suggests that the amplitude of solace in the sickroom rests on its reductive relation to what lies outside of it, while at the same time giving full weight to the nature and significance of what is being excluded.

Moreover, the discontinuity between the world and the sickroom, and between an aesthetic of inclusion and one of exclusion, is marked by the discontinuous relation between the narrative proper and the interpolated tribute to its own foreclosure. For although this apostrophe to the therapeutic balm of the sickroom has as its immediate point of departure Janet's daily ministrations to her husband, it proceeds at once to a general reference which leaves the generating incident behind and puts in its place the nurse–patient relationship as an abstract model of human relations in their purest, most "unpolluted" form. It is only when the narrator returns to Janet's situation that one is made aware of how far from the particular the reader has been led by the generalizing sweep of Eliot's peroration: "Some of this benign result was felt by Janet during her tendance in her husband's chamber." Only "some of this benign result," for the details of Dempster's illness are, in fact, appalling. He is first described in the throes of delirium tremens, shouting imprecations at imaginary persecutors, and subsequently as a figure of "blank unconsciousness and emaciated animalism" (24). Eliot's rigorous particularization of the unpleasantness of suffering and disease, so unusual in Victorian fiction, realistic or otherwise, is put side by side with the vision of its supersession in the realm of feeling divorced from thought. Seeing truly offers one kind of truth, feeling justly another.

The source of the sickroom's healing power lies, then, in the explicit exclusion of those primary concerns of Eliot's realism, at least as she initially defined it in her early work. The "stir and glare of the world," and the self as conscious agent with all its capacity for miscarriage, are eliminated. The purity and ease of action in the sickroom is made possible in effect by the passivity of both nurse and patient in the face of necessity. Like the sufferer who "lies prostrate, thrown on the tender mercies of his fellow," the nurse, too, is, in a sense, thrown upon her own acts of tender mercy. They are both outside of or beyond the entanglements of interest and desire which obstruct the moral relations of man to man in the world of the "healthy." "All the forces of our nature rush towards the channels of pity, of patience, and of love..." The rush and sweep of the energies released by the imperatives of survival are described here as involuntary and instinctive and thus beyond the alloy and confusion of conscious agency; their direction is channeled or restrained from their potential destructive force by the external event or fact that gave rise to them. The circumscription of determining circumstances, the adjustment of desire to external fact, which so often constrain the ardent deeds and ideal aspirations of Eliot's characters ("Indeed, my lot has been a very hard one," Janet offers in partial extenuation of her inability "to be good and to do right" [18]) here shape the enabling medium which would prevent error and illusion. "Here you may begin to act without settling one preliminary question." Within this healing space, one may obey one's impulses without fear of repercussion or of misjudgment, one may yield to the pressure of circumstance without weighing the consequences, one may interpret signs without the fear of misreading them through the distorting filter of individual perspective and motive ("to divine the want that can find no utterance beyond the feeble motion of the hand or beseeching glance of the eye" demands "no self-questionings"). Any reader of George Eliot will recognize in these activities, permitted, even mandated, in the sickroom, that which is dangerous and destructive outside its protective confines. In "Janet's Repentance" alone, to obey one's impulses without weighing the consequences is to marry blindly, to drink uncontrollably, to surrender to fits of passion, and results in abandonment, betrayal, and alienation. To yield to the pressures of circumstance is to give up one's projects for improvement, to be passive in the face of injustice or constraint. And, finally, to interpret signs and act upon the strength of that interpretation without a keen awareness of the inevitable distortions of self-partiality is to act, often disastrously, on the strength of one's own desires. To be able to act without fear of such consequences or without any preliminary self-scrutiny is to inhabit a world in which, as D. A. Miller puts it, "daily experience would have a cognitive transparency, and conduct would immediately translate into the moral necessity of duty, a kind of apocalypse, or foreclosure."[9] It is to such a world that Eliot pays tribute in this passage on the sickroom and in the repeated recourse to it throughout the story.

In her celebration of an ease and clarity of moral conduct which is primarily instinctive and un-self-conscious, Eliot was responding not only to her own private longings but to those of an age weary of "self-questionings," "theories," and "debates." Harriet Martineau writes of her younger self: "I had now plunged fairly into the spirit of my time, that of self-analysis, pathetic self-pity, typical interpretation of objective matters, and scheme-making in the name of God and Man."[10] "Unconsciousness," wrote Thomas Carlyle in his essay "Characteristics," "belongs to pure, unmixed Life; Consciousness to a diseased mixture and conflict of Life and Death."[11] In language that recalls the moral impulse in the sickroom as Eliot describes it, he contends that the good man is one "to whom well-doing is as his natural existence... there, like a thing of course, and as if it could not but be so." And in a remark which addresses the central paradox in Eliot's moral aesthetic Carlyle notes that "[s]elf-contemplation is, on the other hand, infallibly the symptom of disease, be it or be it not the sign of cure" (53).

In Eliot's later fiction the discovery of national identity provides a less painful, but no less "organic," alternative to "primitive mortal needs" (*MF* vii, 5) as a basis for moral action. In *The Spanish Gypsy*, for instance, Fedalma, the heroine, torn, as I have already mentioned, between her love for a Spanish nobleman and her duty to the larger national aspirations of her gypsy tribe (neither of which alone can satisfy her yearnings) characterizes the unity of the life of Hinda, a gypsy girl, in the following terms:

> For her, good, right and law are all summed up
> In what is possible: life is one web
> Where love, joy, kindred, and obedience
> Lie fast and even, in one warp and woof
> With thirst and drinking, hunger, food, and sleep.
> She knows no struggles, sees no double path.
> Her fate is freedom for her will is one
> With her own people's law, the only law
> She ever knew.   (XXIV:277–278).

In this vision of unity one loves and obeys with the same instinctive impulse as one thirsts or hungers. "Life is one web" in which the demands of the self are one with the demands upon the self and, by extension, as easily satisfied. In another evocation of a similar unity based on national identity in *Daniel Deronda*, Eliot contrasts the attachment to others through "sentimental effort and reflection" with that which spreads "as a sweet habit of the blood" (*DD* 3). These are certainly more positive conditions under which man's "well-doing is as his natural existence," but, as Fedalma ruefully notes, Hinda's untroubled medium is only made possible by the absence of change:

"Within her world / The dial has not stirred since first she woke : / No changing light has made shadows die / And taught her trusting soul sad difference" (xxiv:277). Fedalma's comments place Hinda's world in the blissful childhood world celebrated in *The Mill on the Floss* "before we had known the labour of choice and where the outer world seemed only an extension of our own personality; we accepted and loved it as we accepted our own sense of existence and our own limbs" (ii, 1). They also identify Hinda's relation to the world with that which exists in the symbiotic relation of mother and infant ("The dial has not stirred since first she woke"), while the orality of the needs mentioned in connection with love and kindred ("thirst and drinking") reinforces this identification.

The desired reconciliation between self and other, duty and desire, in terms of, or inseparable from, the instinctive life of the body depicted in *The Spanish Gypsy* as a childhood idyll, is, in fact, not very far removed from its depiction as a sickroom idyll. Although the bliss of childhood is prior to the fall into time and change, while the sickroom is a refuge from it, and although the ease of relations in the one are those of a healthy child to its mother rather than the dependence of the ill or infirm on a nurse, envisioned in both is an instinctive expression of need and the no less instinctive response to it which banishes desire and frustration, "sad difference," and "the labour of choice." Janet, we are told, finds relief in her nursing from "the burthen of decision" (JR 24), and her duties in the sickroom "to bear up the drooping head, to lift the helpless limbs, to divine the want that can find no utterance" specifically invoke a mother's nursing of her infant. Like Caroline Helstone in Brontë's *Shirley*, Janet is both nurse and patient, mother and child, and as such she is able to combine without opprobrium those two opposing principles in Eliot's moral universe, narcissism, and altruism. It is the special property of the sickroom to reconcile opposites and neutralize their destructive aspects and in Eliot, in a sense, we find the last refinement on the sickroom's reconciliation of desire and repression and of realism's empirical bias and its unifying impulse. To see truly and feel justly with the same instinctive impulse as one hungers or thirsts is to make of the demands of the superego, libidinal drives.

The problem is how to bring the "perfect love and purity" of the sickroom into the larger life of the community, and back into the rhetorical mode which governs the larger narrative. What, for instance, are Janet and Dempster to make of their ensuing life? In his discussion of organic form in "Janet's Repentance," David Carroll contends that the dialectical conflict represented by Tryan's "self-abnegation" and Dempster's "self-will" is absorbed into the rhythm of organic growth evinced by Janet's "crucial change."[12] If there is a change in Janet at all, however, it is not growth but extrication. The organic rhythm that makes itself felt in the story is a fluctuation of urgent dependencies in successive sickroom scenes, until what Carol Christ has called providential death[13] decisively frees Janet from all threats to the self either from within or without.

Once Janet has been relieved "from the burthen of decision," by her husband's collapse and ensuing illness, she begins to imagine their future together as his continuing convalescence: "He would be a long time feeble, needing help, walking with a crutch, perhaps. She would wait on him with such tenderness, such all-forgiving love, that the old harshness and cruelty must melt away for ever under the heart-sunshine she would pour around him" (24). One is reminded here of Jane Eyre's nursing of Rochester, and Caroline Helstone's of Robert Moore, but unlike Brontë's willful egoists Dempster has embodied too starkly the physical and mental devastations of passion, bigotry, and the tyrannies of the will to be restored to pride of place, even as the enfeebled recipient of her Christ-like "all-forgiving love." That place has been taken by Tryan. Eliot permits Janet her conscience-appeasing fantasy of reconciliation ("her bosom heaved at the thought, and delicious tears fell" [24]) but spares her the actuality. Dempster does not survive. A return to health carries with it the threat of a return to the instabilities of identity and relation which the sickroom expunges. The narrative, therefore, having taken the place of the sickroom, eliminates Dempster as it will his successor, the altogether too attractive Mr. Tryan.

After Dempster's death Janet becomes a patient under Tryan's care until her depression and craving for alcohol ("the demon" in her) is cured, and she becomes his nurse when his health begins rapidly to deteriorate. Janet provides a new home for Tryan and within it a new sickroom where she will preside as his constant attendant until his death from consumption (the internalized equivalent to Dempster's delirium tremens). "She made Holly Mount her home, and ... filled the painful days and nights with every soothing influence that care and tenderness could devise ... [her] dark watchful eyes detected every want and ... supplied the want with a ready hand" (27). These are familiar words, just as this is the counterpart to her husband's sickroom, which more fully realizes the ideal posited by the earlier tribute. The exchange between nurse and patient is again put in the place of more threatening or censorious entanglements.[14] Tryan's illness protects her from his desire for her and her own for him. (Consonant with the capacity of illness to satisfy both moral and libidinal forces, to make them, in a sense, equivalent, Tryan's illness also allows Janet to move in with him, just as Dempster's illness permitted her a form of disguised revenge.)

The thought of Mr. Tryan, according to the narrator, was "associated for her with repose from that conflict of emotion, with trust in the unchangeable, with the influx of a power to subdue self" (27). Tryan, in other words, was associated for her with the sickroom and to retain that association he must become an inhabitant of it, himself the object of an "unchangeable" duty that offers Janet repose from doubt, from conflict, and from "clamorous, selfish desires." Janet retains the much desired repose even after Tryan's death. "Janet felt a deep stillness within. She thirsted for no pleasure; she craved no worldly good. She saw the years to come stretch before her like an autumn afternoon, filled with resigned memory" (28). In this, she joins the main characters of the other *Scenes of Clerical Life*, Mr. Gilfil and Amos Barton, who, having nursed the objects and incarnations of their guilt and passion, live on as memorials to their own dead selves.[15] In these first fictional productions the sickroom relation is repeatedly called upon to plug the gap between subject and object, between aggression and love, between truth and feeling. And in each instance the sickroom scene functions as a prelude to detachment. The achieved reconciliations, the higher feelings, the chastened desires reside in the private consciousness of a solitary figure.

In "Janet's Repentance," the isolated virtues of the sickroom achieve their final apotheosis in this concluding evocation of Janet. Disencumbered of all objects of desire and will, she has become as indefinite a figure as the anonymous "watcher in the sick-room," particular ties having given way to the more generic and impersonal bond of fellow-feeling. (Janet, we are told, looks back "on years of purity and helpful labour" [28].) She has, in essence, gone from one death-like limbo to another which passes for its opposite. From her initial isolation resulting from the breakdown of essential bonds she passes to the disengaged, unindividuated world of the sickroom, which is then reinstated at the end of the story by the remoteness of her attachments and the "deep still-ness" of her being. The impersonal nature of the connections affirmed through reciprocal nurturing in the works of Eliot in general marks a striking difference from the bonds formed in the sickrooms of Dickens and Brontë, which, however denuded those bonds may be of passion and energy, nonetheless represent the reunion of specific men and women bound by ties of kinship, love, and a shared past. Eliot's more acute and tense awareness of the possibilities of infection through interdependence requires in response a more exclusive quarantine and one which claims for itself a more general reference. In *Romola* the sickroom will engulf the entire world of the novel in all of its painstakingly depicted detail and intricacy.

Like "Janet's Repentance," *Romola* offers a redemptive vision of sustaining human interaction in terms of nursing and being nursed, once more set against a background of a holy war precipitated by the man who will become the heroine's spiritual guide and example. The widening of the scope of Eliot's ambitions in the novel is indicated by the fact that the small-town pastor, Mr. Tryan, is replaced by no less than Savonarola, and Milby's social and religious strife over the advent of Evangelicism by the chaos of Florence following the death of Lorenzo de Medici, the "Magnificent." Following the general outline of the earlier story, the diseased state of Florentine society, figured in the outbreak of pestilence which engulfs the city in direct consequence of internal disorder, is ministered to by the example of Romola's sojourn in a plague-stricken village rather than by political, religious, or dynastic settlements. Romola's nursing of the ailing villagers, like Janet's of her ailing husband, ministers to her own internal disorders as well. The episode to which I refer is, as Eliot herself avowed, frankly and deliberately symbolic (*GEL* IV:104), serving the same ostensible purpose as the sickroom's clarification of "the moral relation of man to man" in "Janet's Repentance." It reveals, as the narrator of *Romola* puts it, "the simpler relations of the human being to his fellow-men" (*R* 69). Yet this avowed use of the symbolic mode suggests even more forcibly Eliot's difficulty in imagining for her heroine and representing, within the techniques of realism, social forms and relations sufficiently coherent and reliable to serve as guides to the self in its choices and actions. "Where were the beings with whom she could work and endure with the belief that she was working for the right?" Romola asks (52). The fact that Romola nurses and is nursed by an anonymous and undifferentiated population in an undisclosed location and that she, in turn, is known to them as the equally anonymous and unindividuated Madonna "who came over the sea" (68) is a measure of the pervasive doubt in the novel that such beings can, in reality, be found.[16]

The relentless depiction of the withdrawal or inadequacy of external supports for identity in the novel is accompanied by a commensurate increase in the demands made upon the individual self for purity of motive as well as deed, which in turn engenders a sense of guilt and incapacity. Romola and Savonarola are the central figures in the drama of the self, and if they share, as George Eliot puts it, "a chief problem" (*GEL* IV:97), it is not only that of "where the sacredness of obedience ended, and where the sacredness of rebellion began" (56) but also, and perhaps most poignantly for Eliot, it is, as it was for Janet, their agonizing fluctuation between blaming and justifying the integrity of their own motives and conduct, their "continued colloquy with that divine purity with which [they] sought complete reunion; it was the outpouring of self-abasement; it was one long cry for inward renovation" (71).

Romola's continued colloquy assumes the proportions of the entire narrative, with each character taking part in representing that aspect of self which separates her from the complete reunion she desires.[17] Romola's history is characterized by her relationships with men, each of whom fails to provide Romola with the authority she seeks as a ground for her own moral life. Although she devotes herself to her natural father, Bardo, the blind scholar, he denies her larger intellectual capacity to serve him in his researches: "For the sustained zeal and unconquerable patience demanded from those who would tread the unbeaten paths of knowledge are still less reconcilable with the wandering, vagrant propensity of the feminine mind than with the feeble powers of the feminine body" (5). Savonarola, her spiritual father, teaches her to bend her will to her duties as a wife and citizen of Florence, and yet betrays her by himself yielding to expedience and the pursuit of power. Her brother, Dino, offers as example devotion to the religious life, but at the expense of the more intimate ties of family. And, her husband, Tito, offers her sensuality and then betrays her by his liaison with a simple village girl, Tessa. Each of these putative authorities is also engaged in parricidal acts of self-definition and ambitious rivalry and, as such, represent in differing ways Romola's own feared tendencies and longings, her own "disposition to rebel against command" (15). Like Janet, the otherwise exemplary Romola has a "proud tenacity and latent impetuousness" (5). Her father's sterile competitive intellectualism, her brother's excessive spirituality and consequent estrangement from Bardo, Tito's self-love and denial of his adoptive father, Baldassare, and, of course, Savonarola's titanic struggle with the Holy Father in Rome for prominence and domination, each embodies Romola's own suppressed desires and destructive impulses – the parricidal wishes which fuel her paternal piety: "But the sense of something like guilt towards her father in a hope that grew out of his death, gave all the more force to the anxiety with which she dwelt on the means of fulfilling his supreme wish" (17). While Romola "strangle[s] every rising impulse" (27) these men enact those impulses and are punished or destroyed by them. When Romola entreats her godfather to "trust no one. If you trust, you will be betrayed" (54) she expresses the novel's abiding distrust of both inner and outer authority.

It is no wonder then that Romola, in flight from Florence and the men who have betrayed or abandoned her, is "half in love with easeful death," seeking to efface, in her escape to the sea in a small fishing boat, both self and other as sources of authority and of narrative.

The imagination of herself gliding away in that boat on the darkening waters was growing more and more into a longing, as the thought of a cool brook in sultriness becomes a painful thirst. To be freed from the burden of choice [Janet's "burthen of decision"] when all motive was bruised, to commit herself, sleeping, to destiny which would either bring death or else new necessities that might rouse a new life in her! (61)

As Carole Robinson notes, "Unlike Maggie Tulliver, Romola does not find death by water." The comparison with Maggie is pertinent, for Romola's surrender to her "sensuously conceived death-wish" (Robinson, 36) gratifies the same impulses that Maggie's sleeping journey down the river with Stephen gratifies – a relaxation of the moral consciousness in a surrender to the pleasures of corporeal ease. "[Romola] longed for that repose in mere sensation which she had sometimes dreamed of in the sultry afternoons of her early girlhood, when she had fancied herself floating naiad-like in the waters" (61). Maggie's two journeys down the river – the libidinal drifting and the purposeful response to "primitive, moral needs" – are conflated in Romola's journey to the "new necessities" that await her at her destination, necessities that are hardly distinguishable from her surrender to the instinctive life in the boat. Romola is awakened from

her "Lethe...without memory and without desire" by the cry of a
child in distress and to the claims of an entire village dying of the
plague. The poverty of options that precipitated her crisis becomes
the means of her salvation; being unable to choose becomes under the
pressure of circumstances the liberating condition of having no choice
at all: "She felt no burden of choice on her now, no longing for death.
She was thinking how she would go to the other sufferers" (68).[18]
Here is one "rising impulse" that she need not "strangle." Illness has
again worked its transformative magic, making the dangerous
impulse benign, the passive active, and determining circumstances
the enabling medium for a full and moral existence. As in "Janet's
Repentance," illness offers the possibility of instinctive moral conduct
with its salubrious effects on the worn and wounded spirit.
"[Romola] had not reflected...she had simply lived with so energetic
an impulse...that the reasons for living, enduring, labouring, never
took the form of argument" (69). But what was confined to the
sickroom in "Janet's Repentance" has in *Romola* been extended to
embrace the entire visible world, dissolving it in all of its historical,
geographical, and social specificity.

Given the well-known difficulty George Eliot experienced in the
composition of *Romola* and the vast accumulation of historical
information and detail by which she continually postponed its
commencement, there is something almost breathtaking about the
way she so utterly levels the huge, variegated edifice built up by her
own labors and renders its complexity nugatory in her symbolic
representation of human relations in the stricken village. The formal
disjunction between these narrative sequences recapitulates the
relation between the sickroom passage in "Janet's Repentance" and
the surrounding narrative. The painstaking realism of *Romola*, its
sheer mimetic density and psychological intricacy, seems to have
precipitated its own foreclosure in the nursing scenes – scenes whose
scope needed to be commensurate with the ambitious inclusiveness to
which they put an end. It is as if Eliot looked upon the *quattrocento*
world she had created, as Dorothea would later look upon Rome, and
saw "all this vast wreck of ambitious ideals, sensuous and spiritual...
spreading itself everywhere like a disease of the retina" (*MM* 20).
Like the diseased participation in other people's consciousnesses
from which Latimer suffered, the disease of perception finds its cure
in the elimination from perception and representation of all the
divisive elements in human relationships, including the necessity

even to distinguish among the objects of one's own feelings and actions.

A similar harmony and its underlying cost is fleetingly depicted earlier in the novel during a time of civic emergency when, as in the plague-stricken village, the survival of the whole community is at stake. Romola (returning from the hospital where she has been volunteering her services) witnesses a procession of the various trades, fraternities, and authorities of Florence calling for divine intercession to forestall the imminent destruction of the city by war, pestilence, and famine. The members of one of these groups wears "a garb which concealed the whole head and face except the eyes."

[N]o member now was discernible as son, husband, or father. They had dropped their personality, and walked as symbols of a common vow. Each company had its colour and its badge, but the garb of all was a complete shroud, and left no expression but that of fellowship. (43)

Again moral relations are revealed in clear, immediately apprehensible form. Differences of rank, profession, and family identity have been masked in order to reveal their common humanity and purpose. The description of "things as they are," it would seem, works against rather than in support of the values of sympathy and community that Eliot wishes to promote through her fiction. "Seeing truly" in order to feel justly depends upon piercing through the mass of particulars to a realm of meaning which remains unmolested by them. Despite the manifest idealism of such a notion, Eliot retains her allegiance to the empirical and ethical continuity upon which the kind of mimetic realism she espouses in chapter 17 of *Adam Bede* rests by grounding the independence from particulars in the leveling imperatives of bodily crisis and the homely tasks of feeding and caring for the sick.

There is, nonetheless, something sinister about these shrouded figures, particularly in view of the virtual elimination of the specific sons, fathers, and husbands who harass and betray each other during the course of the novel. One need not accuse Eliot of parricidal longings to see at the heart of such strenuous assertions of anonymous fellowship Romola's wish to be free of "a sense of confusion in human things which made all effort a mere dragging at tangled threads" (61); but there does seem to be an unspoken aggressiveness at the root of many of the "simple direct acts of mercy," like Janet's nursing of her husband, Maggie's attempted rescue of Tom, and the submergence of the particular sufferer into the undifferentiated mass. The narrator provides an illuminating gloss of the passage I have just quoted in terms of Romola's own situation: "All that ardour of her nature which could no longer spend itself in the woman's tenderness for father and husband, had transformed itself into an enthusiasm of sympathy with the general life" (45).

Not surprisingly, Romola's nursing of the suffering multitude in Florence proves far less engrossing and revelatory of simple human relations than her activities in the village. Frankly compensatory for the failures of her more primary relationships, sympathy for the "general life" remains an insufficient prop for the self. "She had no innate taste for tending the sick and clothing the ragged ... and if she had not brought to them the inspiration of her deepest feelings, they would have been irksome to her" (45). The "new necessities" in the village seem to satisfy where the old necessities failed because the needs of the collective are made wholly consistent, even identical, to her own. Her efforts on behalf of the dying villagers are, like Florence Nightingale's on behalf of the British army, put into the service of asserting and gratifying her need for love. It is only in this circuitous manner that Eliot can imagine for her heroine an acceptable form of self-assertion and fulfillment, given her stern Victorian insistence that all acts be acts which nourish rather than attenuate the collective life – a nourishment which, more often than not, is gauged by a corresponding attenuation of self.[19] The birth imagery used in describing Romola's immersion in the sea and ultimate retrieval from it is followed by the cry of a child, as if her newly reborn self were crying out for succor. As Laura Comer Emery observes, Romola's nurturing of the abandoned child reveals her "underlying wish to be nurtured by a mother."[20] Carlyle's dictum that the good man's "well-doing is as his natural existence" again finds an appropriate expression in the conflation of egoism and altruism, a maternal symbiosis in which one is both nurse and patient, mother and child.

The essentially self-reflexive nature of Romola's experience in the village is suggested further when Romola herself falls ill and is nursed "by a woman whom the pestilence had widowed" (68). Romola, by this time, has also been widowed by the pestilence of subsequent Florentine struggles. At last, a full and acknowledged beneficiary of the "joys of convalescence," Romola lies on a "delicious bed" with the baby she has rescued, being fed "honey, fresh cakes, eggs and polenta" by the villagers: "She always gave [the baby] a bit of what she took, and told them if they loved her they must be good to Benedetto" (68). Like her nursing, Romola's convalescence is hardly distinguishable from "the repose in mere sensation" which she seems briefly to experience before fully waking in "a sheltered nook" in her boat (68). Nursing and convalescence, however, have the virtue of camouflaging retreat as moral engagement, pleasure as pain – the virtue, in other words, of being virtuous. "O the bliss," Eliot once wrote in a letter to a friend, "of being in a very high attic in a romantic continental town...and then to return to life, and work for poor stricken humanity and never think of self again" (*GEL* 1:261). Romola manages simultaneously to obey both needs – to appease her conscience with good works and to minister to her own stricken self in a romantic refuge from "the confusion in human things."

It seems pertinent that *Silas Marner*, the book that "thrust itself" (*GEL* III:384) in the midst of Eliot's agonizing preparation for *Romola* like the new necessities that thrust themselves upon that novel's heroine, features a psychosomatic illness whose primary attribute is a loss of consciousness. If *Silas Marner* is more idyllic than the narrative which its composition interrupted, it is in part because Silas is spared the "inner colloquy" concerning the integrity of motive and intent that threatens to paralyze all acts of volition in *Romola*, by his cataleptic absence of consciousness at crucial moments of desire and transition. Catalepsy, the central image in the novel of discontinuity and alienation, is also a form of self-preservation – a means of insulating the patient from contamination from within and without; it is both disease and antidote.

Silas's cataleptic fit at the bedside of the ailing deacon of Lantern Yard absolves him of guilt for the deacon's death and for the theft of his belongings, and definitively designates Silas as innocent victim rather than the perpetrator of another's betrayal and treachery. (This sequence of events, incidentally, seems in direct response to the problem of Romola's guilt concerning the death of her father and the loss of the collection she promised to preserve in his name.) In a similar fashion, Silas's fit during which Eppie enters his cottage absolves him from any imputation of blame for Milly's death and his gain at her expense. Like Benedetto, whose needs awaken Romola from her unconscious drifting, Eppie, as Jonathan Quick puts it, "comes to [Silas] as an outright gift, unencumbered by association with his wretched history,"[21] or, it seems pertinent to add, with hers.

Although Silas is "cured" of catalepsy by his adoption of Eppie and his gradual reconnection to the life of the community, his rearing of her takes the place of his former disease by providing protective sequestration or quarantine from the corruption of communal life:

The tender and peculiar love with which Silas had reared her in almost inseparable companionship with himself, aided by the seclusion of their dwelling, had preserved her from the lowering influences of the village talk and habits, and had kept her mind in that freshness which is sometimes falsely supposed to be an invariable attribute of rusticity... (*SM* 15)

Silas has constructed for himself and for Eppie an exile within the "Lethean...exile" (2) that is Raveloe. Lantern Yard, the site of his troublesome past and failed expectations, has conveniently disappeared. Eliot's sly dig here at the idealization of the rustic mind both invokes by implicit contrast her realist principles of representation and masks her own more marked departure from those principles in the same passage. Eppie is being sequestered, with the narrator's apparent approval, not only from the people among whom she is to make her home, but also from the same "village talk and habits" whose authenticity the readers have been implicitly asked to appreciate and to profit by through the extension of their sympathies.

Just as the problem of how to protect the integrity of the self against inner and outer forces of fragmentation is "resolved" for Silas through further alienation and the obliteration of the past, so Romola's loss of consciousness in the boat marks a decisive break with an intolerable past and a reversal of its conditions. And both of these solutions necessitate a decisive separation between seeing truly and feeling justly, between mimeticism and the preservation of value. The nursing scenes in the village seem to consecrate and to dream into wholeness what had been experienced in the midst of her own community as separation and loss. Moreover, like Brontë's sickroom romances, the village is a female world. As I discussed briefly in my introductory chapter, the apotheosis of Romola derives not only from her struggle with internal contradictions and perceptions, but also from the frustrated aspirations of a woman of large capacities constrained by her gender to the role of subordinate to a commanding and censorious male. In a reversal of the hierarchy that obtained in Florence, where her father deprecated her ability to apply herself to intellectual tasks and the imperious Savonarola guided the humble Romola's actions, Romola reigns supreme in the village, assisted by her loyal subordinate, the somewhat comical Padre, who believes her to be the Holy Mother. When Romola returns to Florence determined to resume the ties and reassume the burdens from which she has twice fled, she recreates in small her role in the village by presiding over a female household containing her somnolent and helpless Aunt Brigida, Tito's illegitimate children, and his babyish mistress, Tessa, who, in her easy, submissive childishness and maternal intensity, seems an unintentional parody of the values proffered as redemptive. Romola's newly found strength and assertiveness as the head of a diminished household of dependants is best characterized by the quotation from *Felix Holt* which I cited earlier in connection to Jane Eyre's relation to Rochester: "Strength is often only another name for willing bondage to irremedial weakness" (*FH* 6). This seems a peculiarly Victorian definition in its full defensive alert against the supervening self – justifying even the limited supremacy of the nurturer – and in its attempt to see strength as a form of renunciation and the exercise of the will as a sacrifice to the helpless. (This formula can, of course, serve to justify an empire as well as underwrite a form of quietism.)

Although Florence, unlike Lantern Yard, has not disappeared, those nearest to Romola, to whose needs she had meant to dedicate herself upon her return, have been conveniently purged by the violence to which her own benevolence in the village provided an antidote and example. Just as Janet at the end of her story lives on as "another memorial to Edgar Tryan which bears a fuller record" of his "true compassion" and "fervent faith" (JR 28), Romola remains as memorial and memorialist to the dead objects and embodiments of her own desires and aspirations. In a well-upholstered retreat from the complications of social relations, *Romola* concludes with the heroine giving a carefully expurgated version of the novel we have just read as cautionary tale to Tito's children, anticipating, as Susan Greenstein points out, "the later George Eliot" as "sybil, mother, storyteller."[22] Like Janet and even Silas, weaving his "tale of Mrs. Osgood's table linen" (*SM* 2) and dispensing medicinal herbs to an ungrateful populace, Romola is identified with the author in her professional capacity as healer–storyteller and, in more personal terms, as a separated figure whose separation is both self-protective and communally mandated. The sickroom, explicitly offered as a mode of interaction based on sympathy and shared understanding, emerges more and more clearly as a retreat for the alienated figure of the narrator.

In Eliot's explicit treatments of the artist (in particular female artists) – Armgart in her verse drama by the same name and the Princess Halm-Eberstein in *Daniel Deronda* – the "insoluble problem" of duty is depicted in a less idealized fashion. Both women, as other commentators have noted,[23] enact George Eliot's own guilt-ridden defiance of the constrictions of womanhood and of family and social ties, her own fears about the egoistic energies of "the performed self."[24] The usual oscillation between guilt and victimization is decided in favor of self-lacerating guilt, and Eliot afflicts her artistic surrogates with diseases which chasten their presumption rather than assist the reconciliation of their opposing impulses and provide a means of strategic withdrawal. In effect, Eliot exposes the disabling terms upon which the reconciliation of the sickroom had always rested.

Both women assert the priority of their artistic gifts over familial concerns, "a rebel's right" (*Armgart* x:127) to resist the common lot of women, the right "not to be hampered by other lives" (*DD* 51). Armgart's cousin and companion, Walpurga, expresses the opposing voice of conscience in her accusations against the woman she has served so faithfully: "Where is the rebel's right for you alone? / Noble rebellion lifts a common load /... / Say rather, the deserter's" (x:130–131). She charges Armgart with her claimed exemption from suffering and failure, for her "monstrous Self / Which, smiling down upon a race oppressed / Says, 'All is good'..." (x:133), and for her failure to reciprocate love and devotion. Just as Silas's art of weaving verges on onanism (Eliot calls it "a mere pulsation of desire and satisfaction that had no relation to any other being" [*SM* 2]), Armgart's singing is shown to have narcissism as its underlying impulse: "I love in singing, and am loved again" (x:75). In this disciplinary rather than exculpatory version of the same conflict about the motives for one's actions and the aims of one's artistry, egoism is not conveniently made synonymous with altruism through the imperatives of illness, but rather just the opposite.

The Princess and Armgart are ultimately forced to acknowledge, though not embrace, communal and family ties by illnesses which rob them of their voices and, with that loss, their sense of power and independence. In more conspicuously punitive ways than we have seen in the cases of Janet, Romola, and Silas, who were, on balance, more sinned against than sinning, Armgart's and the Princess's alienation from family is transformed into another kind of alienation which passes for reintegration. Under the influence of her "gathering illness" (*DD* 52) the Princess reluctantly reconciles herself to her past by acknowledging her son and restoring him to his heritage and to his communal destiny. The cure for Armgart's illness deprives her of her voice, while the cure for her resulting despair becomes the nursing of others who suffer as she does: "Were there one / This moment near me, suffering what I feel, / And needing me for her comfort in her pang – / Then it were worth the while to live; not else" (x:131). Her voice now "lame" (x:133), she reciprocates the care she received from the lame Walpurga by exiling herself to the small provincial town of Freiburg, which Walpurga had left in order to follow her illustrious cousin. For both of these women illness constitutes a loss of self and a reduction of potential, even if that loss (in social and moral terms) is presented as a condition for survival – both personal, and, in the case of the Princess, cultural. These two artists are the female counterparts of Robert Dempster in "Janet's Repentance," whose alienation was the product of his own tyrannical will and desire and whose illness both punished and humbled him before the victim of his own monstrous selfhood. The "satisfaction of self" is again set at irreconcilable odds with the "idea of duty." Illness simply incapacitates one from pursuing the former and by virtue of that incapacity determines the latter. We might read in this reversal of the earlier benignities of sickroom consolation the possibilities for which the sickroom's representation of loss as gain manages to substitute. We might imagine, on the one hand, a Janet Dempster who left her husband and town and found a new life elsewhere, a Romola who separated from Tito and became a scholar of antiquities. Or we might find, on the other hand, a hopelessly alcoholic Janet forced by circumstances to return to her abusive husband, and a diminished Romola silently enduring her husband's neglect and infidelity. We would not, in other words, find in the exceptionality of the first, nor the bleak helplessness of the second, the moderating conventions of realism.

If Armgart's and the Princess Halm-Eberstein's reluctant submission to the exigencies of illness undoes the sickroom's reconciliation of competing imperatives by explicitly exposing the terms upon which it is achieved, the fate of the Princess's son, Daniel, seems to reassert the possibility of such coherence on less debilitating grounds; but they are grounds which leave us at the threshold of another mode of representation. In Deronda's case the determining fact that unifies self and other, desire and duty is not the ailing body, but physical being itself. Deronda's dedication to self-culture is made identical to the larger national culture, and both are determined by birth and certified by physiognomy.[25]

As I stated at the outset of this chapter, the breadth of Eliot's intellectual and moral concerns led her beyond the personal lot, which so preoccupied Brontë, to "the wider public life" (*FH* 3), by which the private life is determined and which it in turn determines in small but ultimately significant ways. Sickroom relations – essentially private, internal, and reductive, despite their exemplary value – are necessarily inadequate in their therapeutic benefit to Eliot's larger aims and her more pressing moral ambitions, although their attraction lay, as I have shown, precisely in that reductiveness. National identity, to which she turned in *Daniel Deronda*, afforded her a means of combining the irresistible imperatives of the physical with a wide political scope of reference more in keeping with her conception of her own role as diagnostician and healer of social ills. Deronda's simultaneous discovery of his Jewish identity and his destiny – the spiritual and physical recuperation of the "torn and soiled and trodded on" people of Israel (*DD* 42) – allows for both a reduction of his paralyzing inner conflicts and "many-sided sympathy" and an expansion of his significance and possible affect within his own community – indeed, in the world at large. Deronda, in short, nurses an entire nation, one whose life has made "half the inspiration of the world" (42). The task of national resuscitation is figured in the novel by his nursing of the ailing Mordechai, apostle and visionary of Zionism. The sickroom, appropriately enough, inscribes in the terms available to traditional realism the eclipse of realism's methodological usefulness.

The messianic fantasy which concludes *Deronda*, like the sickroom solace it carries to its farthest limit, undoes the premises of Eliot's realism in the process of authenticating the values of fellow-feeling and "higher worthiness" that realism was meant to promote. As Catherine Gallagher puts it, by the mid-1860s Eliot "could no longer believe in the automatic facts–values continuity that once guaranteed the significance of representing the social."[26] The distance is not as far as it might seem between Deronda, whose mission is to restore the homeland of an indistinct multitude in an exotic location, and Eliot's last *alter ego*, Theophrastus Such, who asserts in his unpublished didactic essays his fellowship with "a far-off, hazy, multitudinous assemblage" (IX:17) of his own imagining. "The balance of separateness with communication" upon which, according to Deronda's grandfather, "the strength and wealth of mankind depend[s]" (*DD* 60) is in the one book a belated if exemplary ideal, and in the other frankly an illusion. "The real step that has been taken," wrote Raymond Williams of Eliot's later novels, "is withdrawal from any full response to an existing society... All that is left is a set of personal relationships and of intellectual and moral insights, in a history that for all valuing purposes has, disastrously, ended."[27] It is difficult to predict precisely where Eliot's experimentation with realism would have led her had she lived, but *The Impressions of Theophrastus Such*, first published in 1879, is presented as just such a set of intellectual and moral insights divorced from the representation of an "existing society." This withdrawal had always been implicit in Eliot's fiction in the sickroom's intensely private mediations of public weal and woe, but in *Theophrastus Such* it is frankly manifested in the solitary sickroom of the dyspeptic observer of the moral and cultural foibles of his age.

There is an obvious diffidence expressed in the title about the general validity and application of these "impressions," accentuated still further by the painstaking attempt in the initial autobiographical chapters to situate the private consciousness and sensibilities from which they have issued. Even the possibility of a sustaining "set of personal relationships" is called into question in Eliot's final work. Theophrastus Such, who, as he tells us, lives alone and loveless, cannot even bear to particularize his own imaginary audience without posing a threat to the authority of his moral discourse and to his own rather fragile *amour-propre*. He writes: "If any physiognomy becomes distinct in the foreground, it is fatal... " He "shudders at his too corporeal auditor" (IX:17). Like the expressionless and indistinct Florentine procession in *Romola*, their faces covered by hoods, fellowship is figured as an absence of visual particularity. The indemnification of "a binding theory" (*DD* 61) through the subordination and devaluation of physical reality is also evident in Such's meditation on the England of affectionate memory: "Perhaps this England... is a dream in which things are connected according to my well-fed, lazy mood, and not at all by the multitudinous links of graver, sadder fact" (IX:42). He concludes, nevertheless, that in loving such illusions "we strengthen the precious habit of loving something not visibly, tangibly existent, but a spiritual product of our visible tangible selves" (IX:42). Despite the attempt in this statement, as in Eliot's sickrooms, to preserve the visible and tangible by locating the spiritual within our own bodies, there is a manifest shift from the importance of the knowledge conferred by the observed ("graver, sadder fact") in favor of the quality of the sensibility of the observer and his products. This shift from the perceived object to the perceiving subject is characteristic of late-Victorian aestheticism and Theophrastus, for all his moral earnestness, resembles not a little the Paterian aesthete in his high-strung sensitivity, his retreat from the collisions and compromises of everyday life, and his stance as disengaged commentator on culture. The sickroom quarantine which had been pressed into the service of providing a salutary compromise between individual perception and communal forms of being and knowing perhaps reaches both its inevitable conclusion and its point of refiguration in the private impressions of a sickly and alienated bachelor.

Afterword

The fate of the sickroom scene as literary convention and code was tied to the generic exigencies of the realist mode that made it requisite – the obligation to find and assert affirmative links between circumstance and consciousness, between self artd society, between beginnings, middles, and ends. Illness and its succor provided a fragile organic link between felt oppositions, while doubling as the sign of what in fact could neither be accommodated nor redressed within the moderating tonalities of realist discourse. The explanatory malady conjured by Mr. Utterson in *Dr. Jekyll and Mr. Hyde* could provide shelter from the exorbitant alarms inscribed in Hyde's baffling deformities by yielding itself to known remedies and consolations. The unendurable agonies of loss, of self-estrangement, of alienation, or even of physical pain itself could be figured within the sickroom and then assuaged by the hallucinated appurtenances of cushioned beds, basins of weak tea, familial intimacies, and lavish kindness. If there was pain, there was reward, if there was loneliness, there was sanctuary, if there was loss there was restitution, if there was confusion, there was clarification – but until inner necessities conformed with outer circumstances – a realist requirement – the sickroom remained the necessary venue for the representation of such harmonies.

According to Harriet Martineau, her own emergence from the sickroom was enabled by a newly discovered law of nature which restored the harmony between her constitution and its environment.[1] During the course of the century, however, the search for the grounds of continuity sanctioned by natural law ended in the exploration of inevitable disjunction. Separation, which in the sickroom scenes was a provisional condition pending a cure, became itself the newly discovered law of nature.

The sickroom scene did not, therefore, suddenly disappear in the

fiction of the last decades of the century. As late as 1884 George
Meredith was still generously laying on the conventionally climactic
sickroom scenes, while at the same time ridiculing the sentiments on
which they relied for their emotional and narrative significance.
Diana's and Emma's rapturous reciprocation of illness and ministration in *Diana of the Crossways* presents "a new vision of the world
and our life" (26), but Constance Asper's offer to nurse Diana's
estranged husband back to health in the uniform of a "Sister of
Charity" provides a risible instance of hypocrisy. "[Redworth]
laughed to himself, when alone, at the neatly implied bitter reproach
cast on the wife by the forsaken young lady, who proposed to nurse
the abandoned husband of the woman bereaving her of the man she
loved. Sentimentalists enjoy these tricks, the conceiving or the doing
of them – the former mainly, which are cheaper and equally
effective" (29). Although *Diana of the Crossways* presents a new kind
of heroine willing to brave social prejudice to live as she chooses, it
remains a Victorian novel, puncturing with one hand what it sustains
and enobles with the other. False compassion is juxtaposed to true
compassion, sentimental highmindedness to genuine moral conduct.
The sickroom is still called upon to figure rupture and to heal it
through the assertion of the enduring bond of mutual dependency,
and to claim even for the social misfit a place within the ethical norms
of the status quo.

More often, however, the sickroom in late Victorian realism was
the object of a demystifying scrutiny as useful in exposing contradictions as it had once been in reconciling them. In Henry James's
Wings of a Dove and Joseph Conrad's *Nigger of the Narcissus*, for
instance, the sickroom is expressly portrayed as the site of ma-
nipulation in the service of individual needs. Although both authors
still inhabit the world of Victorian realism, with its dramas of social
conduct and moral choice, and its plotting of the self along the graph
of gratification and renunciation, the solidarity engendered by
suffering is exposed as a sentimental, even a murderous lie. Moreover,
their sick protagonists, Milly Theale and Jimmy Wait, generate (in a
sense, exist to generate) the ethical ambiguities, psychological
complexities, and abysses of subjectivity that the earlier sickrooms
sought to coerce through physical urgency and instinctive sympathy
into the "utmost clearness and simplicity" (JR 24).

Like their invalided predecessors in mid-Victorian fiction, Jimmy
and Milly draw about them a society of attentive nurses, a sickroom

setting as snug or as grand as the forecastle of a ship or a Venetian villa allows, and compel through their privileged status the special powers and consolations of debility. Operating within the established conventions of the sickroom scene, Conrad and James reverse the earlier ideal of interaction and demonstrate the collusion between nurses and patients to achieve their own consolatory ends, to sustain their illusions, to enjoy their surreptitious pleasures. Those who surround and assist Milly to "live" until she dies are "working" her and each other for all they desire to be worth, just as Milly herself performs her own vulnerability as a means of forestalling its consequences. At the center of these stratagems is the combined refusal of all the partipants to acknowledge the occasion for their machinations: "It was a conspiracy of silence... to which no one had made an exception, the great smudge of mortality across the picture, the shadow of pain and horror, finding in no quarter a surface of spirit or of speech that consented to reflect it."[2] Kate and Merton reassure themselves that Milly would never "smell of drugs, that she wouldn't taste of medicine" (33). In a manner characteristic of the late-nineteenth-century rewriting of Victorian fiction, a narratorial expedient is enacted at the level of character and in the process turns sinister rather than consoling.

If Milly brokers a saving shift in Merton Densher's consciousness through the magnificence of her renunciation, we are still far from the mediational pathologies of mid-Victorian realism and the effort to imagine reconciliations within the established forms of a representative community. Milly, whose illness and death we never witness, becomes an effect of consciousness, an incitement to speculation, and Merton, her spiritual beneficiary, the sole votary at her shrine. Leo Bersani writes: "Densher's paroxysm of moral scruples... affects us as the creative strategy meant to veil the fact that we are no longer in the kind of novelistic world where such scruples would be relevant. In this novel in which social truth is essentially social brutality, James allows Densher, finally, to die to the world as completely as Milly has died."[3]

Milly still retains the Victorian sick person's odor of sanctity and power to redeem, though on a drastically reduced scale. *The Nigger of the Narcissus* presents instead a grotesquely comic version of the sickroom community in the crew's fierce abjection before a man they despise. Although in the famous preface to the novel the artist is said to speak to the "latent feeling of fellowship with all creation," the novel itself exposes "the latent egoism of tenderness to suffering" and the divisiveness and hostility aroused by the sufferer.[4] Jimmy is a "sick tyrant" whom his shipmates serve "with rage and humility"; (2) he is the locus of mortal anxiety and horrified fascination. The fellow-feeling of the crew in its combined efforts to nurse and comfort Jimmy is vitiated by their fear that he is not really dying and by their fear that he really is. Belfast, the lachrymose Irishman, is a parody of the devoted nurse spending every spare minute by the sickbed, intuiting every want "as sentimentally careful of his nigger as a model slave-owner," and "never so brutal as when most sorrowful" (5). The "sick-bay" conveniently situated next to the galley is "a nice little cabin opening on deck...with two berths" (3). It replicates the cozy sufficiency of the Victorian sickroom, but becomes a deathtrap during the storm that capsizes the ship, and a prison cell when the captain confines Jimmy to it for malingering. Immobilized within its once restorative space, Jimmy is at the mercy first of Podmore, the cook who tries to save him from hellfire, and Donkin who torments him about his impending death. And in the final travesty of Victorian solemnity Jimmy's corpse is caught on a protruding ship's nail and an ungreased plank, refusing at the appropriate rhetorical moment to acquiesce to the ceremonies of bereavement, and revealing even in his death the disorder he has brought to the shipboard community and its appointed tasks. Even so, we are told, something has been lost, if not of transcendent then certainly of instrumental value. The narrator says of the crew following Wait's death, "a common bond was gone; the strong, effective and respectable bond of a sentimental lie" (5).

In the process of decoding the Victorian sickroom scene into its constituent disingenuities Conrad and James still take illness and the obligations it confers as the context for staging powerful moral and metaphysical dilemmas. They render enigmatic but still richly significant the imponderables to which the Victorian scenes sought to give substantial and homely form – the meaning of human suffering, "the moral relation of man to man" (JR 24). But in Ford Madox Ford's *The Good Soldier*, written on the eve of the First World War, the fictional ethos of the Victorian sickroom scene is made to represent the pretenses and blindness of a culture on the verge of collapse. Nauheim, the German health spa to which the Dowells and Ashburnhams retreat for nine years of "uninterrupted tranquillity," sustained by the "beautiful intimacies" of nursing and being nursed, is revealed at last to the blandly credulous Dowell as "a prison full of screaming hysterics."[5] Weak hearts cover for infidelity, nursing is merely impotent connivance at or against the pleasures of others, and the regularity and civil decorum of the spa's health regimen facilitates the clandestine and ultimately catastrophic expression of private hungers.

The discontinuity that was always implicit in the sickroom scenes' narrative positioning is figured here as an absolute and openly avowed disjunction between two incompatible versions of the same reality. The reconciliatory efforts of the Victorian narrator are explicitly psychologized in Dowell's desperate efforts to make sense of allegiances and narrative modes that simply won't, to use the Dowell-like Utterson's words, "hang well together."[6] Or to offer an earlier prototype, King Charles's head keeps intruding on narrative continuity. "Is there then any terrestrial paradise," Dowell asks, "where, amidst the whispering of the olive-leaves, people can be with whom they like and have what they like and take their ease in shadows and in coolness? Or are all men's lives like the lives of us good people... broken, tumultuous, agonized, and unromantic lives, periods punctuated by screams, by imbecilities, by deaths, by agonies? Who the devil knows?" (204–205).

Dowell's two superimposed narrative accounts – the "terrestrial paradise" or the prison of "screaming hysterics" – reconstruct for modernism the relation between the Victorian sickroom and the narrative possibilities that it attempts to foreclose within the sequential form of realist fiction. The relation between, for instance, the utopian sickroom of marital reconciliation in the passage in "Janet's Repentance" and the convulsive violence of the dying Robert Dempster; between the cozy familial sickroom at La Terrasse and Lucy's lonely, bleak agony of abandonment in the deserted pension (or between Jane in the sickroom and Bertha in the attic); between the infantile paradise of passivity, nurturance, and love that is Dick Swiveller's or Pip's convalescence and the desperate and shameful struggles of an impoverished child or an impassioned adult.

Dowell not only wrestles with two narrative versions of his own lived experience, but also presents the reader with alternative narrative settings, imagining for himself and his reader a cozy fireside chat in a cottage by the sea, while "in fact" writing in the bleak, deserted Ashburnham mansion in attendance upon the mad Nancy – the now blighted object of his desire. ("[W]hat I wanted most," he says, "was to cease being a nurse-attendant. Well, I am a nurse-attendant" [204].) Here too one can discern the Victorian equivalents to these doubled sites of narration in Jane Eyre's seclusion at Ferndean with the maimed and blinded Rochester ("Leave sunny imaginations hope") or in the roving narrator in *The Old Curiosity Shop* building his castles in the air and the sick man immured in St. Martin's Square, or in the lonely and embittered Theophrastus Such addressing his "far-off, hazy, multitudinous assemblage." Irrecuperable separation was always an incipient possibility embedded in the consolatory forms, the "binding theories," and conventions of order of Victorian realism and nowhere more so, as these late Victorian and Edwardian authors seem to take for granted, than in the recuperative compromise of the sickroom quarantine.

The late nineteenth century also saw the transformation of the representation of illness as adaptation to illness as deviance. Illness increasingly became the badge of the outsider who disdained normalcy and all it implied of bourgeois Philistinism or else the epithet directed at such "misfits" in defense of an endangered status quo.[7] As Barbara Spackman puts it in her study of "the rhetoric of sickness" in *fin de siècle* literature, "decadent writers place themselves on the side of pathology and valorize physiological ills and alteration as the origin of psychic alterity."[8]

The rise of biomedicine, which began in the late nineteenth century, also had its effects on the descriptive relation of illness to social and cultural phenomena. The growing distinction between rational, empiricist theories of knowledge and issues of value and ethical consciousness, a distinction which struck at the root of realism's explanatory force, made itself felt as well in the etiological models and treatment practises of modern medicine. Jean Comaroff writes: "As a discrete corpus of knowledge and technique, biomedicine has become progressively disengaged from the language of cosmology and morality, from a system of knowledge addressing the relationship of man to his fellow man, and to nature and spirit."[9] Not only has the sick body been decontextualized in modern medical theory, as well as physically removed from the personal and communal domain to clinics and hospitals, but the body itself has been fragmented, as E. Gartly Jaco puts it, into "laboratory artifacts and research objects." According to Jaco "the physician began increasingly to concern himself with more minute aspects of the human body, such as organs, tissues, and cells."[10] Norman Jewson goes farther in describing the decomposition of the patient: "the universe of discourse of medical theory changed from that of an integrated conception of the whole person to that of a network of bonds between microscopical particles."[11] The body may still be considered a register of truth, but that truth is no longer available to the sufferer or to his lay caregivers. Our bodies and our psyches constitute a "terrain our own senses can never traverse but which are interpreted and controlled by the techniques of empirical science."[12]

These developments (including the rapid improvement in the effectiveness of medical interventions in disease) have led to a general deference to medicine and to the institutions that administer medical care in matters of physical and mental distress. The negotiation of diagnoses and treatment strategies between doctor and patient based on the latter's particular needs is, for the most part, a thing of the past.[13] The drama played out in many contemporary accounts of illness is very often the attempt in the face of the sometimes terrible mercies of an impersonal and bureaucratic health care system to reassert personal control over one's body – even over its own demise. In the era of the persistent vegetative state, death itself has become an ambiguous condition determined and redetermined by legal and medical criteria. If illness once served as a desperate and poignant form of affirming communal ties while preserving the integrity of one's own impulses and desires, its current lack of availability to that office speaks just as poignantly of what ails us now.

Notes

INTRODUCTION

1 Sandra M. Gilbert and Susan Gubar, *The Madwoman in the Attic*: *The Woman Writer and the Nineteenth-Century Literary Imagination* (New Haven: Yale University Press, 1979) 54.
2 The literature on these subjects has become too extensive to list here. Many articles and books dealing with women and disease are cited in my notes and bibliography.
3 Leonard Huxley, *Thomas Henry Huxley*: *Life and Letters* (London: Macmillan, 1903) 1:154.
4 Dorothy and Roy Porter, *In Sickness and in Health*: *The British Experience 1650–1850* (London: Fourth Estate, 1988) 8.
5 Bryan S. Turner, *Medical Power and Social Knowledge* (London: Sage Publications, 1987) 214.
6 See, for instance, Roger Cooter, "Anticontagionism and History's Medical Record" in *The Problem of Medical Knowledge*: *Examining the Social Construction of Medicine*, eds. P. Wright and A. Treacher (Edinburgh University Press, 1982) 107n; or Dorothy and Roy Porter, *Patients' Progress*: *Doctors and Doctoring in Eighteenth-Century England* (Stanford University Press, 1989) 11.
7 See Christopher Lawrence, "Incommunicable Knowledge: Science, Technology and the Clinical Art in Britain 1850–1914," *Journal of Contemporary History* 20 (1985): 512–514.
8 "Incommunicable Knowledge," 510.
9 Lawrence Rothfield's fine book *Vital Signs*: *Medical Realism in Nineteenth-Century Fiction* (Princeton University Press, 1992) offers an account of the constitutive role played by clinical discourse in the development of the "realistic novel and its allied genres" (14). We obviously disagree about the relative importance of the epistemic biases of clinical medicine on realism. His choice of French novelists (Balzac, Flaubert, Zola) and the later writings of George Eliot and Henry James to demonstrate his case indicates, I would argue, the difference between the continental receptiveness to clinical medicine and British resistance to it, and the difference among "realisms," early and late, French and British. The

"medical-authorial subject" Rothfield focuses on is, as I contend throughout, more an authorizing metaphor for intimate scrutiny than the declaration of a specific discursive procedure in most mid-Victorian fiction.

10 What I take to be the central attributes of realism will be presented in my study, but a brief summary would include the emphasis on the ordinary, the normative, the particular as it shapes the whole, the moderate over the extreme gesture, and the ultimate intelligibility of human experience.

11 Suzanne Graver, *George Eliot and Community* (Berkeley: University of California Press, 1984) 75.

12 Jean-Jacques Rousseau, *Emile* (London: Dent, 1948) 22.

1 LIFE IN THE SICKROOM

1 Charles Kingsley, *Alton Locke: Tailor and Poet* (New York: Harper & Row, 1856) 35. Hereafter cited in the text.

2 William Makepeace Thackeray, *The History of Pendennis* (New York: Harper, 1900) 53. Hereafter cited in the text.

3 Frank Harris, *Oscar Wilde* (New York: Dell, 1960) 210.

4 Elizabeth Barrett Browning, *Aurora Leigh* (New York: Crowell, 1900) iii:1117–18. Hereafter designated by book and line numbers in the text.

5 Elizabeth Gaskell, *Ruth* (Oxford University Press, 1985) 29. Hereafter cited in the text.

6 Sir Edward Cook, *The Life of Florence Nightingale*, 2 vols. (London: Macmillan, 1913) 1: 283.

7 *The George Eliot Letters*, ed. Gordon S. Haight, 9 vols. (New Haven: Yale University Press, 1954–1978) 1: 283. Hereafter cited in the text as *GEL*.

8 Charles Lamb, *Elia and the Last Essays of Elia* (Oxford University Press, 1987) 210–211.

9 *The Correspondence of Maria Edgeworth*, ed. C. Colvin (Oxford: Clarendon Press, 1974) 297.

10 Gwen Raverat, *Period Piece* (New York: Norton, 1953) 121, 122.

11 This view is most closely identified with Talcott Parsons, who defines somatic health as "the state of optimum capacity for the effective performance of valued tasks." "Definitions of Health and Illness in the Light of American Values and Social Structure" in *Patients, Physicians and Illness: Sourcebook in Behavioral Science and Medicine*, ed. E. Gartly Jaco (New York: The Free Press, 1958) 168.

12 Comaroff, "Medicine: Symbol and Ideology," in Wright and Treacher, eds., 51.

13 *Patients and Practitioners: Lay Perceptions of Medicine in Pre-Industrial Society*, ed. Roy Porter (Cambridge University Press, 1985) 22.

14 See for instance Horacio Fabrega, Jr., *Disease and Social Behavior: An Interdisciplinary Perspective* (Cambridge: MIT Press, 1974) 136.

15 M. Jeanne Peterson, *The Medical Profession in Mid-Victorian London* (Berkeley: University of California Press, 1978) 38–39.

16 See Norman Jewson, "The Disappearance of the Sick Man from Medical Cosmology 1770–1870," *Sociology* 10 (1976): 232–234.

17 See Dorothy and Roy Porter, *In Sickness and In Health: The British Experience 1650–1850* (London: Fourth Estate, 1988) 30–38.

18 Herzlich and Pierret, *Illness and Self in Society*, trans. Elborg Forster (Baltimore: The Johns Hopkins University Press, 1987) 29.

19 Susan Sontag, *Illness as Metaphor* (New York: Farrar, Straus, Giroux, 1978) 30.

20 Talcott Parsons, *The Social System* (New York: The Free Press, 1951).

21 Herzlich and Pierret, *Illness and Self*, 25.

22 Boyd Hilton, *The Age of Atonement: The Influence of Evangelicalism on Social and Economic Thought, 1795–1865* (Oxford: Clarendon Press, 1988) 13.

23 *Life in the Sick-room: Essays by an Invalid*, 2nd ed. (London: Edward Moxon, 1844) 7. Hereafter cited in the text as *LSR*.

24 Gillian Avery, *Nineteenth Century Children* (London: Hodder and Stoughton, 1965) 83.

25 *Memoirs and Letters of Sir James Paget*, ed. Stephen Paget (New York: Longmans, 1901) 294.

26 Thomas Hughes, *Tom Brown's Schooldays* (London: J. M. Dent, 1906) 213.

27 William Thackeray, *The Newcomes*, 2 vols. (London: Dent, 1962) II:3.

28 Raverat, *Period Piece*, 122.

29 See, for instance, Richard Sennett, *The Fall of Public Man* (New York: Alfred Knopf, 1977) 179–180.

30 *The Diary of Alice James*, ed. Leon Edel (New York: Dodd, Mead, 1964).

31 Max Nordau, *Degeneration* (New York: Howard Fertig, 1968) 324.

32 What Cecil Jenkins says of the French realists and naturalists is true for British realism as well: "[T]here was a broad consensus as to the more obvious features of Realism: the need for observation and documentation, for fictional characters to be constituted as typical or representative, and for the writer to regard as his rightful territory the whole range of society and experience..." "Realism and the Novel Form," in *The Monster in the Mirror: Studies in Nineteenth-Century Realism*, ed. D. A. Williams (Published for the University of Hull by Oxford University Press, 1978) 7.

33 Robert Louis Stevenson, *The Strange Case of Dr. Jekyll and Mr. Hyde* and *The Suicide Club* (London: Penguin, 1985) 70. Hereafter cited in the text.

34 Elizabeth Ermarth, *Realism and Consensus in the English Novel* (Princeton University Press, 1983) 47.

35 Leo Bersani, *A Future for Astyanax: Character and Desire in Literature* (Boston: Little, Brown, 1976) 61.

36 John Kucich, *Excess and Restraint in the Novels of Charles Dickens* (Athens: University of Georgia Press, 1981) 55.

37 Garrett Stewart, *Death Sentences: Styles of Dying in British Fiction* (Cambridge: Harvard University Press, 1984) 5.

38 The gratuitous sickness and near-death of Rose Maylie in *Oliver Twist* has been credited to Dickens's desire to imagine the restoration of Mary Hogarth to life. The many illnesses and recoveries in Charlotte Brontë's novels seem to originate in a purely personal desire to bring back her lost family.

39 See, for instance, Harriet Martineau, *Autobiography* (London: Smith, Elder, 1877) II:148: "Every book, tract, and narrative which sets forth a sick-room as a condition of honour, blessing, and moral safety, helps sustain a delusion and corruption which have already cost the world too dear." She, of course, did just that in her *Life in the Sick-room*.

40 Talcott Parsons and Renée Fox, "Illness, Therapy and the Modern Urban American Family" in Jaco, 236.

41 Comaroff, "Medicine," 51–52.

42 Mrs. Leslie Stephen, *Notes from Sick Rooms* (London: Smith, Elder, & Co., 1883) 2.

43 Catherine Gallagher, *The Industrial Reformation of English Fiction* (University of Chicago Press, 1985) 115.

44 Charlotte Mary Yonge, *The Daisy Chain, or Aspirations, a Family Chronicle* (London: Macmillan, 1908) 17.

45 Valerie Sanders, *Reason over Passion: Harriet Martineau and the Victorian Novel* (New York: St. Martin's Press, 1986) 83.

46 Florence Nightingale, *Cassandra* (Old Westbury, New York: The Feminist Press, 1979). Gillian Avery (*Nineteenth Century Children*) gives another view of the same situation: "It was an era when the upper-middle class middle-aged woman had erected a vast structure of time-consuming devices about her to conceal from herself how much time she had on her hands" (109).

47 Stephen, *Notes from Sick Rooms*, 2.

48 *Selected Writings of Florence Nightingale*, compiled by Lucy Ridgley Seymer (New York: Macmillan, 1954) 352.

49 See, for instance, M. Jeanne Peterson, *Family, Love, and Work in the Lives of Victorian Gentlewomen* (Bloomington: Indiana University Press, 1989) 58–84; and Peter Gay, *The Tender Passion*, vol. II (*The Bourgeois Experience: Victoria to Freud*) (Oxford University Press, 1986).

50 Raverat, *Period Piece*, 104.

51 Anthony Trollope, *The Small House at Allington* (Oxford University Press, 1970) 42. Hereafter cited in the text.

52 Jean Strouse, *Alice James: A Biography* (Boston: Houghton Mifflin, 1980) 100–101.

53 E. Lynn Linton, "In Sickness" in *The Girl of the Period and Other Social Essays*, vol. II (London: Richard Bentley & Son, 1883) 211–212.

54 John Forster, *The Life of Dickens* (New York: Doubleday, 1928) 640.

55 This accords with Richard Sennett's contention that the nineteenth

century inaugurated an "ideology of withdrawal" from public life in which "people behave, and manage their behavior, only through withdrawal, 'accommodation,' and 'appeasement'" (*The Fall of Public Man*) 36.

56 Michel Foucault, *Discipline and Punish: The Birth of the Prison*, trans. Alan Sheridan (New York: Vintage, 1979) 28.

57 Sam Schulman, "Basic Functional Roles in Nursing: Mother Surrogate and Healer," in Jaco, 528–537.

58 Lamb, "The Convalescent," *Elia*, 210.

59 Nightingale, *Notes on Nursing: What It Is and What It Is Not* (London: Harrison, 1860) Preface.

60 See Carroll Smith-Rosenberg, *Disorderly Conduct: Visions of Gender in Victorian America* (New York: Alfred A. Knopf, 1985) 198–199.

61 Gilbert and Gubar, *Madwoman in the Attic*, 54.

62 Peterson, *Family, Love, and Work*, 66.

63 Raverat, *Period Piece*, 123.

64 Ann Douglas, "'The Fashionable Diseases': Women's Complaints and Their Treatment in Nineteenth-Century America," in *Clio's Consciousness Raised: New Perspectives on the History of Women*, eds. Mary Hartman and Lois W. Banner (New York: Harper and Row, 1974).

65 Carroll Smith-Rosenberg, *Disorderly Conduct*, 207.

66 Jessica Gerard, "Lady Bountiful: Women of the Landed Classes and Rural Philanthropy," *Victorian Studies* 30: 2 (1987): 206, 194.

67 See, for instance, the excerpts in Janet Horowitz Murray, *Strong-Minded Women: And Other Lost Voices from Nineteenth-Century England* (New York: Pantheon, 1982) 93–107.

68 Jessica Gerard points out in "Lady Bountiful" that for "women of intelligence, energy, and initiative, those with a thirst for power," the role of Lady Bountiful offered opportunities for "independent action and unfettered power over the lives of others" (206).

69 Nancy Cott, *The Bonds of Womanhood: "Woman's Sphere" in New England 1780–1835* (New Haven: Yale University Press, 1977) 201.

70 Florence Nightingale, *Selected Writings*, 351.

71 E. Lynn Linton, "In Sickness," 213.

72 Florence Nightingale, *Cassandra*, 37.

73 Martineau, *The Sickness and Health of the People of Blaeburn* (Boston: Crosby, Nichols, and Company, 1853). "As she passed along the street, the children at play ran into the houses to say that the Good Lady was coming; and the healthy and the convalescent came out on their doorsteps, to bid God bless her; and the sick who were sensible enough to know what was going on, bade God bless her from their beds" (75).

74 Cecil Woodham-Smith, *Florence Nightingale 1820–1910* (London: Collins, 1955) 9. Hereafter cited as W-S in the text.

75 Cook, *Life*, 1: 52.

76 F. F. Cartwright, *A Social History of Medicine* (London: Longman, 1977) 154.

77 See Anne Summers's discussion of the hired nurse in "The Mysterious Demise of Sarah Gamp: The Domiciliary Nurse and Her Detractors c. 1830–1860," *Victorian Studies* 32 (1989): 365–386.

78 Cartwright, *Social History of Medicine*, 154.

79 Nightingale, *Cassandra*, 42.

80 Cook, *Life*, 1:52.

81 As she put it in a letter to her brother-in-law, Sir Harry Verney, "What is wanted is to drain India, to water-supply India, to cleanse India by something more than surface-cleansing." *Ever Yours, Florence Nightingale: Selected Letters*, eds. Martha Vicinus, Bea Nergaard (Cambridge: Harvard University Press, 1990) 244.

82 *Ever Yours*, 92.

83 Zymosis is a process analogous to fermentation by which, it was once thought, diseases were produced and which required as a disease-prevention measure the constant cleaning and ventilation of the dirt and effluvia from which disease arose. The obvious advantage for Nightingale in believing such a theory was the crucial curative importance it gave to the nurse's special duties.

84 See Charles Rosenberg, "Florence Nightingale on Contagion: The Hospital as Moral Universe," in *Healing and History: Essays for George Rosen*, ed. Charles Rosenberg (London: Dawson & Sons, 1979) for a discussion of Nightingale's anti-contagionism.

85 Nightingale, *Selected Writings*, 372.

86 Poovey, *Uneven Developments: The Ideological Work of Gender in Mid-Victorian England*. (University of Chicago Press, 1988) 195.

87 Steven Marcus, *Dickens: From Pickwick to Dombey* (New York: Basic Books, 1965) 261.

88 Sally Mitchell, "Sentiment and Suffering: Women's Recreational Reading in the 1860's," *Victorian Studies* 21 (1977): 37.

89 Elaine Showalter considers the "permanently handicapped man" to represent the desire to provide a "healthy and instructive" experience of "dependency, frustration, and powerlessness for the hero" in *A Literature of Their Own: British Women Novelists from Brontë to Lessing* (Princeton University Press), 1977) 150.

90 Carol Christ, "Victorian Masculinity and The Angel in the House," in *The Widening Sphere: Changing Roles of Victorian Women*, ed. Martha Vicinus (Bloomington: Indiana University Press, 1977) 160.

91 Alfred Tennyson, *The Princess*, in *The Poems of Tennyson: A Selected Edition*, ed. Christopher Ricks (Berkeley, University of California Press, 1989) VII: 264. Hereafter designated by section and line numbers in the text.

92 See, for instance, Christopher Craft, "'Descend, and touch, and enter': Tennyson's Strange Manner of Address," *Genders* 1 (1988): 83–101; and Carol Christ, "The Feminine Subject in Victorian Poetry," *ELH* 54: 2 (1987): 385–405.

93 Edward Marston, *Athenaeum*, 1 January 1848, quoted in Christopher Ricks, *Tennyson* (New York: Macmillan, 1972) 190.

94 Both Daniel Albright and Herbert Tucker, Jr. see this fascination with indeterminacy as crucial in Tennyson's poetry. "[H]is poetry is caught between the desires of the self and the demands of a power whose recognition exacts, in one way or another, the dissolution of the self," (Tucker, *Tennyson and the Doom of Romanticism* [Cambridge: Harvard University Press, 1988] 15). "Indeed much of Tennyson's best poetry is a kind of contest of authorship between Tennyson and his shadow, a lurking anonymity," (Albright, *Tennyson: The Muses' Tug-of-War* [Charlottesville: University Press of Virginia, 1986] 5).

95 See Ricks, *Tennyson*: "*The Princess* manifests great skill – directed, though, not to poetic achievement but to a therapy of evasion... [Tennyson] created a complicated series of evasions such as could temporarily stave off his dilemmas and disasters" (190).

96 Ida's instinctive recoil from the study of anatomy is particularly ironic if we take into account the extent to which nineteenth-century studies in comparative anatomy were used to ground the social and political inequality of women in the supposedly incontrovertible evidence of the body. More pertinently, given Ida's decision not to teach her maids medicine, the exclusion of women from the practise of medicine prevented any possible refutation of this anatomical evidence of their inequality. In her discussion of this issue Londa Schiebinger, ("Skeletons in the Closet: The First Illustrations of the Female Skeleton in Nineteenth-Century Anatomy," *Representations* 14 [1986]: 72) comments: "In the absence of women... nineteenth-century science defined feminine nature as essentially incommensurate with masculine nature." On this see also in the same issue Thomas Laqueur, "Orgasm, Generation, and the Politics of Reproductive Biology."

97 James Turner, *Reckoning with the Beast: Animals, Pain, and Humanity in the Victorian Mind* (Baltimore: The Johns Hopkins University Press, 1980) 102, 87, 88.

98 Eve Kosofsky Sedgwick, *Between Men: English Literature and Male Homosocial Desire* (New York: Columbia University Press, 1985) 126.

99 See Elliot L. Gilbert, "The Female King: Tennyson's Arthurian Apocalypse," *PMLA* 98 (October, 1983) 863–878. Gilbert refers to the "maenad" view of women with reference to the change to domestic angel manifested in Tennyson's *Idylls of the King*. See also Nancy F. Cott, "'Passionless': An Interpretation of Victorian Sexual Ideology, 1790–1850," *Signs* 4 (1978): 221: "Between the seventeenth and the nineteenth centuries, the dominant Anglo-American definition of women as especially sexual was reversed and transformed into the view that women were less carnal and lustful than men."

100 Herbert Tucker, Jr., "Tennyson and the Measure of Doom," *PMLA* 98 (January 1983): 15.

101 Sedgwick, *Between Men*, 123; see also James R. Kincaid, *Tennyson's Major Poems: The Comic and Ironic Patterns* (New Haven: Yale University

Press, 1975) 73–74: "The basic relationship imaged here is clearly not that between man and woman but between mother and child. Men expose their childlike natures to trap women and perhaps form them into children too."
102 Sarah Gilead, "Trollope's Orphans and the 'Power of Adequate Performance,'" *Texas Studies in Language and Literature* 27 (1985): 100.

2 CHARLOTTE BRONTË: "VARIETIES OF PAIN"

1 Terry Eagleton, *Myths of Power: A Marxist Study of the Brontës* (New York: Harper and Row, 1975) 9. Hereafter cited in the text.
2 Quoted in Winifred Gérin, *Charlotte Brontë: The Evolution of Genius* (Oxford University Press, 1969) 144. Hereafter cited in the text.
3 Elizabeth Gaskell, *The Life of Charlotte Brontë* (Harmondsworth: Penguin, 1975) 267. Hereafter cited in the text.
4 Karen Chase, *Eros and Psyche: The Representation of Personality in Charlotte Brontë, Charles Dickens, and George Eliot* (New York: Methuen, 1984) 56. Hereafter cited in the text.
5 Sontag, *Illness as Metaphor*, 43.
6 Janet Oppenheim, *"Shattered Nerves": Doctors, Patients, and Depression in Victorian England* (Oxford University Press, 1991) 142. Athena Vrettos writes of this scene: "By transforming the king's body into a signifier, reading symbolic meaning into the 'peculiar and painful fold' of the king's furrowed brow, Lucy enacts her own corporeal dilemma... In this way, the king appears as both an independent sufferer of immediate pain and a symbolic extension of Lucy over which she wields hermeneutic control." "From Neurosis to Narrative: The Private Life of the Nerves in *Villette* and *Daniel Deronda*," *Victorian Studies* 33 (1990): 566.
7 Carol Christ, "Imaginative Constraint, Feminine Duty, and the Form of Charlotte Brontë's Fiction," *Women's Studies* 6 (1979): 294.
8 T. J. Wise and J. A. Symington, *The Brontës: Their Lives, Friendships, and Correspondence* (Oxford: Shakespeare Head, 1933).
9 Gilbert and Gubar, *The Madwoman in the Attic*, 375.
10 "She represents that troubled, restlessly subjective dimension which the novel's optimistic politics expel" (Eagleton, *Myths of Power* (57)).
11 In my discussion of George Eliot's novel *Romola* in chapter 4, I discuss the disjunction between nursing that is an unsatisfactory substitute for more intimate ties, and nursing that assuages the yearning for a secure identity.
12 "I often wonder," Caroline tells Shirley, "whether most men resemble my uncle in their domestic relations; whether it is necessary to be new and unfamiliar to them... and whether it is impossible to their natures to retain a constant interest and affection for those they see every day." Shirley replies, "I don't know... But... if I were convinced that they are ...fickle, soon petrifying, unsympathetic – I would never marry" (12).

13 See, for instance, Karen Chase, *Eros and Psyche*, 83–84; Helene Moglen, *Charlotte Brontë: The Self Conceived* (New York: Norton, 1976) 52; and Philip Momberger, "Self and World in the Works of Charlotte Brontë," *ELH* 32 (1965): 365.

14 Elizabeth Rigby, "An Anti-Christian Composition," *The Quarterly Review* (December 1848); excerpted in *Jane Eyre*, ed. Richard J. Dunn (New York: Norton, 1971) 60.

15 Parsons, *The Social System*, 478.

16 The full quotation from *Villette* is as follows: "Besides, I seemed to hold two lives – the life of thought and that of reality; and, provided the former was nourished with a sufficiency of the strange necromantic joys of fancy, the privileges of the latter might remain limited to daily bread, hourly work, and a roof of shelter."

17 Tony Tanner, "Introduction," in *Villette* (Harmondsworth: Penguin, 1979) 49.

18 John Kucich, *Repression in Victorian Fiction: Charlotte Brontë, George Eliot, and Charles Dickens* (Berkeley: University of California Press, 1987), 91.

19 Kucich, *Repression*, 91.

20 "Bedridden," in this context, is a revealing way of transliterating the otherwise designated Bedreddin Hassan of *The Arabian Nights*.

21 See Vrettos, "The Private Life of the Nerves," 551–579, for an extended discussion of nervous disorder and somatic disease in *Villette*.

22 George Meredith, *Diana of the Crossways* (New York: Scribner's, 1909) 36.

23 See also Dianne Sadoff, *Monsters of Affection: Dickens, Eliot, and Brontë on Fatherhood* (Baltimore: John Hopkins University Press, 1982) 54: "This wood with the ruins of a nunnery at its center is, like Maggie Tulliver's red deeps, a female sexual landscape complete with metaphorical vagina at its center." It is interesting that the idea of a female refuge, which also appears in *Jane Eyre* as Ferndean, has an early appearance in the Angria tales. The following is from "Caroline Vernon": "Trust me, Caroline, you shall never want a refuge…I have a little retreat, my fairy, somewhere near the heart of my kingdom, Angria, sheltered by Ingleside and hidden in a wood…You shall live there. Nobody will ever reach it to disturb you" (*Legends of Angria*, ed. Fannie E. Ratchford and William Clyde Devane (New Haven: Yale University Press, 1933), excerpted in *Jane Eyre*, ed. Dunn, 437.

24 Dianne Sadoff notes that Caroline's recollection of her father "associates the father with seduction and punishment" (*Monsters*, 133).

25 George Levine, *The Realistic Imagination: English Fiction from Frankenstein to Lady Chatterley* (University of Chicago Press, 1981) 15.

26 Robert Keefe (*Charlotte Brontë's World of Death* [Austin: University of Texas Press, 1979]) argues that it is Mrs. Pryor, not Robert Moore, who Caroline was after in the first place (160).

27 Nancy Armstrong also identifies Ferndean as "feminine turf": in "The

Rise of Feminine Authority in the Novel," *Novel: A Forum in Fiction* 15 (1982): 143.

28 For the mythic point of view see Richard Chase, "The Brontës, or Myth Domesticated," in *Forms of Modern Fiction*, ed. William Van O'Connor (Minneapolis: University of Minnesota Press, 1948). For two views of the social aspects of Rochester's wounds, see Eagleton, *Myths of Power*, 32; Gilbert and Gubar, *The Madwoman in the Attic*, 36.

29 M. Heger is the obvious model for M. Paul, but in significant respects M. Paul also resembles James Taylor – a suitor for Charlotte's hand – whom she once described as a "stern and abrupt little man" (Clement Shorter, *The Brontës: Life and Letters* [Oxford University Press, 1932] II: 202). Taylor, like M. Paul, went on a long journey across the sea (to India) and Charlotte's remarks about the possibility of their ever marrying seem pertinent to Paul's failure to return in *Villette* and Charlotte's general fears about "otherness." "An absence of five years – a dividing expanse of three oceans – the wide difference between a man's active career and a woman's passive existence – these things are almost equivalent to an eternal separation. But there is another thing which forms a barrier more difficult to pass than any of these. Would Mr. Taylor and I ever suit?" (Shorter 203).

30 Wise and Symington, *The Brontës: Their Lives*, I: 232.

31 Jessica Gerard comments in "Lady Bountiful": "In their role as Lady Bountiful, women of the nineteenth-century gentry and aristocracy reinforced the landed classes' rule over the rural poor, implementing paternalism and enforcing deference ... They made the personal contacts so crucial for maintaining the system of patriarchal control and deference" (182).

32 Elaine Scarry, *The Body in Pain: The Making and Unmaking of the World* (Oxford University Press, 1985) 207.

33 Louis's fever, for instance, and Shirley's nervous suffering as a result of a dog bite and her fear of hydrophobia.

3 CHARLES DICKENS: "IMPOSSIBLE EXISTENCES"

1 The patient draws to his bedside a loving nurturing community. In *Little Dorrit*, for instance, "Maggy and Mrs. Plornish and Mr. Baptist took care of [Arthur] by turns" (ii, 33). Similarly, Jenny Wren, Morimer Lightwood, and Lizzie Hexam nurse Eugene Wrayburn in *Our Mutual Friend*.

2 Garrett Stewart, *Dickens and the Trials of Imagination* (Cambridge: Harvard University Press, 1978) 196. Hereafter cited in the text. Although I take issue with some of Stewart's conclusions, I am much indebted to his examination of feverish states in Dickens.

3 See George Levine, *The Realistic Imagination*, 209: "[T]ransformation ... has something of the quality of dream, as in Pen's recuperation from his

fever, or Lucy Snowe's or Pip's, or Eugene Wrayburn's...and is accompanied, as for Oliver Twist in the Maylie's garden, by a passivity not much different from death."

4 See also Chase, *Eros and Psyche*, 94.

5 Forster, *Life of Dickens*, 76. Hereafter cited in the text.

6 F. M. L. Thompson, *The Rise of Respectable Society: A Social History of Victorian Britain 1830–1900* (Cambridge: Harvard University Press, 1988) 197.

7 Sennett, *The Fall of Public Man*, 140.

8 Oppenheim, "*Shattered Nerves*," 155.

9 Peterson, *Family, Love, and Work*, 117, 118.

10 Oppenheim, "*Shattered Nerves*," 154.

11 Alexander Welsh, *From Copyright to Copperfield: The Identity of Dickens* (Cambridge: Harvard University Press, 1987) 158.

12 Oppenheim, "*Shattered Nerves*," 157.

13 Charles Lamb, *Elia and The Last Essays of Elia*, "The Convalescent," 209.

14 Patrick Creevy, "In Time and Out: The Tempo of Life in *Bleak House*," *Dickens Studies Annual: Essays on Victorian Fiction* 12 (1983): 75.

15 Judith Wilt also notes the partial effacement of Esther's encounter with her dead mother "with the help of an illness that blurs," in "Confusion and Consciousness in Dickens's Esther," *Nineteenth-Century Fiction* 32 (1977): 302.

16 See Cynthia Northcutt Malone, "Flight and Pursuit: Fugitive Identity in *Bleak House*," *Dickens Studies Annual: Essays in Victorian Fiction* 19 (1990): 107–124, for a different view of such oscillations among representations of the self. She argues that the multiple and fugitive selves in the novel figure the ontological status of identity itself.

17 Garrett Stewart notes of Pip's delirium that Pip "has never known what was good for him, and this nightmarish transformation of ministration into murder is his imagination's retributive parable," *Trials*, 194. The hallucinations of Pip's fever also obliquely confirm Orlick's status as the dark double of Pip's own violent impulses. During his fever "the vapor of a limekiln would come between" Pip and the distinctions he struggles to make between himself and his own hallucinatory image, "disordering them all" (57). It is near the limekiln and its choking vapors that Orlick attacks Pip.

18 One of Dickens's fondest memories of childhood was of being nursed by his father. "By me, as a sick child, he has watched night and day, unweariedly and patiently, many nights and days" (John Forster, *Life of Dickens* [New York: Doubleday, 1928] 10).

19 On this see also Philip Rogers, "The Dynamics of Time in *The Old Curiosity Shop*," *Nineteenth-Century Fiction* 28 (1973): 127–144.

20 Discussions of the probable identity of the Marchioness can be found in *The Dickensian* 36 (1940): 205–208; *Modern Language Notes* 68 (1953): 162–165; and *Modern Language Review* 65 (1970): 517–518.

21 See also Stewart, *Trials*, 105: "Dick befriends her and, in fact, by naming her almost brings her into being" (105).

22 I base this observation of their "common deformity" upon Master Humphrey's retrospective revelation of his identity as the single gentleman of his tale. Master Humphrey, like Quilp, is humpbacked.

23 For a thorough and interesting discussion of these issues see Audrey Jaffe, "'Never Be Safe but in Hiding': Omniscience and Curiosity in *The Old Curiosity Shop*," *Novel: A Forum in Fiction* 19 (1986): 118–134.

24 Jaffe, "Omniscience and Curiosity," 125.

25 Robert Kiely, "Plotting and Scheming: The Design of Design in *Our Mutual Friend*," *Dickens Studies Annual: Essays on Victorian Fiction* 12 (1983): 279.

26 John Kucich's contention that Wrayburn's "sadistic enterprise...in its very gratuitousness springs from and helps confirm his own psychological freedom," seems to me to take Eugene's engagement with Bradley on Eugene's own terms. See Kucich, "Repression and Representation: Dickens's General Economy," *Nineteenth-Century Fiction* 38 (1983): 74.

27 Taylor Stoehr observes of Dicken's novels generally: "At the root of each novel the same sore rankles: a sexual transgression somehow related to the overstepping (or the inability to overstep) class boundaries," *Dickens: The Dreamer's Stance* (Ithaca: Cornell University Press, 1965) 96.

28 See Eve Kosofsky Sedgwick, *Between Men*, 171, for a discussion of this issue.

29 Chase, *Eros and Psyche*, 131.

30 Stewart, *Trials of the Imagination*, 218, 198.

31 Stewart, *Trials of the Imagination*, 220.

32 Robert Garis, *The Dickens Theatre: A Reassessment of the Novels* (Oxford: Clarendon Press, 1965) 250.

33 "I have tried to scud about town at all hours," Jenny tells Riah. "[I]t's the trying-on by the great ladies that takes it out of me" (iii, 1).

34 Although it is customary, following Edgar Johnson's lead, to associate Bella with Ellen Ternan, Lizzie seems to me the more likely candidate. Separated from Dickens by age and class as well as for a time by Dickens's marriage, Ellen, like Lizzie, was a desired but taboo object. Lizzie's dramatically virtuous efforts to separate herself from Eugene seem in keeping with Dickens's published certification of Ellen's blamelessness, and, like Eugene's uneasy obliquity about his intentions toward Lizzie, arose as much from his chivalry toward the girl he was compromising as from his need to disavow the lack of purity in his own intentions toward her. See, for instance, Edgar Johnson, *Charles Dickens: His Tragedy and Triumph* (New York: Simon and Schuster, 1952) II: 917: "In the indignant fervor of his emotion he resented the accusation as a slur on Ellen's purity; swirling in a luminous mist, his feelings presented themselves to him as a shining and sanctified devotion and Ellen as the far-off princess on the unscalable mountain. He was in that lyrical and

anguished state which could not bear having itself imaged, even in its own eyes, as the desire to defile that fair beauty in a libertine embrace. His wife's bitter suspicions enraged him as hideous and degrading."

35 See Dickens, *Our Mutual Friend*, i, 6, for Eugene's flirtation with "the domestic virtues."

36 Eve Kosofsky Sedgwick, *Between Men*, 178.

37 Johnson, *Charles Dickens*, ii:882.

4 GEORGE ELIOT: "SEPARATENESS AND COMMUNICATION"

1 See George Eliot, "The Natural History of German Life: Riehl," *Essays of George Eliot*, ed. Thomas Pinney (New York: Columbia University Press, 1963) 271.

2 *The George Eliot Letters*, ed. Gordon S. Haight 1: 283. Hereafter cited in the text as *GEL*.

3 See Laura Comer Emery, *George Eliot's Creative Conflict: The Other Side of Silence* (Berkeley: University of California Press, 1976)) 95: "Submission has on its side the superego's dependence on duty, and also the instinctual need for love."

4 One may count among their number Romola, Dorothea, Lydgate, Godfrey Cass, and Gwendolyn Harleth Grandcourt.

5 David Carroll, "'Janet's Repentance' and the Myth of the Organic," *Nineteenth-Century Fiction* 35 (1980): 345.

6 Thomas P. Wolfe, "'The Inward Vocation': An Essay on George Eliot's *Daniel Deronda*," *Literary Monographs* 8 (1976): 21.

7 George Eliot's fear of "voluntarily leaving" her father is suggestive in this regard (*GEL* 1: 129). As Ruby Redinger points out, Eliot felt that the act of defiance that had precipitated her expulsion from her father's home and protection "had been both in cause and effect an act of aggression against her father, and that to leave him voluntarily would have been but a continuation of that act" (*George Eliot: The Emergent Self* [New York: Knopf, 1975]) 123.

8 Gilbert and Gubar, *The Madwoman in the Attic*, 474–475.

9 D. A. Miller, *Narrative and Its Discontents: Problems of Closure in the Traditional Novel* (Princeton University Press, 1981) 138.

10 Martineau, *Autobiography*, 1: 157.

11 Thomas Carlyle, "Characteristics," in *Critical and Miscellaneous Essays*, 5 vols. (Boston: James Munroe and Company, 1839) iii: 62. Hereafter cited in the text.

12 Carroll, "'Janet's Repentance,'" 347, 348.

13 Carol Christ, "Aggression and Providential Death in George Eliot's Fiction," *Novel: A Forum in Fiction* 9 (1976): 130–140.

14 Dianne Sadoff notes that "Janet's confessed story to him of her unhappiness and his respondent confession to her about his sexual profligacy create an attraction between them for which Eliot's metaphor

is consumption," *Monsters*, 70. (Consumption is perhaps more a metaphor for denial of attraction than for attraction itself.)

15 See Steven Marcus, *Representations: Essays on Literature and Society* (New York: Random House, 1975) 183–213. Marcus argues that Milly Barton is the victim of the strong sexual attraction which she and Amos have for each other; Mr. Gilfil keeps his wife Tina's room as a shrine and memorial after her death.

16 See Carole Robinson, "*Romola*: A Reading of the Novel," *Victorian Studies* 6 (1962): 31. Hereafter cited in the text.

17 Robinson, "*Romola*," also notes the novel's "curious air of an endless argument" (37).

18 In his essay "*Romola* as Fable," George Levine contends that the symbolic element in the novel – Romola's separation from the determining conditions that hamper choice in Eliot's usual, realistic treatment of decision-making – allows Romola a choice that is "absolutely free and spontaneous" (*Critical Essays on George Eliot*, ed. Barbara Hardy [London: Routledge and Kegan Paul, 1970] 93). I am arguing, to the contrary, that the symbolic nature of the "Drifting Away" episode renders choice unnecessary by making determining conditions coincide with desire.

19 Sara Hennell characterizes this paradox most starkly in her letter to Eliot about *Romola*: "It is only those who want nothing for themselves, that can really be wanted by others" (*GEL* IV:104n).

20 Emery, *Creative Conflict*, 100.

21 Jonathan R. Quick, "Silas Marner as Romance," *Nineteenth-Century Fiction* 29 (1974): 295.

22 Susan M. Greenstein, "The Question of Vocation: From *Romola* to *Middlemarch*," *Nineteenth-Century Fiction* 35 (1981): 504.

23 See for instance, Wolfe, "'The Inward Vocation'," 41–45, and Gilbert and Gubar, *The Madwoman in the Attic*, 454–455.

24 Wolfe, "'The Inward Vocation'," 43.

25 "[T]he thought glanced through Deronda that precisely such a physiognomy as that might possibly have been seen in a prophet of the Exile or in some New Hebrew poet of the medieval time" (*DD* 33).

26 Gallagher, *Industrial Reformation of English Fiction*, 265.

27 Raymond Williams, *The Country and the City* (Oxford University Press, 1973) 180.

AFTERWORD

1 Martineau, *Autobiography*, II:153.

2 Henry James, *The Wings of the Dove* (New York: Signet, 1964).

3 Bersani, *A Future for Astyanax*, 144.

4 Joseph Conrad, *The Nigger of the Narcissus* (New York: Norton, 1979) 5.

5 Ford Madox Ford, *The Good Soldier* (London: The Bodley Head, 1915)

40, 18. References to this novel are by page number and are hereafter cited in the text.

6 Stevenson, *Jekyll and Hyde*, 70.

7 Max Nordau's *Degeneration* has become the *locus classicus* of the latter position, but the association of illness with deviation from the status quo was widespread in the closing years of the century, when anxiety about degeneration was at its height.

8 Barbara Spackman, *Decadent Genealogies: The Rhetoric of Sickness from Baudelaire to D'Annunzio* (Ithaca: Cornell University Press, 1989) "Preface," vii-viii.

9 Comaroff, "Medicine," in Wright and Treacher, 56.

10 Jaco, *Patients, Physicians, and Illness*, 4.

11 Jewson, "The Disappearance of the Sick-Man," 225.

12 Comaroff, "Medicine," in Wright and Treacher, 59. It should be noted that the so-called "medical model" of disease which assumes that ultimately the causes of disease can be located in the body and its biochemical mechanisms (Turner, *Medical Power*, 9) has come under increasingly critical scrutiny by the medical establishment as well as by medical sociologists.

13 Jewson, "The Disappearance of the Sick-Man," 230. See also Porter, *Patients' Progress*, 13: "It is time to acknowledge how far the procedures and outcomes of pre-modern medicine depended upon a dialogue, a co-operative relationship established between the sick person and his medical attendant." The Porters also claim that even today patients are not as passive in relation to medical control as many historians and sociologists contend (15).

Bibliography

Albright, Daniel. *Tennyson: The Muses' Tug-of-War*. Charlottesville: University Press of Virginia, 1986.

Allott, Miriam, ed. *The Brontës: The Critical Heritage*. London and Boston: Routledge and Kegan Paul, 1974.

Armstrong, Nancy. "The Rise of Feminine Authority in the Novel." *Novel* 15 (1982): 127–145.

Avery, Gillian. *Nineteenth Century Children*. London: Hodder and Stoughton, 1965.

Bersani, Leo. *A Future for Astyanax: Character and Desire in Literature*. Boston: Little, Brown, 1976.

Bonaparte, Felicia. *The Triptych and the Cross: The Central Myths of George Eliot's Poetic Imagination*. New York University Press, 1979.

Browning, Elizabeth Barrett. *Aurora Leigh*. New York: Crowell, 1900.

Carlyle, Thomas. "Characteristics." *Critical and Miscellaneous Essays*. 5 vols. Boston: James Monroe and Company, 1839, III: 46–92.

Carroll, David. "'Janet's Repentance' and the Myth of the Organic." *Nineteenth-Century Fiction* 35 (1980): 331–348.

Cartwright, F. F. *A Social History of Medicine*. London: Longman, 1977.

Chase, Karen. *Eros and Psyche: The Representation of Personality in Charlotte Brontë, Charles Dickens, and George Eliot*. New York: Methuen, 1984.

Chase, Richard. "The Brontës, or Myth Domesticated." *Forms of Modern Fiction*. Ed. William Van O'Connor. Minneapolis: University of Minnesota Press, 1948, 102–119.

Christ, Carol. "Aggression and Providential Death in George Eliot's Fiction." *Novel: A Forum in Fiction* 9 (1976): 130–140.

"The Feminine Subject in Victorian Poetry." *ELH* 54:2 (1987): 385–405.

"Imaginative Constraint, Feminine Duty and the Form of Charlotte Brontë's Fiction." *Women's Studies: An Interdisciplinary Journal* 6 (1979): 287–296.

"Victorian Masculinity and the Angel in the House." *The Widening Sphere: Changing Roles of Victorian Women*. Ed. Martha Vicinus. Bloomington: Indiana University Press, 1977, 146–162.

Cohen, Susan R. "'A History and a Metamorphosis': Continuity and

Discontinuity in *Silas Marner.*" *Texas Studies in Language and Literature* 25 (1983): 410–425.

Colp, Ralph Jr. *To Be an Invalid: The Illness of Charles Darwin.* University of Chicago Press, 1977.

Comaroff, Jean. "Medicine: Symbol and Ideology." Eds. Wright and Treacher. 1982, 49–68.

Conrad, Joseph. *The Nigger of the Narcissus.* New York: Norton, 1979.

Cook, Edward. *The Life of Florence Nightingale.* 2 vols. London: Macmillan, 1913.

Cooter, Roger. "Anticontagionism and History's Medical Record." Eds. Wright and Treacher, 1982, 87–108.

Cott, Nancy F. *The Bonds of Womanhood: "Woman's Sphere" in New England 1780–1835.* New Haven: Yale University Press, 1977.

"'Passionless': An Interpretation of Victorian Sexual Ideology, 1790–1850." *Signs* 4 (1978): 219–236.

Craft, Christopher. "'Descend, and touch, and enter': Tennyson's Strange Manner of Address." *Genders* 1 (1988): 83–101.

Creevy, Patrick. "In Time and Out: The Tempo of Life in *Bleak House.*" *Dickens Studies Annual: Essays on Victorian Fiction* 12 (1983): 63–83.

Douglas, Ann. "'The Fashionable Diseases': Women's Complaints and Their Treatment in Nineteenth-Century America." *Clio's Consciousness Raised: New Perspectives on The History of Women.* Eds. Mary Hartman and Lois W. Banner. New York: Harper and Row, 1974.

Dubos, Rene and Jean Dubos. *The White Plague: Tuberculosis, Man, and Society.* Boston: Little, Brown, 1952.

Du Maurier, George. *Trilby.* London: Dent, 1951.

Eagleton, Terry. *Myths of Power: A Marxist Study of the Brontës.* New York: Harper and Row, 1975.

Edgeworth, Maria. *The Correspondence of Maria Edgeworth.* Ed. C. Colvin. Oxford: Clarendon Press, 1974.

Ehrenreich, Barbara, and English, Deirdre. *For Her Own Good: 150 Years of the Expert's Advice to Women.* New York: Anchor Books, 1979.

Eliot, George. "The Natural History of German Life: Riehl." *Essays of George Eliot.* Ed. Thomas Pinney. New York: Columbia University Press, 1963.

The George Eliot Letters. Ed. Gordon Haight. 9 vols. New Haven: Yale University Press, 1963.

Ellis, Sara Stickney. *The Mothers of England: Their Influence and Responsibility.* London: Fisher, 1843.

Emery, Laura Comer. *George Eliot's Creative Conflict: The Other Side of Silence.* Berkeley: University of California Press, 1976.

Ermarth, Elizabeth. "Incarnations: George Eliot and 'Undeviating Law'." *Nineteenth-Century Fiction* 29 (1974): 273–286.

Realism and Consensus in the English Novel. Princeton University Press, 1983.

Fabrega, Horacio, Jr. *Disease and Social Behavior: An Interdisciplinary Perspective.* Cambridge: MIT Press, 1974.

Ford Madox Ford, *The Good Soldier*. London: The Bodley Head, 1915.

Forster, John. *The Life of Charles Dickens*. New York: Doubleday, 1928.

Foucault, Michel. *Discipline and Punish: The Birth of the Prison*. Trans. Alan Sheridan. New York: Vintage, 1979.

Froude, James Anthony, ed. *Letters and Memorials of Jane Welsh Carlyle*. New York: Scribners, 1883.

Gallagher, Catherine. *The Industrial Reformation of English Fiction*. University of Chicago Press, 1985.

Garis, Robert. *The Dickens Theatre: A Reassessment of the Novels*. Oxford: Clarendon Press, 1965.

Gaskell, Elizabeth. *The Life of Charlotte Brontë*. Harmondsworth: Penguin, 1975.

Ruth. Oxford University Press, 1985.

Gay, Peter. *The Tender Passion: The Bourgeois Experience: Victoria to Freud*, vol. II. Oxford University Press, 1986.

Gerard, Jessica. "Lady Bountiful: Women of the Landed Classes and Rural Philanthropy." *Victorian Studies* 30:2 (1987): 183–209.

Gérin, Winifred. *Charlotte Brontë: The Evolution of Genius*. Oxford University Press, 1967.

Gilead Sarah. "Trollope's Orphans and the 'Power of Adequate Performance.'" *Texas Studies in Language and Literature* 27 (1985): 86–105.

Gilbert, Elliot L. "The Female King: Tennyson's Arthurian Apocalypse." *PMLA* 98 (1983): 863–878.

Gilbert, Sandra M. and Susan Gubar. *The Madwoman in the Attic: The Woman Writer and the Nineteenth-Century Literary Imagination*. New Haven: Yale University Press, 1979.

Graver, Suzanne. *George Eliot and Community*. Berkeley: University of California Press, 1984.

Greenstein, Susan M. "The Question of Vocation: From *Romola* to *Middlemarch*." *Nineteenth-Century Fiction* 35 (1981): 487–505.

Haight, Gordon. *George Eliot: A Biography*. Oxford University Press, 1968.

Haley, Bruce. *The Healthy Body and Victorian Culture*. Cambridge: Harvard University Press, 1978.

Hardy, Barbara. *Critical Essays on George Eliot*. London: Routledge and Kegan Paul, 1970.

Harris, Frank. *Oscar Wilde*. New York: Dell, 1960.

Heilman, Robert B. "Charlotte Brontë's 'New' Gothic." *From Jane Austen to Joseph Conrad*. Minneapolis: Minnesota University Press, 1958.

Herzlich, Claudine and Janine Pierret. *Illness and Self in Society*. Trans. Elborg Forster. Baltimore: Johns Hopkins University Press, 1987.

Hilton, Boyd. *The Age of Atonement: The Influence of Evangelicalism on Social and Economic Thought, 1795–1865*. Oxford: Clarendon, 1988.

House, Humphrey. *All in Due Time*. London: Hart-Davis, 1955.

The Dickens World. 2nd ed. Oxford University Press, 1942.

Hughes, Thomas. *Tom Brown's Schooldays*. London: J. M. Dent, 1906.

Huxley, Leonard. *Thomas Henry Huxley: Life and Letters.* 2 vols. London: Macmillan, 1903.

Jaco, E. Gartly, ed. *Patients, Physicians and Illness: Sourcebook in Behavioral Science and Medicine.* New York: The Free Press, 1958.

Jaffe, Audrey. "'Never Be Safe but in Hiding': Omniscience and Curiosity in *The Old Curiosity Shop.*" *Novel: A Forum in Fiction* 19 (1986): 118–134.

James, Alice. *The Diary of Alice James.* Ed. Leon Edel. New York: Dodd, Mead, 1964.

James, Henry. *The Wings of the Dove.* New York: Signet, 1964.

Jenkins, Cecil. "Realism and the Novel Form." *The Monster in the Mirror: Studies in Nineteenth-Century Realism.* Ed. D. A. Williams. Published for the University of Hull by Oxford University Press, 1978, 1–16.

Jewson, Norman. "The Disappearance of the Sick Man from Medical Cosmology 1770–1870." *Sociology* 10 (1976): 225–244.

Johnson, Edgar. *Charles Dickens: His Tragedy and Triumph.* 2 vols. New York: Simon and Schuster, 1952.

Keefe, Robert. *Charlotte Brontë's World of Death.* Austin: University of Texas Press, 1979.

Kenyon, Fredric G., ed. *The Letters of Elizabeth Barrett Browning.* 2 vols. New York: Macmillan, 1898.

Kiely, Robert. "Plotting and Scheming: The Design of Design in *Our Mutual Friend.*" *Dickens Studies Annual: Essays on Victorian Fiction* 12 (1983): 267–283.

Kincaid, James R. *Tennyson's Major Poems: The Comic and Ironic Patterns.* New Haven: Yale University Press, 1975.

King, Lester S. *The Medical World of the Eighteenth Century.* Huntington, New York: Krieger, rpt. 1971.

Kingsley, Charles. *Alton Locke: Tailor and Poet.* New York: Harper & Row, 1856.

Kucich, John. *Excess and Restraint in the Novels of Charles Dickens.* Athens: University of Georgia Press, 1981.

     "Death Worship Among the Victorians: *The Old Curiosity Shop.*" *PMLA* 95 (1980): 58–72.

     "Repression and Representation: Dickens's General Economy." *Nineteenth-Century Fiction* 38 (1983): 62–77.

     Repression in Victorian Fiction: Charlotte Brontë, George Eliot, and Charles Dickens. Berkeley: University of California Press, 1987.

Lamb, Charles. "The Convalescent." *Elia and the Last Essays of Elia.* Oxford University Press, 1987, 208–212.

Laqueur, Thomas. "Orgasm, Generation, and the Politics of Reproductive Biology." *Representations* 14 (1986): 1–41.

Lawrence, Christopher. "Incommunicable Knowledge: Science, Technology and the Clinical Art in Britain 1850–1914." *Journal of Contemporary History* 20 (1985): 503–520.

Levine, George. "George Eliot's Hypothesis of Reality." *Nineteenth-Century Fiction* 35 (1980): 1–28.

The Realistic Imagination: English Fiction from Frankenstein to Lady Chatterley. University of Chicago Press, 1981.

"*Romola* as Fable." *Critical Essays on George Eliot.* London: Routledge and Kegan Paul, 1970.

Linton, E. Lynn. "In Sickness" in *The Girl of the Period and Other Social Essays*, vol.II. London: Richard Bentley & Son, 1883, 208–216.

Malone, Cynthia Northcutt. "Flight and Pursuit: Fugitive Identity in *Bleak House.*" *Dickens Studies Annual: Essays in Victorian Fiction* 19 (1990): 107–124.

Marcus, Steven. *Representations: Essays on Literature and Society.* New York: Random House, 1975.

Dickens: From Pickwick to Dombey. New York: Basic Books, 1965.

Martineau, Harriet. *Autobiography.* 3rd ed. 2 vols. London: Smith, Elder, 1877.

Life in the Sick-room: Essays by an Invalid. London: Edward Moxon, 1844.

The Sickness and Health of the People of Blaeburn. Boston: Crosby, Nichols, and Company, 1853.

Meredith, George. *Diana of the Crossways.* New York: Scribner's, 1909.

Mill, John Stuart. *Essays on Literature and Society.* Ed. J. B. Schneewind. New York: Collier, 1965.

Miller, D. A. *Narrative and Its Discontents: Problems of Closure in the Traditional Novel.* Princeton University Press, 1981.

Miller, J. Hillis. *Charles Dickens: The World of His Novels.* Cambridge: Harvard University Press, 1958.

Mitchell, Sally. "Sentiment and Suffering: Women's Recreational Reading in the 1860's." *Victorian Studies* 21 (1977): 29–45.

Moglen, Helene. *Charlotte Brontë: The Self Conceived.* New York: Norton, 1976.

Momberger, Philip. "Self and World in the Works of Charlotte Brontë." *ELH* 32 (1965): 349–369.

Moynahan, Julian. "The Hero's Guilt: The Case of *Great Expectations.*" *Essays in Criticism* 10 (1960): 60–79.

Murray, Janet Horowitz. *Strong-Minded Women: And Other Lost Voices from Nineteenth-Century England.* New York: Pantheon, 1982.

Nightingale, Florence. *Cassandra.* Old Westbury, New York: The Feminist Press, 1979.

Ever Yours, Florence Nightingale: Selected Letters. Eds. Martha Vicinus and Bea Nergaard. Cambridge: Harvard University Press, 1990.

Notes on Nursing: What It Is and What It Is Not. London: Harrison, 1860.

Selected Writings of Florence Nightingale, compiled by Lucy Ridgley Seymer. New York: Macmillan, 1954.

Oppenheim, Janet. "*Shattered Nerves*": *Doctors, Patients, and Depression in Victorian England.* Oxford University Press, 1991.

Nordau, Max. *Degeneration.* New York: Howard Fertig, 1968.

Paget, Sir James. *Memoirs and Letters of Sir James Paget.* Ed. Stephen Paget. New York: Longmans, 1901.

Parsons, Talcott. "Definitions of Health and Illness in the Light of American Values and Social Structure." Jaco, 165–187.

  and Renee Fox. "Illness, Therapy and the Modern Urban American Family." Jaco, 234–245.

  The Social System. New York: The Free Press, 1951.

Peterson, M. Jeanne. *Family, Love, and Work in the Lives of Victorian Gentlewomen.* Bloomington: Indiana University Press, 1989.

  The Medical Profession in Mid-Victorian London. Berkeley: University of California Press, 1978.

Pickering, George. *Creative Malady.* New York: Oxford University Press, 1974.

Poovey, Mary. *Uneven Developments: The Ideological Work of Gender in Mid-Victorian England.* University of Chicago Press, 1988.

Porter, Dorothy and Roy Porter. *Patients' Progress: Doctors and Doctoring in Eighteenth-Century England.* Stanford University Press, 1989.

  In Sickness and In Health: The British Experience 1650–1850. London: Fourth Estate, 1988.

Porter, Roy. *Patients and Practitioners: Lay Perceptions of Medicine in Pre-Industrial Society.* Cambridge University Press, 1985.

Prichard, James Cowles. *A Treatise on Insanity and Other Disorders Affecting the Mind.* Philadelphia: Haswell, Barrington, 1837.

Quick, Jonathan R. "*Silas Marner* as Romance." *Nineteenth-Century Fiction* 29 (1974): 287–298.

Ratchford, Fannie E. *The Brontës' Web of Childhoood.* New York: Russell and Russell, 1941.

Ratchford, Fannie E. and William Clyde Devane, eds. *Legends of Angria.* New Haven: Yale University Press, 1933.

Raverat, Gwen. *Period Piece.* New York: Norton, 1953.

Redinger, Ruby V. *George Eliot: The Emergent Self.* New York: Alfred Knopf, 1975.

Ricks, Christopher. *Tennyson.* New York: Macmillan, 1972.

Rigby, Elizabeth. "An Anti-Christian Composition." *The Quarterly Review* (December 1848). Excerpted in *Jane Eyre.* Ed. Richard Dunn. New York: Norton, 1971.

Robinson, Carole. "*Romola*: A Reading of the Novel." *Victorian Studies* 6 (1962): 29–42.

Rogers, Philip. "The Dynamics of Time in *The Old Curiosity Shop.*" *Nineteenth-Century Fiction* 28 (1973): 127–144.

Rosenberg, Charles. *Healing and History: Essays for George Rosen.* Ed. Charles Rosenberg. London: Dawson & Sons, 1979.

Rothfield, Lawrence. *Vital Signs: Medical Realism in Nineteenth-Century Fiction.* Princeton University Press, 1992.

Rousseau, Jean-Jacques. *Emile.* London: Dent, 1948.

Sadoff, Dianne F. *Monsters of Affection: Dickens, Eliot and Brontë on Fatherhood.* Baltimore: Johns Hopkins University Press, 1982.

Sanders, Valerie. *Reason over Passion: Harriet Martineau and the Victorian Novel.* New York: St. Martin's Press, 1986.

Scarry, Elaine. *The Body in Pain: The Making and Unmaking of the World.* Oxford University Press, 1985.

Schiebinger, Londa. "Skeletons in the Closet: The First Illustrations of the Female Skeleton in Nineteenth-Century Anatomy." *Representations* 14 (1986): 42–82.

Schulman, Sam. "Basic Functional Roles in Nursing: Mother Surrogate and Healer." Jaco, 528–537.

Sedgwick, Eve Kosofsky. *Between Men: English Literature and Male Homosocial Desire.* New York: Columbia University Press, 1985.

Sennett, Richard. *The Fall of Public Man.* New York: Alfred Knopf, 1977.

Shalvi, Alice, ed. *Daniel Deronda: A Centenary Symposium.* Jerusalem: Jerusalem Academic Press, 1976.

Shorter, Clement. *The Brontës: Life and Letters.* 4 vols. Oxford University Press, 1932.

Showalter, Elaine. *A Literature of Their Own: British Women Novelists from Brontë to Lessing.* Princeton University Press, 1977.

Smith-Rosenberg, Carole. *Disorderly Conduct: Visions of Gender in Victorian America.* New York: Alfred A. Knopf, 1985.

Sontag, Susan. *Illness as Metaphor.* New York: Farrar, Straus, Giroux, 1978.

Spackman, Barbara. *Decadent Genealogies: The Rhetoric of Sickness from Baudelaire to D'Annunzio.* Ithaca: Cornell University Press, 1989.

Stephen, Karin. *The Wish to Fall Ill: A Study of Psychoanalysis and Medicine.* Cambridge University Press, 1960.

Stephen, Mrs. Leslie. *Notes from Sick Rooms.* London: Smith, Elder, 1883.

Stevenson, Robert Louis. *The Strange Case of Dr. Jekyll and Mr. Hyde* and *The Suicide Club.* London: Penguin, 1985.

Stewart, Garrett. *Dickens and the Trials of Imagination.* Cambridge: Harvard University Press, 1974.

    Death Sentences: Styles of Dying in British Fiction. Cambridge: Harvard University Press, 1984.

Stoehr, Taylor. *Dickens: The Dreamer's Stance.* Ithaca: Cornell University Press, 1965.

Strouse, Jean. *Alice James: A Biography.* Boston: Houghton, Mifflin, 1980.

Summers, Anne. "The Mysterious Demise of Sarah Gamp: The Domiciliary Nurse and Her Detractors c. 1830–1860." *Victorian Studies* 32 (1989): 365–386.

Tanner, Tony. "Introduction." *Villette.* By Charlotte Brontë. London: Penguin, 1979.

Tennyson, Alfred. *The Poems of Tennyson: A Selected Edition.* Ed. Christopher Ricks. Berkeley: University of California Press, 1989.

Thackeray, William M. *The Newcomes.* 2 vols. London: Dent, 1962. *Pendennis.* New York: Harper & Row, 1900.

Thompson, F. M. L. *The Rise of Respectable Society: A Social History of Victorian Britain 1830–1900.* Cambridge: Harvard University Press, 1988.

Tooley, Sarah A. *The History of Nursing in the British Empire.* London: Bousfield, 1906.

Trollope, Anthony. *The Small House at Allington.* Oxford University Press, 1970.

Tucker, Herbert, Jr. *Tennyson and the Doom of Romanticism.* Cambridge: Harvard University Press, 1988.

"Tennyson and the Measure of Doom." *PMLA* 98 (1983): 8–20.

Turner, Brian S. *Medical Power and Social Knowledge.* London: Sage Publications, 1987.

Turner, James. *Reckoning with the Beast: Animals, Pain, and Humanity in the Victorian Mind.* Baltimore: The Johns Hopkins University Press, 1980.

Vicinus, Martha. *The Widening Sphere: Changing Roles of Victorian Women.* Bloomington: Indiana University Press, 1977.

Vrettos, Athena. "From Neurosis to Narrative: The Private Life of the Nerves in *Villette* and *Daniel Deronda.*" *Victorian Studies* 33 (1990): 551–579.

Welsh, Alexander. *The City of Dickens.* Oxford: Clarendon, 1971.

From Copywright to Copperfield: The Identity of Dickens. Cambridge: Harvard University Press, 1987.

Williams, D. A., ed. *The Monster in the Mirror: Studies in Nineteenth-Century Realism.* Published for the University of Hull by Oxford University Press, 1978.

Williams, Raymond. *The Country and the City.* Oxford University Press, 1973.

Wilt, Judith. "Confusion and Consciousness in Dickens's Esther." *Nineteenth-Century Fiction* 32 (1977): 285–309.

Winnifrith, Tom. *The Brontës.* New York: Macmillan, 1977.

Winslow, John H. *Darwin's Victorian Malady: Evidence for its Medically induced Origin.* Philadelphia: American Philosophical Society, 1971.

Wise, T. J. and J. A. Symington. *The Brontës: Their Lives, Friendships, and Correspondence.* 4 vols. Oxford: Shakespeare Head, 1932.

Wolfe, Thomas P. "'The Inward Vocation': An Essay on George Eliot's *Daniel Deronda.*" *Literary Monographs* 8 (1976), 1–46.

Woodham-Smith, Cecil. *Florence Nightingale 1820–1910.* London: Collins, 1955.

Wright, P. and A. Treacher, eds. *The Problem of Medical Knowledge: Examining the Social Construction of Medicine.* Edinburgh University Press, 1982.

Yonge, Charlotte Mary, *The Daisy Chain, or Aspirations, a Family Chronicle.* London: Macmillan, 1908.

Zwerdling, Alex. "Esther Summerson Rehabilitated." *PMLA* 88 (1973): 429–439.

Index

Printed in the United States
130114LV00006B/3/A